Verbal Art,
Verbal Sign,
Verbal Time

Roman Jakobson

'Verbal Art,
Verbal Sign,
Verbal Time

Krystyna Pomorska and Stephen Rudy, editors

With the assistance of Brent Vine

University of Minnesota Press   Minneapolis

Published by the University of Minnesota Press,
2037 University Avenue Southeast, Minneapolis MN 55414

Printed in the United States of America

Library of Congress Cataloging in Publication Data
Jakobson, Roman, 1896–1982.
 Verbal art, verbal sign, verbal time.
 "Based on a special issue of Poetics today . . . Autumn 1980"—Verso t.p.
 Includes bibliographical references and index.
 1. Philology—Addresses, essays, lectures. 2. Semiotics—Addresses, essays, lectures. 3. Space and time in language—Addresses, essays, lectures. 4. Space and time in literature—Addresses, essays, lectures.
I. Pomorska, Krystyna. II. Rudy, Stephen. III. Poetics today. IV. Title.
P49.J35 1984   808'.00141   84-7268
ISBN 0-8166-1358-3
ISBN 0-8166-1361-3 (pbk.)

This book is based on a Special Issue of *Poetics Today,* Vol. 2, No. 1a, Autumn 1980. Information on sources is given in a note on the opening page of each chapter.

The University of Minnesota is an equal-opportunity educator and employer.

Contents

Preface

Roman Jakobson—innovative explorer of the science of language, literary scholar, and semiotician—ranks among the seminal thinkers who shaped the "human sciences" in the twentieth century. Born in Moscow in 1896, Jakobson identified himself with the generation of great artists and writers born in the 1880s and 1890s, such as Picasso (1881–1973), Joyce (1882–1941), Braque (1882–1963), Stravinsky (1882–1971), Xlebnikov (1885–1922), Le Corbusier (1887–1965), and Majakovskij (1893–1930). The major influence of his youth was the pictorial and poetic experiments of the European avant-garde, especially Cubism, which radically posed the question of the relationship between the sign and reality, and between the material and intelligible parts of the sign (*signans* and *signatum*). In characterizing this generation, which reached maturity before the catastrophe of World War I and the cataclysms that ensued, and which managed to leave its creative mark upon twentieth-century thought, Jakobson stresses "the extraordinary capacity of these discoverers to overcome again and again the faded habits of their own yesterdays, together with an unprecedented gift for seizing and shaping anew every older tradition or foreign model without sacrificing the stamp of their own permanent individuality in the amazing polyphony of new creations."[1] This statement about his generation is at the same time an extremely apt self-characterization.

A poet himself (writing under the nom de plume Aljagrov), Jakobson was active in the Russian Futurist movement and was a friend of the leading artists and poets of the period between 1913 and 1919—Kazimir Malevič and Pavel Filonov, Velimir Xlebnikov and Vladimir Majakovskij. The bold experimentation in the arts, as exemplified especially in the work of the Cubo-Futurists, impressed upon Russian students of literature and language the need for a thorough revision of the basic tenets of both literary theory and linguistics, a revision necessitating the discarding of the old absolutes and an insistence on

[1] R. Jakobson, "Retrospect," in his *Selected Writings I: Phonological Studies* (The Hague-Paris: Mouton, 1971, 2nd ed.), p. 632.

the dynamic view of art and reality. It is characteristic of the avant-garde approach that these problems were tackled in collective scientific work and discussion. As a first-year student at Moscow University, in 1915, Jakobson was a founding member and president of the Moscow Linguistic Circle and played an active part in its Petersburg counterpart, the "Society for the Study of Poetic Language" or OPOJAZ, as it is known by its Russian acronym. These two circles, which insisted upon the autonomy of literary studies and the immanent analysis of literary works, produced a revolution in the study of literature: their collective endeavors, which today go under the name of Russian Formalism, resulted in the reformulation of both the object of literary study and its methodology.[2]

After leaving Russia for Czechoslovakia in 1920, Jakobson, with Prince N. S. Trubetzkoy, elaborated the new discipline of phonology, the structural study of speech sounds. In 1926, with Vilém Mathesius and other prominent Czech and Russian scholars, he founded the Prague Linguistic Circle, the center of modern structural linguistics. After the Nazi invasion of Czechoslovakia in 1939, Jakobson was forced to flee, via Scandinavia, to the United States, where he arrived in 1941. In New York, Jakobson taught first at the École Libre des Hautes Études, the Free French and Belgian university hosted by the New School for Social Research, where his colleagues included the anthropologist Claude Lévi-Strauss and the medievalist Henri Grégoire. Later, as a professor at Columbia (1945–1949), Harvard (1949–1965), and the Massachusetts Institute of Technology (1957–1982), Jakobson trained two generations of American linguists and Slavists, and was largely responsible for the growth of these disciplines in the United States.

An issue of the journal *Poetics Today,* edited by Benjamin Hrushovski and dedicated to Roman Jakobson on his eighty-fifth birthday, forms the core of this book.[3] Before his death in 1982, Jakobson elaborated the basic table of contents for the volume and provided the title—*Verbal Art, Verbal Sign, Verbal Time*—which eloquently echoes the spirit of his scholarly work. In Jakobson's view, the literary work is first and foremost a linguistic fact, a special use of language that engages linguistic structure maximally, radically, and—it should be stressed—often unconsciously. Indeed, Jakobson's scholarly feat consists as much in enlivening linguistic science by confronting the creative use of language as in bringing to bear upon literary texts the precise methods of linguistics. As Roland Barthes astutely wrote: "Roman Jakobson has given us a marvelous gift: he has given linguistics to artists. It is he who has opened up the live and sensitive juncture between one of the most exact of the sciences of man and the creative world. He represents, both for his theoretical thought and his actual accomplishments, the meeting of scientific thought and the creative spirit."[4]

[2] See V. Erlich, *Russian Formalism: History—Doctrine* (New Haven-London: Yale University Press, 1981, 3rd ed.).
[3] *Roman Jakobson: Language and Literature = Poetics Today,* vol. 2, no. 1a (Autumn 1980).
[4] R. Barthes, "Avant-Propos," *Cahiers CISTRE,* vol. 5 (Lausanne: Editions L'Age d'Homme, 1978), p. 9.

Moreover, in keeping with his belief in the necessity of a global approach to language, poetry, and the arts, Jakobson views the literary work as a semiotic phenomenon, one that must be examined within the context of the entire universe of signs. Finally, the dynamism of verbal art and of language in general is a cardinal point of his theory: time is viewed as a constitutive, rather than extraneous, factor in language and literature, one that produces momentum and change.

In the introductory article included here, "My Favorite Topics," Jakobson presents in lapidary fashion the diversity of his interests and achievements, marks the path of their development, and, characteristically, outlines further tasks and possibilities for the science of language. Originally presented at the Accademia dei Lincei in Rome in 1980, on the occasion of his receiving the Antonio Feltrinelli Prize for Linguistics and Philology, the article points to "invariance in the midst of variation" as the leitmotif unifying the author's work in such diverse domains as phonology, versification, grammar of poetry, language acquisition and loss, the Slavic oral tradition, and semiotics. As becomes clear from reading this article, what is remarkable about Jakobson's work is its essential unity despite the variations in topics he addressed, the vicissitudes of his actual biography, and the enormous volume and temporal span of his scholarly output. One theme he particularly singles out, the role of time and space in language and society, is the subject of the first section of the present book.

All his life Jakobson remained a man of the avant-garde, and his emphasis on the dynamic role of time reflects that legacy. As he says in the opening "Dialogue on Time in Language and Literature," Futurism, with the theory of relativity, exercised a profound influence on his ideas about time and space as factors intrinsic to language. They prompted him to challenge the formulation of this problem given in Ferdinand de Saussure's classic *Cours de linguistique générale* (1916). According to Saussure, language as a system (synchrony) is opposed to its historical development (diachrony) as static versus dynamic moments. In Jakobson's view such an opposition is false, since it excludes the role of time in the present moment of language and thus creates an erroneous disruption between the past and the present in linguistic processes. Although the article included here reassessing Saussure's doctrine, "Sign and System of Language," was originally published in 1959, it is the fruit and continuation of ideas Jakobson introduced as early as 1929, in his pathbreaking monograph on the evolution of the Russian phonological system, *Remarques sur l'évolution du russe comparée à celle des autres langues slaves.*[5] The application of the principle of dynamics to literary studies is advocated in "Problems in the Study of Language and Literature" on which Jakobson collaborated in 1929 with Jurij Tynjanov, one of the most brilliant members of OPOJAZ. Written at a time when Russian Formalism was coming under increasing attack in the Soviet Union for its supposed "ahistoricism," this manifesto anticipates the structural

[5] See *Selected Writings I,* pp. 7–116.

approach to literary history which evolved in the 1930s in the Prague Linguistic Circle. The entire section on time dispels the tenacious belief that Structuralism has ignored the historical dimension in favor of synchronic analysis; on the contrary, as Jakobson's work shows, the problem is one of integrating the two dimensions in their interaction.

The central part of this book is devoted to one of Roman Jakobson's major contributions to poetics, his theory of "grammar of poetry." In his celebrated essay of 1960, "Linguistics and Poetics," Jakobson postulates that in poetry "equivalence is promoted to the constitutive device of the sequence."[6] As the etymology of the word suggests, verse consists of recurrent returns. Nowhere is this more apparent than in the basic principle underlying any system of versification, which Jakobson qualifies as "the superinducing of the equivalence principle upon the word sequence or, in other terms, the *mounting* of the metrical form upon the usual speech form."[7] In one of his earliest works, *On Czech Verse—Primarily in Juxtaposition with Russian* (1923),[8] Jakobson demonstrates, using the methods of phonology, how the different prosodic features of the Slavic languages affect the type of versification systems that evolved historically in those languages. In going from metrics, where one deals with recurrence of equivalent units of sound, to grammar, Jakobson establishes yet another level at which the interrelationship of linguistic material and poetic form should be studied.

The core of Jakobson's theory is presented with examples from several languages in the opening essay of the second section of the present book, the English abstract of his longer Russian paper "Poetry of Grammar and Grammar of Poetry."[9] Grammatical categories, which are purely relational and obligatory in everyday speech, become, in poetry, wide-ranging expressive devices. In other words, in poetry such abstract language "fictions," to use Jeremy Bentham's term, become reified and take on a life of their own. Grammar is a particularly semioticized part of language, one constantly experienced in our everyday mythology in such basic aspects as gender, for example. It becomes even more highly charged in the context of poetry: as Jakobson writes, "*in fiction,* in verbal art, *linguistic fictions* are fully realized."[10]

The results of Jakobson's investigation into the role of grammar in poetry are contained in the third volume of his *Selected Writings,* a work of more than 800 pages.[11] Included there are Jakobson's theoretical articles on the subject as well as thirty-four analyses of poems ranging in period from the eighth to the twentieth century and representing the most diverse cultural, aesthetic, and

[6] R. Jakobson, "Linguistics and Poetics," in his *Selected Writings III: Poetry of Grammar and Grammar of Poetry* (The Hague-Paris-New York: Mouton, 1981), p. 27.

[7] *Ibid.,* p. 37.

[8] See *Selected Writings V: On Verse, Its Masters and Explorers* (The Hague-Paris-New York: Mouton, 1979), pp. 3–130.

[9] The Russian version was first delivered as a lecture at the International Conference on Poetics, Warsaw, 1960; it is reprinted in *Selected Writings III,* pp. 63–86.

[10] See below, p. 39.

[11] See footnote 6 above.

linguistic environments. Jakobson has clearly succeeded in proving that the creative exploitation and patterning of grammatical categories are poetic universals. In certain poems, styles, or periods, they may in fact become the dominant poetic device. The section on grammar of poetry in the present volume contains some of Jakobson's most accessible and persuasive analyses. The Russian nineteenth-century poet Aleksandr Puškin wrote entire poems devoid of the usual poetic tropes and figures but structured on the skillful use of grammatical tropes. A classic example is his "Ja vas ljubil . . ." ("I loved you . . ."), the most famous short lyric poem in the Russian language. Jakobson's analysis, which shows beyond any doubt the full poetic efficacy of grammar, is published here in its first English translation. This example is, of course, a rarity; far more usual are poems in which imagery, tropes, and figures are intertwined with grammatical figures in a complex network of equivalences and contrasts. Such a play on the literal and metaphorical, the concrete and abstract, is elegantly analyzed in the same study on the basis of another of Puškin's poems, "Čto v imeni tebe moem . . ." ("What is in my name for you . . .").

Both "Subliminal Verbal Patterning in Poetry" and "On Poetic Intentions and Linguistic Devices in Poetry" address a question that is often asked by readers confronted with the astounding poetic ordering of linguistic materials that structural analysis reveals: are these consciously applied devices? Do they reflect the author's intention? Some critics of Jakobson's theory go so far as to argue that if such devices are not intentional, not part of a conscious poetic "code" shared by poet and audience, then they cannot be considered as poetic devices properly speaking. Jakobson's reply is that while some poets may be highly conscious of such devices, this need not be the case at all. If one examines oral literature, one finds the same striking structural regularities that characterize the written tradition, while the "tellers of tales" are as a rule totally ignorant of the structural code they so assiduously follow. Indeed, much of the evocative power of oral and written poetry is due precisely to the fact that its patterns are perceived subliminally. It remains for the analyst to pinpoint the concrete linguistic patterns that the poet has created; if some of them prove to be below the threshold of individual readers' perceptions, it hardly means that they do not exist or fail to have an effect on readers.

The study concluding the section on grammar of poetry, "Yeats' 'Sorrow of Love' through the Years," written in collaboration with Stephen Rudy, is in many respects a paradigmatic Jakobsonian analysis. It demonstrates how all levels of language—phonology, grammar, lexicon, and syntax—are exploited in the creation of poetic structure and meaning. It is unique among Jakobson's studies, however, in addressing the diachronic problem of structural change across time, thus complementing the articles in the first section of this book. Yeats' later reworkings of his poems have been a subject of controversy in literary studies, with some critics even charging that he spoiled his early poems by rewriting them. In the case in point, the reworking was so radical that Yeats retained only a few words. An objective and painstaking analysis discloses, however, the futility of applying such arbitrary judgments to Yeats' work: the two poems share certain structural features at the same time that they reveal essentially different principles of organization reflecting the changes in Yeats' poetics. Jakobson's concern here is hardly a question of textology in the traditional sense of the term. The problem of variation emerges in a double aspect: what is rejected by a poet at a later stage of development cannot be viewed judgmentally; moreover, the poet's workshop, his creative experimentation, is as important for establishing the invariance characterizing his work as are the canonic versions of his poems. This study also contains one of Jakobson's most interesting analyses of the role of "sound symbolism" in poetry, a realm in which Yeats was the consummate master.

The third section of this book, "Poetry and Life," demonstrates Jakobson's versatility as a literary scholar. Many of his critics have accused Jakobson of trying to "reduce" poetry to parallelisms in sound and grammar. On the contrary, as an attentive reading of his work shows, the wider questions that traditionally occupy the student of literature are ones Jakobson also addressed. Although he disliked the term "literary critic," Jakobson possessed one of the finest critical intelligences that has been brought to bear on problems of nineteenth- and twentieth-century literature, and especially of Russian poetry. In 1930, when Vladimir Majakovskij took his own life, Roman Jakobson responded to this tragic event with an article under the symptomatic title "On a Generation that Squandered Its Poets." Contemporaries rightly considered this impassioned piece of literary criticism one of the best articles he had written: Osip Mandel'štam, for example, is said to have called it "a thing of biblical power." On the one hand, this essay is, as Jakobson's writes in "My Favorite Topics," "a wide adoption of the invariance test": its central concern is to isolate the invariant thematic core of Majakovskij's poetry. On the other hand, Majakovskij's act, which Jakobson considered symbolic for the entire generation, turned his thoughts toward the problem of "poetic myth," i.e., the particular link between a writer's life and work. The article on Majakovskij was followed by four studies in a similar vein: "What Is Poetry?" (1933–1934), "Marginal Notes on the Prose of the Poet Pasternak" (1933), "Notes on Erben's Work" (1935), and "The Statue in Puškin's Poetic Mythology" (1937).[12] All five works are linked by the same idea: in the life of a poet the border line between the "hard facts" of biography and the symbolic expression of poetry becomes obliterated, and the traditional division between "Dichtung und Wahrheit" proves to be invalid. Summarizing his ideas from that epoch half a century later, Jakobson said: "In these circumstances the question of our loss and the lost poet forced itself upon us. Majakovskij had more than once stated that for him, the poet's realism did not consist in picking up the crumbs of the past, nor in reflecting the present, but rather in creatively anticipating the future. And we

[12] See R. Jakobson, "What Is Poetry?" *Selected Writings III*, pp. 740–750; "Marginal Notes on the Prose of the Poet Pasternak," in *Pasternak: Modern Judgments*, ed. D. Davie and A. Livingstone (Glasgow, 1969), pp. 131–151; "Poznámky k dílu Erbenovu," *Selected Writings V*, pp. 510–537; "The Statue in Puškin's Poetic Mythology," *Selected Writings V*, pp. 237–280.

did indeed discover that the poet had recounted his destiny in advance, had foreseen his fateful end, and had even precisely guessed and described all the absurd and unpitying reactions of his contemporaries to his 'unexpected,' but timely, death. . . . Throughout the course of his poems, Majakovskij had sketched out the monolithic myth of the poet, a zealot in the name of the revolution of the spirit, a martyr condemned to cruel and hostile incomprehension and rejection. . . . When this myth entered the sphere of life, it became impossible to trace a limit between the poetic mythology and the curriculum vitae of the author without committing terrible forgeries."[13]

"The Language of Schizophrenia: Hölderlin's Speech and Poetry" is a selection from a monograph written in collaboration with Grete Lübbe-Grothues, entitled "Ein Blick auf *Die Aussicht* von Hölderlin." It deals with the effect of the poet's madness on his work, in particular a late lyric entitled "The View." One constant concern of Jakobson's work in poetics was his battle against what he termed "aesthetic egocentrism." In his analyses of medieval poetry, of so-called primitives (Blake, Rousseau, Janko Král'), and of the oral tradition, Jakobson has revealed poetic swans where earlier critics, biased by their own aesthetic orientation, saw only "ugly ducklings." Hölderlin's poem is a vivid case in point. Rather than analyzing the poet's late verse objectively, previous critics had labeled it the incoherent ravings of a madman. Jakobson's meticulous structural analysis of "The View" discloses its aesthetic merits and will doubtless spark a critical revision of the poet's work. The selection published here, however, concentrates more on the theoretical conclusions to be drawn from the actual analysis of the verse of a madman. The language of schizophrenia is revealed to be not an aberration but a linguistic system in which the capacity for dialogue is lost. The monologic orientation led, in Hölderlin's case, to bizarre everyday speech behavior and a radical shift in his poetic style, both of which cease to be mysterious when analyzed from a linguistic point of view.

The present volume concludes with three essays that provide a perspective on Jakobson's work as a whole. Theoretically minded readers may wish to turn to them first, before sampling Jakobson's own works published here. Linda Waugh, who collaborated with Jakobson on his crowning work on phonology, *The Sound Shape of Language*,[14] has contributed a fine study tracing the ways in which Jakobson's theory of poetics grows out of and is organically bound to his general theory of language. In an essay of particular interest to students of literature, Krystyna Pomorska shows how Jakobson's theory of poetics and analytical method can be applied to prose. Finally, Igor Mel'čuk analyzes Jakobson's work in morphology and in the process draws wider conclusions about Jakobson's contribution to humanistic scholarship in general.

The author of over 600 books and articles, of which more than half are

[13] R. Jakobson and K. Pomorska, *Dialogues* (Cambridge, Mass.: The MIT Press, 1982), pp. 138–139.
[14] R. Jakobson and L. Waugh, *The Sound Shape of Language* (Bloomington-London: Indiana University Press, 1979).

included in the seven monumental volumes of his *Selected Writings,*[15] Jakobson can hardly be represented adequately by a single volume. Nevertheless, the present book, one of the last he himself planned and worked on, may be regarded as a fitting introduction to certain of his linguistic theories and especially to his pathbreaking work in poetics. Several of the articles included here are obligatory reading for anyone interested in poetics or in the history of twentieth-century literary criticism, but they have not been available previously in a convenient edition addressed to the wider reading public.

Krystyna Pomorska and Stephen Rudy

[15] Volumes I, III, and V are referred to in footnotes 1, 6, and 8 above. The other volumes of the *Selected Writings* are *II: Word and Language* (1971); *IV: Slavic Epic Studies* (1966); *VI: Early Slavic Paths and Crossroads* (1984); and *VII: Contributions to Comparative Mythology. Studies in Linguistics and Philology, 1972-1982* (1985). For a complete listing of Jakobson's works see *A Complete Bibliography of Roman Jakobson's Writings, 1912-1982*, compiled and edited by S. Rudy (Berlin-Amsterdam-New York: Mouton, 1984).

Verbal Art,
Verbal Sign,
Verbal Time

My Favorite Topics

Roman Jakobson

The question of invariance in the midst of variation has been the dominant topic and methodological device underlying my diversified yet homogeneous research work since my undergraduate attempt of 1911 to outline the formal properties of the earliest Russian iambs. The interplay of invariance and variation continued to attract my attention ever more insistently. Versification, with its diaphanous dichotomies of downbeat—upbeat, break—bridge, and with its correlation of two fundamental metrical concepts, namely design and instance, offered the self-evident possibility of determining the relational invariance that the verse retains across its fluctuations, and of defining and interpreting the scale of the latter.

A monograph of 1923, *On Czech Verse, Primarily in Comparison with Russian* (in Russian), which was later included, together with a few subsequent papers on metrics, in my *Selected Writings* (henceforth abbreviated as *SW*), (*V*/1979:3–223, 570–601), initiated a long and detailed discussion about the relationship between poetic forms and language. This investigation required a careful delineation of the diverse functions assigned by a given language to its prosodic elements, a delineation that plays a substantial role in the relative application of those elements in the corresponding system of versification.

The continued inquiry into this problem, which ties together metrics and linguistics, impelled me to elucidate and exemplify such essentially topological questions as, for instance, the invariants retained and the variations experienced throughout the diverse works of one and the same poet or of different poets within the same literary school, as well as the question of the metrical cleavage between single literary genres. The transformation undergone by certain verse types all along the history of a given poetic language called for

The Italian version of this self-portrait was presented at the awarding of the "Antonio Feltrinelli" Prize, and was published by the Accademia Nazionale dei Lincei in the *Premio Internazionale per la Filologia e Linguistica,* 1980. The English translation will appear in Roman Jakobson, *Selected Writings VII: Contributions to Comparative Mythology. Studies in Linguistics and Philology, 1972-1982* (Berlin-Amsterdam-New York: Mouton, 1985).

the same kind of treatment. I used chiefly Slavic, especially Czech, verse types as experimental material (see *SW VI/*1984: *Early Slavic Paths and Crossroads*).

The convergent and divergent metrical rules in a set of similar languages, whether cognate or remote, brought me within the reach of comparative metrics in its two aspects, the historical and the typological. By collating the oral traditions of the different Slavic peoples, I ventured to uncover the rudiments of Proto-Slavic versification (*Oxford Slavonic Papers III/*1952, pp. 21–66, republished in *Selected Writings IV/*1966: 414–463), thereby contributing to Meillet's search for Indo-European verse. Concurrently, advances in metrical typology led me to an ever more detailed extraction of invariants and thus towards a closer insight into metrical universals, as was emphasized in my study "Linguistics and Poetics" (*SW III/*1981). An examination of distant metrical phenomena, such as Germanic alliteration, the admissive rules of Mordvinian meters, or the modular design of Chinese regulated verse, enhanced my search for the universal foundations of versification (see *SW V/*1979: *On Verse, Its Masters and Explorers*).

It was the difference between the two classes of prosodic elements, the sense-discriminative function on the one hand, and the delimitative one on the other, that naturally became a topic of discussion in my metrical monograph of 1923, along with the simultaneous application of the same functional approach to the entire sound pattern of language. The book in question proposed the name "phonology" for the study of speech sounds with regard to meaning and asserted the strictly relational character of the sense-discriminative entities, linked to each other by binary oppositions as components of the ever-hierarchical phonological systems. Since my first steps in phonology I have been continuously attracted to the search for the ultimate constituents of language and the powerful structural laws of the network they comprise. I endeavored to trace the allusions to the existence of such ultimate entities in the wisdom of antiquity and the emergence one century ago of the concept "phoneme" in the perspicacious works of a few bold linguistic pioneers (see "Toward a Nomothetic Science of Language," *SW II/*1971:369–602).

The breaking-down of the phoneme into "distinctive features" as the actually ultimate components of the phonological system suggested itself and was achieved toward the end of the 1930s (cf. *Phonological Studies, SW I/*1962: 221–233, 272–316, 418–434, and *Six leçons sur le son et le sens,* (1976). This task demanded a rigorous insight into the common denominator of multiple variables; the notion of contextual variants gradually became more pertinent and more precisely elaborated, and the consistent segmentation of speech proved to be feasible (cf. Jakobson & Linda Waugh, *The Sound Shape of Language,* 1979).

The structure of phonological systems is of great linguistic interest; the typological comparison of such systems reveals significant underlying laws and prompts the final conclusion that "the sound patterns of single languages are varying implementations of universal invariants" (Jakobson & Waugh 1979:

234). Through the argument of the incompatibility and equivalence of certain distinctions, we arrived at the conclusion of the highly limited number of valid distinctive features.

The phonological quest for relational invariants proved to be applicable to the other levels of language as well, and especially to the fundamental question of the interconnection between general and particular (more properly speaking, contextual) meanings of the grammatical categories. This is apparent, e.g., in my treatment of grammatical cases and of the duplex overlapping structures labeled "shifters," which separate verbs and pronouns from nouns (*SW II*/1971, section A: 3–208). In the paper "Russian Conjugation" (*SW II*, sec. A: 119–129) the same criterion of invariance is seen to underlie the grammatical form and makes it possible to predict the entire paradigm. The entangled morphonology of Gilyak required a similar treatment (pp. 72–102).

Similar to the way in which the realization of the intimate relation between the sound level of language and verse led to new insights in the field of metrics, the new approach to grammatical categories enabled me and my collaborators of the last two decades to outline the significant, but until recently underrated, role of grammatical tropes in poetry. Cf. *Poetry of Grammar and Grammar of Poetry* (*SW III*/1981), with many analyzed ("parsed") poems of varied tongues and centuries.

The grammatical parallelism widespread in world poetry (*SW III*/1981: 98–135) consists in a combination of invariants and variables that speaks eloquently to the users of the given poetic canon but that still demands closer scientific analysis, a technique that should prove equally fruitful for both linguistics and poetics, particularly as regards the intricate syntactic questions involved.

The elaboration of a linguistically oriented inquiry into verbal art necessitated a wide adoption of the invariance test. It was with this in mind that I tentatively approached the question of poets' myths, e.g., "The Statue in Puškin's Poetic Mythology" and the monolithic build-up of Majakovskij's mythic imagery (see *SW V*/1979: 237–281, 355–413; cf. the present volume, 111–132).

In defiance of the accustomed mechanistic effacement of the boundary between the writer's individualized production and the collectivistic orientation of oral traditions, Petr Bogatryev's and my lengthy fieldwork in folklore permitted us to insist on the different correlation of invariance and variability in oral tradition as the latter's specific feature, fraught with consequences. It was precisely this point of departure that gave the impetus to my volume of studies prepared for the most part during the 1940s and devoted to the Slavic, especially Russian, oral and written epic tradition, *Slavic Epic Studies* (*SW IV*/1966; cf. *SW VI*/1984: *Early Slavic Paths and Crossroads*), as well as to my still only partly published deliberations on comparative Slavic and Indo-European mythology and especially on its vestiges in languages and folklore.

Returning to the inferences I have made on the basis of my phonological and grammatical research, I should like merely to list several further areas that belong among my favorite themes of investigation.

Time and space, usually regarded as extrinsic factors in relation to the verbal code, prove to be veritable constituents of the latter. In the speaker's and listener's code, any change in progress is simultaneously present in its initial and final forms as stylistic variants, one more archaic and the other more advanced, both being mutually interchangeable in the speech community and even in the use of its individual members (as I remarked, e.g., about the Common Slavic accentual evolution in my three essays included in the expanded edition of *SW I*/1971: 664–699). Since my earliest report of 1927 to the then newborn Prague Linguistic Circle, I have pleaded for the removal of the alleged antinomy synchrony/diachrony and have propounded instead the idea of permanently dynamic synchrony, at the same time underscoring the presence of static invariants in the diachronic cut of language (cf. *SW I*/ 1971: 1–116, 202–220).

The verbal code is convertible also with respect to the factor of space. It contains a set of variants serving for different degrees of adaptation to interlocutors of diverse dialectal and social distance. Diffusion of linguistic characters results from such variations, and during the 1930s I devoted several essays (reproduced in *SW I*/1971: 137–201, 234–246) to one of the extreme manifestations of the space factor in the life of languages, the interlingual rapprochement termed *Sprachbund* by Nikolaj Trubetzkoy. Later I repeatedly, though so far in vain, appealed for phonological atlases of vast territories, a task with undoubtedly surprising vistas.

A concentration on questions of the hitherto neglected, ontogenetic aspect of our science occupied my sojourn of 1939–1941 in three Scandinavian countries and resulted in the book *Kindersprache, Aphasie und allgemeine Lautgesetze* (Uppsala, 1941), as well as in many later observations and reflections on the nearly regular order of children's verbal acquisitions and of aphasic losses (see *Studies on Child Language and Aphasia,* 1971). The intimate connection between mastering language and metalanguage was for me an instructive conclusion from observations of children's linguistic development, observations which induced me to propose a revision in the network of verbal functions (cf. my Presidential Address of 1956 to the Linguistic Society of America, "Metalanguage as a Linguistic Problem," reproduced in *The Framework of Language,* Ann Arbor, 1980, pp. 81–92).

My continuous studies in aphasia can be summed up as follows: "The basic binary concepts viewed in the linguistic quest as the key to understanding the obvious dichotomy of aphasic disturbances, namely dyads such as encoding/decoding, syntagmatic/paradigmatic, and contiguity/similarity, gradually found access to the advanced neuropsychological treatment of aphasic enigmas" (*Brain and Language,* Columbus, Ohio, 1980). The multifarious linguistic and poetic manifestations of the last dyad, which may be outlined as metonymy/metaphor (cf. *SW II*: 239–259), urgently demand a deeper and wider scrutiny.

The ever increasing recognition of the biological roots of *language* does not cancel out the equally relevant social premises of *languages*—the coaction of an interlocutor and the indispensability of learning. Since the 1920s, spent in Prague, I have perused one of the most impressive displays of the creative power of language, the history of Slavic self-determination, which was supported from the beginning by linguistic incentives such as the Pentecostal miracle and the vernacularization of the Holy Communion. (My various contributions to this topic are gathered in *SW VI*/1984: *Early Slavic Paths and Crossroads.*)

I have actively looked forward to the development of semiotics, which helps to delineate the specificity of language among all the various systems of signs, as well as the invariants binding language to related sign systems (cf. *Framework* and *Lo sviluppo della semiotica,* Milan, 1978).

To conclude, I avow that binary solutions attract me and I believe in the mutual salutary influence of *linguistics and philology.* No doubt my linguistic reasonings often profited from my painstaking philological excurses, treating such intricate sources as Old Church Slavonic songs and poems, both related to and autonomous from their Byzantine models. The interplay of linguistic theory and philological art proved helpful in treating the most peculiar displays of Slavic verbal culture, such as vestiges of the earliest Russian vernacular, or the *ornatus difficilis* of the Old Russian *Igor' Tale,* or the Czech (labeled Canaan) glosses in early medieval Hebrew texts, or the Czech mock mystery of the XIVth century with its daring interlacing of sacred, secular, and lascivious motifs, or the Hanseatic manual of colloquial Russian compiled in Pskov on the threshold of the Times of Trouble.

Yet what must have primarily influenced my approach to poetics and linguistics was my proximity to the poets and painters of the avant-garde. Thus, my programmatic monograph on Khlebnikov's verbal art, written in 1919 and printed in 1921 (see *SW V*: 299–354), owes certain of its arguments to my meetings with this unparalleled poet, which began on the eve of 1914. A few weeks later, in a Moscow cafe the "Alpine Rose," I endeavored to elucidate the essentials of Khlebnikov's poetics to the unyielding Italian guest Filippo Tommaso Marinetti. I would like to add that my article "Futurism," published August 2, 1919 in the Moscow newspaper *Iskusstvo,* praised the Italian painters of that trend for their expulsion of absolutes and for dispensing once and for all with one-way static perception: the paths leading toward experimental art and toward the new science appealed to us precisely because of their common invariants.

The Dimension
of Time

Dialogue on Time in Language and Literature

Roman Jakobson and Krystyna Pomorska

KP   In one of your most recent theoretical works on the aims of the science of language among contemporary sciences—a short essay on the history of linguistics that appeared in 1972 in *Scientific American*—you referred briefly to the doctrine of the neo-grammarians, whose methodology was basically concerned only with the history of language. One of the achievements of Ferdinand de Saussure was to overcome these theories that had ruled for so long. But later, in his *Course in General Linguistics,* he in turn reduced the object of study of the system of language to only one of its aspects, namely its static synchrony. The two approaches—the historicism of the neo-grammarians and the static studies of Saussure—prove to be clearly one-sided. How can one surmount these limitations?

RH   Time as such has been and, it seems to me, remains the vital question of our period. In the Moscow journal *Iskusstvo* (Art), which came out for a few months in 1919, I wrote in an article devoted to Futurism: "The overcoming of statics, the expulsion of the absolute—here is the essential turn for the new era, the burning question of today." Our thoughts on time were directly inspired by the current discussions of the theory of relativity, with its rejection of time as an absolute and its linking of the problems of time and space. With its percussive slogans and pictorial experiments, Futurism, too, exercised an influence. "Static perception is a fiction"—this was my reaction in this same article to the traditional efforts of painting to "decompose movement into a series of separate static elements."

This chapter previously appeared in *Poetics Today,* Vol. 2, No. 1a (1980): 15–27, and as Chapter 7, "The Time Factor in Language and Literature," in Roman Jakobson and Krystyna Pomorska, *Dialogues* (Cambridge, Mass.: M.I.T. Press, 1983). Reproduced with permission of the M.I.T. Press.

Such were the preconditions of my first contact with the theory of Saussure on the antinomy between status and history, that is to say, between synchrony and diachrony. My attention was immediately drawn to the fact that synchrony, which is the ensemble of the phenomena of language existing in a community of speakers, was equated by Saussure both terminologically and theoretically to a static state, and was contrasted by him to another equivalence, that of dynamism and diachrony. In criticizing this conception, I referred, by no means accidentally, to the example of cinematographic perception. If a spectator is asked a question of synchronic order (for example, "What do you see at this instant on the movie screen?"), he will inevitably give a synchronic answer, but not a static one, for at that instant he sees horses running, a clown turning somersaults, a bandit hit by bullets. In other words, these two effective oppositions, synchrony/diachrony and static/dynamic, do not coincide in reality. Synchrony contains many a dynamic element, and it is necessary to take this into account when using a synchronic approach.

If synchrony is dynamic, then diachrony, which is the analysis and juxtaposition of different stages of a language over an extended period of time, cannot and must not be limited to the dynamics of the alterations of language alone. One must take static elements into consideration as well. The questions of what has changed and what has remained constant in the French language over its many centuries of development, or of what has not changed in the different Indo-European languages during the several thousand years of migration undergone by the Indo-European tribes since the breakup of the protolanguage, merit deep and detailed study.

It is to Saussure's great credit that he placed primary importance on the study of the system of language both as a whole and in the relation of each of its constituent parts. On the other hand, and here his theory demands significant revision, he attempted to suppress the tie between the system of a language and its modifications by considering the system as the exclusive domain of synchrony and assigning modifications to the sphere of diachrony alone. In actuality, as indicated in the different social sciences, the concepts of a system and its changes are not only compatible but indissolubly tied. The attempts to equate change with diachrony profoundly contradict our entire linguistic experience.

In a linguistic community, it is inconceivable that modifications take place overnight, all at once. The beginning and end of each change are always recognized as such during a period of coexistence in the community. The point of departure and the end point may, however, be distributed in different ways. The older form may be characteristic of an older generation and the new one of a younger, or both forms may belong from the outset to two different styles of language, different subcodes of a single common code, in which case all members of the community have the competence to perceive and choose between the two variants. In other words, I repeat that coexistence and modification not only do not exclude each other, but are instead indissolubly linked.

Inasmuch as the start and the finish of a change simultaneously belong to the common code of a system of language, one must necessarily study not only the meaning of the static constituents of the system but also the meaning of the changes which are *in statu nascendi*. Here the Saussurian idea of changes that are "blind and fortuitous" (*"aveugles et fortuits"*) from the point of view of the system loses ground. Any modification takes place first at the synchronic level and is thus a part of the system, while only the *results* of the modifications are imparted to the diachronic dimension.

Saussure's ideology ruled out any compatibility between the two aspects of time, simultaneity and succession. As a result, dynamism was excluded from the study of the system and the *signans* was reduced to pure linearity, thus precluding any possibility of viewing the phoneme as a bundle of concurrent distinctive features. Each of these mutually contradictory theses sacrificed one of the two dimensions of time, one by renouncing succession in time and the other by renouncing coexisting temporal elements. We insist on the discussion of these notorious attempts to impoverish the object of linguistic analysis, because the danger of such illegitimate reductionism has not yet been overcome.

It must be emphasized that the members of the speech community themselves contradict both of these restrictive measures by their behavior. The speech community tends to include the temporal axis among the linguistic factors which are directly perceived. For example, obsolete elements of a linguistic system are felt as archaisms and new elements as the latest in fashion. This phenomenon can be observed at the phonic, grammatical, and lexical levels of language. The temporal interpretation here should be understood as a metalinguistic fact. Convincing examples of conscious or unconscious behavior on the part of a speech community regarding distinctive features and their combination are provided by the productive processes of vowel harmony, which consists of extending the value of a feature of a given vowel to all the vowels in a word. The opposition of grave and acute vowels is treated in this way in the majority of Finno-Ugric and Turkic languages, as is the opposition of tense and lax vowels in certain African languages.

I have become increasingly convinced that a consistently synchronic conception of the process of linguistic change would permit one to avoid most of the errors and misunderstandings that arise in establishing and interpreting change in linguistic systems, especially sound systems. I became especially aware of this during the sixties when working on the apparently labyrinthine question of prosodic relations and their evolution during the period when Common Slavic was decomposing into separate historical languages. The fact of the original coexistence of various stages of development lent explanation and direction to the seeming confusion, and enabled me to sketch the phonological evolution of the relations of quantity and accent in the Slavic languages at the dawn of their existence. The cardinal questions that had been raised by such experts as Christian Stang (1900–1977) and Jerzy Kuryłowicz (1895–1978) in their work on historical Slavic accentology therefore had to be reformulated in light of these two indissolubly linked criteria, simultaneity and succession in time.

KP It is paradoxical how certain critics do not understand this new attitude towards history. In Bohemia, they accused your approach of being static in character, of giving a "purely immanent" analysis of linguistic and artistic phenomena, rather than an historical interpretation. This was, by the way, the first reproach addressed to the members of the OPOJAZ by the official literary establishment in the 1930s in the Soviet Union. It seemed to these critics that the idea of development was necessarily tied to a separation of the chain of events into "old" events, identified with movement, and current events, which for some reason were not supposed to contain any movement. By the same token they saw time as an object that could by analogy be divided into "dynamic time," that is, the past, and "static time," the present. It seems to me that this view reflects a lack of imagination about how time is experienced: for some reason the principle of a single time, constantly flowing and immutably dynamic, remained beyond the grasp of these critics. Hence we are confronted by events of the past and the present both in their totality and in their mutually determined aspect. This was pointed out by Tolstoj as the untenability of viewing "history" as consisting of facts in the flow of life that stand out because of their "dynamism" (that is, wars, the activities of "great men"), in contrast to the rest of life, "everyday life," as if no evolution occurred there. By the way, your introduction of the principle of relativity into your conception of linguistic change leads again to the idea of system in accordance with the binary principle: we cannot imagine the present without the past, nor the future without the present, etc.

The artists of the Russian avant-garde whom you were closest to — Malevič, Majakovskij, Xlebnikov, and others — were similarly fascinated by the problems of the dynamics of time. However, many of them (Majakovskij in particular) drew from the dialectics of time an absolute inference, one particularly characteristic of the avant-garde: they wanted to vanquish time, to overcome its immutable march. Like Kirillov in Dostoevskij's *The Devils*, Majakovskij believed that in the utopian future time would "fade from consciousness" and cease to be experienced by men.

From all that has been said here about the evolution of language, it is clear to what extent this set of problems served as the basis for the methodological principles of the literary studies linked to the OPOJAZ. In 1929 Tynjanov wrote an important study entitled *"O literaturnoj èvoljucii"* ("On literary evolution"), in which he proceeds from the same assumptions in order to treat the question of change in literature and its dual synchronic and diachronic aspect. His article was a continuation of your jointly written declaration *"Problemy izučenija literatury i jazyka"* ("Problems in the study of literature and language"), which was published in *Novyj Lef* (*New Left Front*) in 1928 [see below, 25–27]. How did you come to write this statement?

RJ   It is worth noting that the problem of an historical approach had attracted special interest in the science of the late 1920s. I believed it appropriate that the questions involved in the application of this method to different spheres of human activity and creation should be formulated and presented for discussion in the form of a few succinct theses. In the fall of 1927 I prepared a text on the treatment of phonological systems and their historical changes, with the intention of presenting it to the First International Congress of Linguists that was to take place in The Hague in April, 1928. After securing the written approval of my friends and close collaborators, the linguists N. S. Trubetzkoy and Sergej Josifovič Karcevskij (1884–1955), I sent my theses to the committee of the Congress. Both Trubetzkoy and I were amazed at the positive reaction of the Congress, and especially of W. Meyer-Lübke (1861–1936), the celebrated representative of the older generation of linguists who chaired the meeting that sympathetically discussed the principles we had advanced. My collaborators and I were particularly delighted that our proposals immediately brought the international avant-garde of our science together as a group outside the official meeting halls of the Congress.

It was this success that inspired the manifesto *"Problemy izučenija literatury i jazyka"* ("Problems in the study of literature and language"), which I wrote at the end of the same year in close collaboration with Jurij Tynjanov (1894–1943), who was visiting me in Prague at that time. The short article was published in *Novyj Lef* upon Tynjanov's return to Leningrad and provoked a number of reactions from members of the OPOJAZ. The commentary that accompanies the new (1977) collection of Tynjanov's articles on the history of literature gives some details of this intense discussion. However, none of these reactions was published at the time, because the independent positions of the Society became an object of official sanctions that soon led to the total suppression of this historic association.

In our manifesto we asserted that the immanent character of changes   ⌣

within literature and their close ties to the system of literary values necessarily implied a coordination between synchrony and diachrony in literature: the isolation of the notion of system from that of its transformation lost significance, since there does not and cannot exist an immobile system and, conversely, mobility inevitably presupposes system; evolution possesses a systematic character. This manifesto of ours remained sealed in silence in Russia for more than half a century. It was published only recently, in the collection of Tynjanov's writings mentioned above, long after it had been quoted often in the West, had been translated into a number of languages and had been the subject of an international debate. Our comparative study of language and of literature was important not only for insisting on the common tasks in both fields, but also for drawing attention to the correlation existing between literature (as well as language) and the different contiguous series of the cultural context. And this correlation called for a wider structural analysis, based on the new and fruitful semiotic concept of the "system of systems," in order to explain the link that united the different cultural series without appeal to the confusing idea of a mechanistic sequence of cause and effect.

It is worth mentioning that, in October 1926, shortly after the founding of the Prague Linguistic Circle, when private reflections had given way to fraternal and lively debate, I wrote a long, worried letter to Trubetzkoy asking him to react to an idea that had come to fruition in my mind, the idea that linguistic changes were systematic and goal-oriented, and that the evolution of language shares its purposefulness with the development of other sociocultural systems. Although more than fifty years have elapsed since I wrote that letter, I can still vividly remember my anxiety as I waited for the reactions of that linguist and associate whom I admired above all others.

On December 22, Trubetzkoy answered me with one of his most significant messages: "I am in perfect agreement with your general considerations. Many elements in the history of language seem fortuitous, but history does not have the right to be satisfied with this explanation. The general outlines of the history of language, when one reflects upon them with a little attention and logic, never prove to be fortuitous. Consequently, the little details cannot be fortuitous either—their sense must simply be discovered. The rational character of the evolution of language stems directly from the fact that language is a system." Trubetzkoy went on to add: "If Saussure did not dare to draw the logical conclusion from his own thesis that language is a system, this was due to a great extent to the fact that such a conclusion would have contradicted the widely accepted notion of the history of language, and of history in general. For the only accepted sense of history is the notorious one of 'progress,' that queer concept which as a consequence reduces 'sense' to 'nonsense.' " Trubetzkoy agreed that the other aspects of culture and national life also evolve according to an internal logic of their own and implement their own specific laws which have nothing in common with "progress." It is for this reason that ethnographers and anthropologists do not want to study these laws. . . . Our Formalists have finally started to study the internal laws of the history of literature, and their path will allow us to see the sense and internal logic of literary development. The evolutionary sciences have been so neglected methodologically that today the immediate task of each science is the regulation of its own methods. The moment for synthesis is not yet at hand. Nevertheless, a certain parallelism undeniably exists in the evolution of the different aspects of culture, and thus there must also exist certain laws which determine this parallelism.

KP   The commentaries that accompany the above-mentioned collection of Tynjanov's articles show the extensive reactions and passions your manifesto provoked in the ranks of the OPOJAZ at the time it was about to be dissolved. The commentators quote from the letters of one of the most active members of the OPOJAZ, Viktor Borisovič Šklovskij, in response to your call for a vital revision of the society's positions. Among those who "answered with emotion" were Boris Viktorovič Tomaševskij (1890–1957), the eminent mathematician and specialist on verse, and Sergej Ignat'evič Bernštejn (1892–1970), the phonetician and student of poetry. Also mentioned are the reactions of Boris Isakovič Jarxo (1880–1942), who carried out statistical analyses of poetry, and Boris Mixajlovič Ejxenbaum (1886–1959), the celebrated historian and theoretician of literature, as well as E. D. Polivanov, the remarkable linguist and orientalist.

You said that questions of history were of general concern at the end of the 1920s. This remark is worth developing, as it of course concerns not only scholars but also artists and writers who had very close ties to science at that time. The first example that comes to my mind is the poet Boris Pasternak. It was precisely in the second half of the twenties that he turned to questions of history, which continued to interest him for the rest of his life. Trubetzkoy's remarks on the parallelism of the evolution of the different aspects of culture can just as well be applied to Pasternak's remarkable narrative *"Vozdušnye puti"* ("Aerial Paths"), written in the middle of the 1920s. Pasternak raises the question of the immanent forces in history that are conditioned by the mutual relations between the "particular" and the "general"; he rejects the sterile schema of causal ties into which some would like to force all the phenomena of life, while life inexorably overflows this schema as it would a narrow and inadequate container. In place of a causal chain of determined states, the poet advances the rule of coincidence of circumstances and makes the historical and psychological principles overlap in their function: both equally disarm man in the face of the imposed and arbitrary schema of causality. As for the "historical" principle, Pasternak does not at all conceive of it as a progressive line, an ascending chain of causes and effects, but rather as a coincidence of circumstances that takes place outside of man, on the "aerial paths."

It would seem not to have been accidental that you wrote at almost the same time a manifesto with P. G. Bogatyrev, *"K probleme razmeževanija fol'kloristiki i literaturovedenija"* ("On the problem of delimiting the studies of folklore and literature," 1928–1929), and a manifesto with Tynjanov on the study of literature. Popular oral poetry, acting as a link in the chain connecting phenomena subject to linguistic analysis and those that belong to literary studies, came to occupy its due place in your organizational and research activity.

RJ   The presentation to the Linguistic Congress at The Hague and the articles *"Problemy izučenija literatury i jazyka"* ("Problems in the study of literature and language") and *"K probleme razmeževanija fol'kloristiki i literaturovedenija"* ("On the problem of delimiting the studies of folklore and literature") were followed by yet another declaration of principle prepared on my initiative at the end of the twenties. Bogatyrev and I wrote the last set of theses in 1929, parallel to the article *"Fol'klor kak osobaja forma tvorčestva"* ("Folklore as a special form of [artistic] creation"), and we published them in order to initiate discussion in the Polish ethnographic magazine *Lud słowiański* (*The Slavic People*) of 1931. We questioned whether the "existence of works of folklore and that of works of literature" in fact represented two distinct concepts, and we asked whether the same was not consequently true of the heritage of folklore and the heritage of literature.

We contrasted the continuity of the folklore tradition with the discontinuities within the history of the system of literary values. The common notion of "eternal fellow travellers" was replaced by the idea of constant encounters and partings. The evolution of artistic tastes always resuscitates forgotten authors, who then become participants in the system of literary values of the given period along with its own poets and writers. This implied both a conception of time as discontinuous and the backwards march of time, which allows for a return to the classics or even for including in the modern repertory certain artistic values that originally went unrecognized; in short, their posthumous rehabilitation and revival. This entire set of literary problems sheds light on the character of the time axis in the development of language, in particular the written language, which permits the absorption and restoration of ancient canons, and oral language, which made possible the renewed study and rehabilitation of older words.

KP   When you examine your own ideas on folklore and literature from the perspective of the years that have elapsed, you assign great importance to the question of values. One could even say that you have effected a certain reorientation by transposing (in a perfectly consistent manner, by the way) the idea of evolution into the idea of value. At the same time, Trubetzkoy also was concerned with analogous issues. In his collection of articles, *O russkom samopoznanii* (*On Russian Self-Awareness*), he attempted to define the social mechanism involved in the elaboration and exchange of values. Russian society before the Revolution consisted of two main strata, the upper and the lower. The role of determining and consolidating the hierarchy of values fell to the upper class; the lower class simply accepted it. There existed a certain flow of these concepts of value between the upper and the lower stratum: a value which today is appreciated in the upper class will pass tomorrow into the lower class, later to return to the higher spheres duly transformed. Your declarations no doubt touch upon this transfer of values. The social mechanism for their elaboration as proposed by Trubetzkoy has clearly been superseded: there cannot be found today in either the East or the West a social structure that would lead to this form of creation of values and to such a mechanism for their movement. The situation is somewhat different and more complex, but the principle of such a mechanism can still be of some use when applied to a new order of things.

When the issue of the successive stages of literature and returns to earlier stages (that is, temporary returns to the artistic values of another period) is raised, there reappears the question of the coexistence of linguistic phenomena from different stages in the history of a language, a question that was posed in relation to Saussure's theories as well. The time factor seems to take a remarkable number of forms in language. Couldn't one say that the essential creative force of language is manifest in precisely this diversity? As I recall, you emphasized more than once in your lectures that the essential power of language, and consequently the privilege of the speaker, lies in the fact that language is capable of transporting us across both time and space.

RJ   It would be difficult to find a domain in which the concepts of coexistence and succession are as intertwined as they are in the life of language and literature. A few clear examples will suffice. One of them refers to the perception of spoken language. Speech is transmitted at a rapid rate and demands that the auditor grasp a considerable part, if not all, of the elements that are needed for comprehension of the utterance. The listener becomes conscious of the words after the units of which they are composed have already been pronounced, and he understands the sentences after the words of which they are composed have already been uttered. In order for the utterance to be understood, attention to the flow of speech must be combined with moments of "simultaneous synthesis," as they were called a hundred years ago by the Russian neurologist and psychologist I. M. Sečenov (1829–1905) in his *Èlementy mysli* (*Elements of Thought*). This is the process of unifying the elements that have already disappeared from immediate perception with those that already belong to memory. These elements are then combined into larger groupings: sounds into words, words into sentences, and sentences into utterances.

I would say that the role of short- and long-term memory constitutes one of the central problems of both general linguistics and the psychology of language, and much in this domain should be reconsidered and thought through more carefully, taking into account the entire range of consequences.

In one of his last novels, the poet Aragon quite appropriately mentioned the idea put forward by a few isolated linguists of the last century concerning the intermittence of recollecting and forgetting in the development of language, and the historical role of oblivion which is compensated for by verbal creativeness.

Over the centuries, the science of language has more than once addressed the question of ellipsis which manifests itself at different verbal levels: sounds, syntax, and narration. One must admit that for the most part these questions, too, have been elaborated only episodically and fragmentarily. A technique which today receives even less consideration is that of elliptical perception, by which the listener fills in (again on all linguistic levels) whatever has been omitted by him as listener. We have also failed to appreciate properly the subjectivism of the hearer, who fills in the elliptic gaps creatively. Here lies the heart of the issue of disambiguation, which has been the object of considerable debate for the past few years within the science of language.

From this angle one of the essential differences between spoken and written language can be seen clearly. The former has a purely temporal character, whereas the latter connects time and space. While the sounds that we hear disappear, when we read we usually have immobile letters before us and the time of the written flow of words is reversible: we can read and re-read, and, what is more, we can be ahead of an event. Anticipation, which is subjective in the listener, becomes objective in the reader, who can read the end of a letter or novel before reading the earlier parts.

We have dwelt on the question of the mutual relation between phonemes and their constituent elements, that is, distinctive features, and this relation is essential for the comprehension of the *signans*. Phonemes as a kind of phonic chord (that is, bundles of concurrent distinctive features) have analogs on the plane of the *signatum*. These are bundles of simultaneous grammatical meanings ("cumulations of signata," as they were called by Charles Bally, Saussure's disciple and successor at Geneva). To give an elementary example: the desinence -o of the Latin *amo* simultaneously designates the person of the verb, its number, and its tense. The transmission of such bundles of concurrent semantic elements by means of a single segment within the flow of discourse is a characteristic of the grammatical systems of the so-called synthetic languages. On the other hand, the agglutinative systems (for example, the Turkic languages) furnish each suffix with a single grammatical signification, and accordingly transform these factually coexisting meanings into a temporal succession of suffixes, each with its own value. The capacity of two competing and essentially contrary factors, namely simultaneous co-occurrence on the one hand and temporal succession on the other, accounts for what is perhaps the most typical manifestation of the idea of time in the structure and the life of language.

A variety of conflicts arises between the two aspects of time. There is on the one hand the time of the speech event and on the other hand the time of the narrated event. The clash of these two facets is particularly evident in verbal art. Since discourse, and especially artistic discourse, is deployed in time, doubts have been expressed more than once over the centuries as to whether it is possible to overcome in verbal art this fact of the uninterrupted temporal flow, which opposes poetry to the stasis of painting. The question was also raised of whether painting is capable of showing movement and poetry—static description. Can one transmit through the means afforded to us by the flow of speech the image of a knight in armor sitting on his horse, or do the laws of language require that such a scene be presented as a narrative about the process of dressing the knight and saddling the horse? This was the argument of the German author Gotthold Ephraim Lessing (1729–1781), who proposed to replace, in poetic description, coexistence in space with succession in time. Lessing's younger fellow writer, Johann Gottfried Herder (1744–1803), answered with a defense of simultaneous phenomena that permit poetry to overcome the linear succession of the events it renders.

Tadeusz Zieliński (1859–1944), the Polish classical philologist, has shown that the impossibility of reconciling in language the constant progress of the narrative with the fact that a number of actions occur in different places at the same time was already realized in the epic tradition of the *Iliad*. In that work, the action of a given person necessarily entails the simultaneous disappearance and passive inaction of all the other personages. By contrast, other poetic approaches make it possible to render several simultaneous actions dispersed in space. The time in a narrative can be reversed. The story may have recourse to retrospective reminiscences, or may simply start with the dénouement and then go back in time. Moreover, the narrator may directly attribute an inverse order of events to the fictional reality itself, as did the great Russian poet of our century, Velimir Xlebnikov. In a Xlebnikov tale the two heroes pass from the ends of their lives to the beginnings but continue to speak of the past and future in the normal and uninverted order of these times.

Finally, in the Easter play of the Middle Ages, which combines the mystery of the saints with a conventional farce of grotesque figures, the characters experience simultaneous existence in two temporal sets. On the one hand they participate in the unfolding of the events of the gospel story that preceded the Resurrection of Christ, while on the other hand they anticipate with pleasure the annual Easter meal. Thus the events of the gospel story appear simultaneously as facts of the distant past and as phenomena that are repeated every year. In short, narrative, especially poetic, time can be unilinear as well as multilinear, direct as well as reversed, continuous as well as discontinuous; it can even be a combination of rectilinearity and circularity, as in the last example. I believe that it would be difficult to find another domain, except perhaps for music, where time is experienced with compatible acuity.

I am convinced that the most effective experience of verbal time occurs in verse, and this holds just as true for oral, folkloric verse as it does for written, literary verse. Verse, whether rigorously metrical or free, simultaneously carries within it both linguistic varieties of time: the time of the speech event and that of the narrated event. Verse pertains to our immediate experience of speech activity, both motor and auditory. At the same time, we experience the structure of the verse in close connection with the semantics of the poetic text—regardless of whether there is harmony or conflict between the structure of the verse and the semantics of the text—and in this way the verse becomes an integral part of the developing plot. It is difficult even to imagine a sensation of the temporal flow that would be simpler and at the same time more complex, more concrete and yet more abstract.

KP   The feelings of the great poets of the beginning of our century towards the time factor are very characteristic. Blok and Majakovskij, otherwise so different, both considered the element of time as the determining principle in the creative act of making poetry. For them, rhythm was primordial and the word secondary. In Majakovskij's well-known pamphlet, *Kak delat' stixi* (*How to Make Verse*), the author described the beginnings of his work on any new poem:

> I walk along gesticulating and muttering—there are almost no words yet—I slow my pace in order not to impede this muttering, or else I mutter more quickly, in the rhythm of my steps. In this way the rhythm is planed down and takes shape. It is the basis of any poetry and passes through it like a din. Gradually one is able to make out single words in this din. Where this fundamental rhythm-din comes from remains unknown. For me it is every repetition within myself of a sound, a noise, a rocking . . . or any repetition of any phenomenon, which I mark with sounds.

In his article *"Poèzija zagovorov i zaklinanij"* ("The poetry of charms and incantations"), Blok speaks in his turn of the way in which the creative force of rhythm "carries the word on the crest of a musical wave," and how "the rhythmic word is sharpened like an arrow that flies directly toward its goal."

RJ   As the etymology of the Latin term *versus* itself suggests, verse contains the idea of a regular recurrence, in contradistinction to prose, the etymology of whose Latin term *prosa* (*provorsa*) suggests a movement directed forward. Verse involves the immediate sensation of present time as well as a backward glance at the impulse of the preceding verses and a vivid anticipation of the verses to follow. These three conjoined impressions form the active interplay of the invariant and the variations. They suggest to the author, to the reader, to the person reciting the lines, and to the listener the constancy of the verse measure, elaborated upon and enhanced by displacements and deviations.

The child's experience of time takes form in close contact with the development of language. Students of language acquisition by children have only recently noticed that the child often remembers an earlier stage in his progressive mastery of language. A child enjoys talking about language. Metalinguistic operations are an essential instrument in his linguistic development. He recalls the past in this way: "When I was small, I talked like that, and now I speak differently, like this." He also sometimes begins to speak in the manner of a baby, either as a game or in order to solicit more tenderness or affection from adults. The phenomena that the Danish linguist Otto Jespersen (1860–1943), in his penetrating analyses of language, called "shifters" play a tremendous role in the acquisition of language by the child.

The concept of the shifter has seemed to me for some time to be one of the cornerstones of linguistics, although it has not been sufficiently appreciated in the past and therefore demands more attentive elaboration. The general meaning of the grammatical form called "shifter" is characterized by a reference to the given speech act in which the form appears. Thus the past tense is a shifter because it literally designates an event that precedes the given act of speech. The first-person form of a verb, or the first-person pronoun, is a shifter because the basic meaning of the first person involves a reference to the author of the given act of speech. Similarly, the second-person pronoun contains a reference to the addressee to whom the speech act in question is directed. If the addressers and addressees change in the course of the conversation, then the material content of the form *I* and *you* also changes. They shift. The desirability of including grammatical tense in linguistic usage occurs in a fairly early stage in the child's acquisition of language, at the moment when the beginner ceases to be satisfied with a direct verbal reaction to what happens in front of him at a given moment.

At this point, the sentence with subject and predicate first arises in his language. This allows him to attribute different predicates to a subject and to apply any predicate to different subjects. This innovation frees the child, liberating him from the *hic et nunc,* the immediate temporal and spatial circumstances. From this moment on, he can speak of events that take place at a distance from him in time and space. Along with shifts of temporal and spatial points of reference, he acquires the idea of the shifting roles of the participants in the speech events. The notion of time appears in the language of the child, as does that of spatial proximity or distance: *I* and *you, here* and *there, mine* and *yours, now* and *then.*

KP   It follows from what you have said that any verbal act, any phenomenon of language from phonemes to literary works, necessarily enters into a dual temporal frame: linear succession and strict simultaneity. It is here that the force as well as the relative limits of language as a means of expression reside, as noted in the dispute mentioned between Lessing and Herder.

It seems to me that the effort either to overcome these restrictions or, conversely, to utilize this frame for novel effects, determines to an important extent the development of any new form of art. The cinema, one of the most contemporary forms of art, tries most graphically to combine the simultaneous and the linear, and this is all the more striking since the cinema combines both the word and the visual image. A daring attempt in this direction is Alain Resnais's film *Last Year at Marienbad,* in which the frames of the past action "straddle" those of the present in the purely technical and cinematographic sense of the term. In this way a unity of the two components of the sign, its signifying (*signans*) and its signified (*signatum*) aspects, is created. The story is constructed around the constant interweaving of the past and the present as perceived by the heroes. One can find an analogous phenomenon among certain sculptors of today who attempt to overcome the statics of matter itself by using sculptural means to construct a set of narrative symbols that render the flow of time.

Problems in the Study of Language and Literature

Roman Jakobson and Jurij Tynjanov

1.   The immediate problems facing Russian literary and linguistic science demand a precise theoretical platform. They require a firm dissociation from the increasing mechanistic tendency to paste together mechanically the new methodology and old obsolete methods; they necessitate a determined refusal of the contraband offer of naive psychologism and other methodological hand-me-downs in the guise of new terminology.

Furthermore, academic eclecticism and pedantic "formalism" — which replaces analysis by terminology and the classification of phenomena — and the repeated attempts to shift literary and linguistic studies from a systematic science to episodic and anecdotal genres should be rejected.

2.   The history of literature (art), being simultaneous with other historical series, is characterized, as is each of these series, by a complex network of specific structural laws. Without an elucidation of these laws, it is impossible to establish in a scientific manner the correlation between the literary series and other historical series.

3.   The evolution of literature cannot be understood until the evolutionary problem ceases to be obscured by questions about episodic, nonsystemic genesis, whether literary (for example, so-called "literary influences") or extraliterary. The literary and extraliterary material used in literature may be introduced into the orbit of scientific investigation only when it is considered from a functional point of view.

4.   The sharp opposition of synchronic (static) and diachronic cross sections has recently become a fruitful working hypothesis, both for linguistics and for

This chapter was written in Russian during Jurij Tynjanov's visit to Prague in the winter of 1928 (see R. Jakobson, *SW V*, pp. 560ff.). The present English translation by H. Eagle was first published in L. Matejka and K. Pomorska, eds., *Readings in Russian Poetics: Formalist and Structuralist Views* (Cambridge, Mass.: MIT Press, 1971), 79–81, and reprinted in *Poetics Today*, Vol. 2, No. 1a (1980): 29–31, and in Roman Jakobson, *Selected Writings III: Poetry of Grammar and Grammar of Poetry* (The Hague-Paris-New York: Mouton, 1981), 3–6.

history of literature, inasmuch as it has demonstrated that language, as well as literature, has a systemic character at each individual moment of its existence. At the present time, the achievements of the synchronic concept force us to reconsider the principles of diachrony as well. The idea of a mechanical agglomeration of material, having been replaced by the concept of a system or structure in the realm of synchronic study, underwent a corresponding replacement in the realm of diachronic study as well. The history of a system is in turn a system. Pure synchronism now proves to be an illusion: every synchronic system has its past and its future as inseparable structural elements of the system: (*a*) archaism as a fact of style; the linguistic and literary background recognized as the rejected old-fashioned style; (*b*) the tendency toward innovation in language and literature recognized as a renewal of the system.

The opposition between synchrony and diachrony was an opposition between the concept of system and the concept of evolution; thus it loses its importance in principle as soon as we recognize that every system necessarily exists as an evolution, whereas, on the other hand, evolution is inescapably of a systemic nature.

5.   The concept of a synchronic literary system does not coincide with the naively envisaged concept of a chronological epoch, since the former embraces not only works of art which are close to each other in time but also works which are drawn into the orbit of the system from foreign literatures or previous epochs. An indifferent cataloguing of coexisting phenomena is not sufficient; what is important is their hierarchical significance for the given epoch.

6.   The assertion of two differing concepts — *la langue* and *la parole* — and the analysis of the relationship between them (the Geneva school) has been exceedingly fruitful for linguistic science. The principles involved in relating these two categories (i.e., the existing norm and individual utterances) as applied to literature must be elaborated. In this latter case, the individual utterance cannot be considered without reference to the existing complex of norms. (The investigator, in isolating the former from the latter, inescapably deforms the system of artistic values under consideration, thus losing the possibility of establishing its immanent laws.)

7.   An analysis of the structural laws of language and literature and their evolution inevitably leads to the establishment of a limited series of actually existing structural types (and, correspondingly, of types of structural evolution).

8.   A disclosure of the immanent laws of the history of literature (and language) allows us to determine the character of each specific change in literary (and linguistic) systems. However, these laws do not allow us to explain the tempo of evolution or the chosen path of evolution when several theoretically possible evolutionary paths are given. This is owing to the fact that the immanent laws of literary (and, correspondingly, linguistic) evolution form an indeterminate equation; although they admit only a limited number of possible solutions, they do not necessarily specify a unique solution. The question of a specific choice

of path, or at least of the dominant, can be solved only through an analysis of the correlation between the literary series and other historical series. This correlation (a system of systems) has its own structural laws, which must be submitted to investigation. It would be methodologically fatal to consider the correlation of systems without taking into account the immanent laws of each system.

Sign and System of Language

A Reassessment of Saussure's Doctrine

Roman Jakobson

It is remarkable that Saussure's *Cours de linguistique générale* was frequently mentioned in this symposium, as if one wished to establish what has changed in the basic assumptions of general linguistics over the fifty years which separate us from the lectures of the Genevan master. For the theory of language and for linguistics as a whole it was indeed half a century of cardinal transformations. It seems to me that our fruitful discussion conveys a clear notion as to what in this famous heritage requires far-reaching revisions, and which parts of Saussure's teaching—in the version edited by his pupils—remain valid to this day.

Of the two basic principles of the *Cours,* "les deux principes généraux," as Saussure labeled them, one may see today the first basic proposition —*l'arbitraire du signe,* the "arbitrariness" of the sign—as an arbitrary principle. As Benveniste has shown beautifully in *Acta Linguistica I,* from the synchronic point of view of a language community using linguistic signs, one must not ascribe to them an arbitrary nature. It is not at all arbitrary but rather obligatory to say *fromage* for "cheese" in French, and to say *cheese* in English. I believe that one may conclude from the whole discussion on "arbitrariness" and "unmotivated" signs that *l'arbitraire* was a most unfortunate choice of a term. This question was dealt with much better by the Polish linguist M. Kruszewski, a contemporary of Saussure (and highly estimated by the latter), as early as the beginning of the 1880s. Kruszewski made a distinction between two basic factors in the life of a language, two associations: similarity and contiguity. The relation between a *signans* and a *signatum,* which Saussure arbitrarily described as arbitrary, is in reality a habitual, learned contiguity, which is obligatory for all members of a given language community. But along with this contiguity the principle of similarity, *la ressemblance,* asserts itself. As was mentioned here,

This lecture was given in Erfurt, East Germany, 2 Oct. 1959, at the 1st International Symposium "Sign and System of Language," and published in German in Roman Jakobson, *Selected Writings II: Word and Language* (The Hague: Mouton, 1971), 272–279. The translation by B. Hrushovski previously appeared in *Poetics Today,* Vol. 2, No. 1a (1980): 33–38.

and as Kruszewski already realized, this principle plays an enormous role in the area of derivations and in the area of word families, where similarity between words of one root is decisive, and where it becomes impossible to speak about arbitrariness. In morphophonological issues, the question of similar structures is of primary importance when we recognize that there exist certain models, certain structural types of the distribution and selection of phonemes in roots, and other types of prefixes or suffixes of derivation and conjugation. Finally, the issue of sound symbolism, on which I shall not further dwell here, remains, in spite of all skepticism voiced in the past, an important and fascinating problem in the study of language. And so are all questions concerning the foundation of language symbols in image and indication (or, as Charles Sanders Peirce, the pioneer of the theory of signs, would have said: the problem of *iconic* or *indexical* symbols).

It seems to me that the second principle in Saussure's *Cours,* the so-called *linéarité,* must also be seen as a dangerous simplification. Actually, we encounter two-dimensional units not only on the level of the *signatum,* as demonstrated by Ch. Bally, but also in the field of the *signans.* If we recognize that the phoneme is not the ultimate unit of language, but can be decomposed into distinctive features, then it becomes self-evident that we may speak in phonology too about two dimensions (as we have chords in music), the dimensions of successivity and of simultaneity. This, however, must lead to abandoning a number of Saussure's theses on basic laws of language structure. Thus, I believe that the term "syntagmatic" is often misleading, since when referring to syntagmatic relations we think of successivity in time; however, besides the combination in temporal succession, we must deal also with combination of simultaneous features. It would be advisable in this respect to speak simply about combination, seen as contrasted to another factor, namely, selection. Selection of units or of their combinations, in contrast to combination per se, belongs to the paradigmatic level of language. It is substitution, as distinguished from both simultaneity and successivity. In selection, the principle of equivalence, or association by similarity, asserts itself. While observing the paradigmatic axis rather than successivity and simultaneity, I do not believe that we abandon the domain of the objective and plunge into subjectivity. Linguistic studies of recent years have shown that in this area an objective stratification, a hierarchy of components, exists. One encounters here the problem of predictability, the problem of primary and secondary functions, which was outlined brilliantly by Kuryłowicz in the thirties and which has been recently developed in America in the theory of syntactical transformations — one of the most topical problems of linguistic analysis. At the same time, the even more important and indispensable question arises, as to the relationship and the difference between paradigmatic series and combinational series (chains or clusters).

We deal here, apparently, as in all modern sciences, with the significant idea of invariance. We speak about combinational, context-dependent variants on the level of sound as well as on the level of grammar. But it would be impossible to speak about variants as long as we have not clarified the nature of the basic invariant, the unit to which all these variants are related. The search for the invariants is now the most substantial problem not only in phonology, but in grammar as well. When dealing with the sign, the bilateral *signum* as a link between the *signans* and *signatum,* how do we discover such invariants on the one hand in the domain of the *signans* and on the other hand in the field of the *signatum?* The basic difference between the two, from a linguistic point of view, is that the *signans must necessarily be perceptible whereas the signatum is translatable.* In both cases the principle of equivalence obtains. In the domain of the *signans* the relative equivalence must be externally perceivable; it can be ascertained, however, only in respect to the function of these sound relations in a given language. We recognize such distinctive features and, by means of a spectrograph, we are able to translate them from the acoustic field into the visual level. And like the *signans*, the *signatum* too must be studied in a purely linguistic and objective manner. A purely linguistic semantics can and must be constructed, if we agree with Peirce that the basic property of any verbal sign lies in its capability of being translated into another verbal sign, either a more developed, explicit sign, or, on the contrary, a more elliptical sign, of the same language system or of a different one. This translatability lays bare that semantic invariant for which we are searching in the *signatum.* In such a way it becomes possible to submit semantic problems of language to distributional analysis. Metalinguistic identifying sentences, such as "A rooster is a male hen" belong to the text inventory of the English language community; the reversibility of both expressions—"A male hen is a rooster"—demonstrates how the meaning of words becomes a real linguistic problem through a distributive analysis of such common metalingual utterances.

Among the basic features of the *Cours de linguistique générale* is the split nature of linguistics: the separation of synchrony from diachrony. The thorough work done over several decades in both partial areas, as well as the refined methodology developed in this research, brought about a serious danger of a flagrant gap between these two descriptions, and also the necessity of overcoming this gap. Saussure's identification of the contrast between synchrony and diachrony with the contrast between statics and dynamics turned out to be misleading. In actual reality synchrony is not at all static; changes are always emerging and are a part of synchrony. Actual synchrony is dynamic. Static synchrony is an abstraction, which may be useful to the investigation of language for specific purposes; however, an exhaustive true-to-the-facts synchronic description of language must consistently consider the dynamics of language. Both elements, the point of origin and the final phase of any change, exist for some time simultaneously within one language community. They coexist as stylistic variants. When taking this important fact into consideration, we realize that the image of language as a uniform and monolithic system is oversimplified. *Language is a system of systems, an overall code which includes various subcodes.* These variegated language styles do not make an accidental, mechanical aggregation, but rather a rule-governed hierarchy of subcodes.

Though we can tell which of the subcodes is the basic code, it is nevertheless a dangerous simplification to exclude the discussion of the other subcodes. If we consider *langue* as the totality of the conventions of a language, then we must be very careful not to be researching fictions.

I believe that *today our chief task should be to become realists, to build a realistic study of language and combat any fictionalism in linguistics.* We must ask ourselves: what is the real linguistic convention that enables exchange of speech in a given language community and serves effectively the various tasks of communication? Some linguists ask: why should linguistics differ from physics in its methodology? Why could not the scholar of language impose his own system of symbols, his creative model, upon the investigated material, as is common in the natural sciences? Indeed, one observes, in many respects, an ever more meaningful and fruitful contact between the natural sciences and linguistics; nevertheless one must keep in mind the specific differences as well. *In the London school of mathematical information theory the cardinal difference was clearly recognized and the problem of communication was separated from other aspects of information.* First of all, one must distinguish between two classes of signs—indices and symbols, as Peirce called them. Indices, which the physicist extracts from the external world, are not reversible. He transforms these indices given in nature into his own system of scientific symbols. In the science of language the situation is cardinally different. The symbols exist immediately in language. Instead of the scientist, who extracts certain indices from the external world and reshapes them into symbols, here an exhange of symbols occurs between the participants of a communication. Here the roles of addresser and addressee are interchangeable. Hence the task of the science of language is quite different. We are simply trying to translate into metalanguage this code, which is objectively given in the language community. For the natural scientist symbols are a scientific tool, whereas for the linguist they are more than that, and above all, the true object of his research. The physicist Niels Bohr understood perspicaciously this natural realism of the linguist's position.

Having mentioned Niels Bohr, I would like to recall his methodological dictum essential both for physics and linguistics, namely that, when an observation is made, it is imperative to determine exactly the relation between the observer and the observed thing. A description that does not comply with this requirement is imprecise from the point of view of today's physics, as it is from that of today's linguistics. It is our task to clarify the various positions of scholars vis-à-vis language. The so-called crypto-analytical position is the point of view of an observer who does not know the language code, and who could be compared to a military crypto-analyst, attempting to decipher an enemy's encoded message. He tries to break the foreign code through a careful analysis of the text. In the study of unknown languages such devices may obviously bring fruitful results. This, however, is merely the first stage of research, and it is by no means the only, but rather one of many methodologies, a first approximation. Then the observer attempts to reach the second, more advanced stage, the stage of a pseudo-participant in the given language community. He no longer moves from the text to the code, but rather absorbs the code and tries to use the code for a better understanding of the message.

Such is the essential assumption of descriptive linguistics. But here a difference emerges, which is rarely considered. We must not hypostatize the code, but rather envisage it from the point of view of the speech exchange. *One must distinguish sharply between two positions, that of the encoder and the decoder, in other words, between the role of the addresser and that of the addressee.* This seems to be a banality, but indeed, banalities are most often disregarded. The whole mode of observing a message is cardinally different for the two participants in a speech event. The hearer is led through the distinctive features, through the phonemes he recognizes, to the grammatical form and to understanding the meanings. In this process the probability factor plays an enormous role. The probabilities of the transition help one to perceive a text, its phonology and then its grammar; after certain units other units follow, endowed with higher or lower probabilities, and many are excluded a priori. The perceiver is endowed with a subliminal statistical set; homonymy is for him an essential process. On the other hand, for the speaker, the order of the language stages is reversed. His road leads from the sentence through the hierarchy of immediate constituents, and finally through the morphological units to the phonic form in which they are manifested. Both orders occur equally in language exchange; their mutual relations lie, as Bohr would have said, in the principle of complementarity. Both language aspects exist for the encoder as well as for the decoder, but the direction that is primary for one becomes secondary for the other. For the speaker qua speaker no homonymy exists. For example, when he pronounces in English /sʌn/ he knows precisely whether he meant a son or a sun; whereas the hearer must use a different method of probability in order to solve this question. Both attitudes, production and perception, have equal claims to be described by the linguist. It would be a mistake to reduce this two-sided language reality to merely one side. Both methods of description participate and have equal rights. Using only one of the two without keeping in mind whether one represents the position of the speaker or the hearer is like playing the role of Jourdain, who spoke prose without having known that it was prose. The real danger arises when one makes compromises between both positions, contradictory to the rules of each side. For example, if a linguist selects encoding as the point of departure of his language description and analysis, and hence forgoes the use of statistics and probability theory, proceeds with a grammatical analysis of immediate constituents, and observes the primacy of morphology over phonology, then he cannot—if he follows a logical direction—exclude meaning. Meaning can be excluded only when one works from the position of the decoder, since for him meaning emerges only as a conclusion, whereas for the speaker meaning is primary. The speaker proceeds *de verbo ad vocem,* whereas the hearer proceeds in the opposite direction, as Saint Augustine had already stressed in his deliberations on the theory of language.

Many things will become clearer in linguistic descriptions and in the theory of language when a clear demarcation is undertaken and the proper attention paid to the different modes of observation of the encoder and decoder. The modes of observation, however, are not exhausted by those two kinds. One should also take into account the considerable process of "recoding": in this case one language is interpreted in the light of another language, or one style of speech in the light of another one; one code or subcode is translated into another code or subcode. This is a most illuminating problem, since translation is one of the most essential and increasingly important linguistic activities, and the methodology of translation, as well as the consistent analysis of translation, have their place on the agenda of contemporary pure and applied linguistics.

Poetry of Grammar and Grammar of Poetry

Poetry of Grammar and Grammar of Poetry

Roman Jakobson

According to Edward Sapir, the juxtaposition of such sequences as *the farmer kills the duckling* and *the man takes the chick* makes us "feel instinctively, without the slightest attempt at conscious analysis, that the two sentences fit precisely the same pattern, that they are really the same fundamental sentence, differing only in their material trappings. In other words, they express identical relational concepts in an identical manner."[1] Conversely, we may modify the sentence or its single words "in some purely relational, nonmaterial regard"[2] without altering any of the material concepts expressed. When assigning to certain terms of the sentence a different position in its syntactic pattern and replacing, for instance, the word order '*A* kills *B*' by the inverse sequence '*B* kills *A*', we do not vary the material concepts involved but uniquely their mutual relationship. Likewise a substitution of *farmers* for *farmer* or *killed* for *kills* alters only the relational concepts of the sentence, while there are no changes in the "concrete wherewithal of speech"; its "material trappings" remain invariable.

Despite some borderline, transitional formations, there is in language a definite, clear-cut discrimination between these two classes of expressed concepts—material and relational—or, in more technical terms, between the lexical and grammatical aspects of language. The linguist must faithfully follow this objective structural dichotomy and thoroughly translate the grammatical concepts actually present in a given language into his technical metalanguage, without any imposition of arbitrary or outlandish categories upon the language observed. The categories described are intrinsic constituents of the verbal code, manipulated by language users, and not at all "grammarian's conveniences," as

This chapter is the author's English version of a paper presented in Russian at the First International Conference of Poetics in Warsaw, 1960, and revised for the volume of *Lingua* (XXI, 1968) in honor of A. Reichling.
[1] E. Sapir, *Language* (New York, 1921), p. 89.
[2] *Ibid*, p. 89.

even such attentive inquirers into poets' grammar as, e.g., Donald Davie were inclined to believe.[3]

A difference in grammatical concepts does not necessarily represent a difference in the state of affairs referred to. If one witness asserts that "the farmer killed the duckling," while the other affirms that "the duckling was killed by the farmer," the two men cannot be accused of presenting discrepant testimonies, in spite of the polar difference between the grammatical concepts expressed by active and passive constructions. One and the same state of affairs is presented by the sentences: *A lie* (or *lying* or *to lie*) *is a sin* (or *is sinful*), *To lie is to sin, Liars sin* (or *are sinful* or *are sinners*), or with a generalizing singular *The liar sins* (or *is sinful, is a sinner*). Only the way of presentation differs. Fundamentally the same equational proposition may be expressed in terms of actors (*liars, sinners*) or actions (*to lie, to sin*) and we may present these actions "as if" abstracted (*lying*) and reified (*lie, sin*) or ascribe them to the subject as its properties (*sinful*). The part of speech is one of the grammatical categories which reflect, according to Sapir's manual, "not so much our intuitive analysis of reality as our ability to compose that reality into a variety of formal patterns."[4] Later, in his preliminary notes to the planned *Foundations of Language,* Sapir outlined the fundamental types of referents which serve as "a natural basis for parts of speech," namely *existents* and their linguistic expression, the *noun; occurrents* expressed by the *verb;* and finally *modes of existence and occurrence* represented in language by the *adjective* and the *adverb* respectively.[5]

Jeremy Bentham, who was perhaps the first to disclose the manifold "linguistic fictions" which underlie the grammatical structure and which are used throughout the whole field of language as a "necessary resource," arrived in his *Theory of Fictions* at a challenging conclusion: "To language, then—to language alone—it is that fictitious entities owe their existence; their impossible, yet indispensable existence."[6] Linguistic fictions should neither be "mistaken for realities" nor be ascribed to the creative fancy of linguists: they "owe their existence" actually "to language alone" and particularly to the "grammatical form of the discourse," in Bentham's terms.[7]

The indispensable, mandatory role played by the grammatical concepts confronts us with the intricate problem of the relationship between referential, cognitive value and linguistic fiction. Is the significance of grammatical concepts really questionable or are perhaps some subliminal verisimilar

[3] Cf. D. Davie, *Articulate Energy: An Inquiry into the Syntax of English Poetry* (London, 1955), p. 144.
[4] E. Sapir, *op. cit.,* p. 125.
[5] Cf. E. Sapir, *Totality* (= *Language Monographs,* No. 6, Linguistic Society of America. Baltimore, 1930), p. 3.
[6] J. Bentham, *Theory of Fictions,* ed. and introduced by C. K. Ogden (London, 1932), pp. 73, 15.
[7] *Ibid.,* pp. 38, 15, 12.

assumptions attached to them? How far can scientific thought overcome the pressure of grammatical patterns? Whatever the solution of these still controversial questions is, certainly there is one domain of verbal activities where "the classificatory rules of the game"[8] acquire their highest significance; *in fiction,* in verbal art, *linguistic fictions* are fully realized. It is quite evident that grammatical concepts—or in Fortunatov's pointed nomenclature, "formal meanings"[9]—find their widest applications in poetry as the most formalized manifestation of language. There, where the poetic function dominates over the strictly cognitive function, the latter is more or less dimmed, or as Sir Philip Sidney declared in his *Defence of Poesie,* "Now for the Poet, he nothing affirmeth, and therefore never lieth." Consequently, in Bentham's succinct formulation, "the Fictions of the poet are pure of unsincerity."[10]

When in the finale of Majakovskij's poem *Xorošo* we read—*"i žizn'/ xorošá,//i žit'/ xorošó//"* (literally "both life is good, and it is good to live')—one will hardly look for a cognitive difference between these two coordinate clauses, but in poetic mythology the linguistic fiction of the substantivized and hence hypostatized process grows into a metonymic image of life as such, taken by itself and substituted for living people, *abstractum pro concreto,* as Galfredus de Vino Salvo, the cunning English scholar of the early thirteenth century, explains in his *Poetria nova.*[11] In contradistinction to the first clause with its predicative adjective of the same personifiable, feminine gender as the subject, the second clause with its imperfective infinitive and with a neuter, subjectless form of the predicate, represents a pure process without any limitation or transposition and with an open place for the dative of agent.

The recurrent "figure of grammar" which along with the "figure of sound" Gerard Manley Hopkins[12] saw to be the constitutive principle of verse, is particularly palpable in those poetic forms where contiguous metrical units are more or less consistently combined through grammatical parallelism into pairs or, optionally, triplets. Sapir's definition quoted above is perfectly applicable to such neighbor sequences: "they are really the same fundamental sentence, differing only in their material trappings."

There are several tentative outlines devoted to different specimens of such canonical or nearly canonical parallelism, labeled carmen style by J. Gonda in his monograph,[13] full of interesting remarks about "balanced binary word groups" in the Veda and also in the Nias ballads and priestly litanies. Particular attention has been paid by scholars to the biblical *parallelismus membrorum* rooted in an archaic Canaanite tradition and to the pervasive, continuous role of parallelism in Chinese verse and poetic prose. A similar pattern proves to

---

[8] E. Sapir, *Language,* p. 104.
[9] F. Fortunatov, *Izbrannye trudy* (Moscow, 1956), I, p. 124.
[10] J. Bentham, *op. cit.,* p. 18.
[11] See E. Faral, *Les arts poétiques du XIIe et XIIIe siècle* (Paris, 1958), pp. 195, 227.
[12] G. M. Hopkins, *Journals and Papers,* ed. by H. House (London, 1959), p. 289.
[13] J. Gonda, *Stylistic Repetition in the Veda* (Amsterdam, 1959).

underlie the oral poetry of Finno-Ugric, Turkic, and Mongolian peoples. The same devices play a cardinal role in Russian folk songs and recitatives;[14] cf., e.g., this typical preamble of Russian heroic epics (*byliny*):

Kak vo stól'nom górode vo Kíeve,	How in the capital city, in Kiev,
A u láskova knjázja u Vladímira,	Under the gracious prince, under Vladimir,
A i býlo stolován'e počótnyj stól,	There was banqueting, an honorable banquet,
A i býlo pirován'e počéstnyj pír,	There was feasting, an honorary feast,
A i vsé na pirú da napiválisja,	Everyone at the feast was drunk,
A i vsé na pirú da porasxvástalis',	Everyone at the feast was boasting,
Úmnyj xvástaet zolotój kaznój,	The clever one boasts of his golden stock,
Glúpyj xvástaet molodój ženój.	The stupid one boasts of his young wife.

Parallelistic systems of verbal art give us a direct insight into the speakers' own conception of the grammatical equivalences. The analysis of various kinds of poetic license in the domain of parallelism, like the examination of rhyming conventions, may provide us with important clues for interpreting the make-up of a given language and the hierarchical order of its constituents (e.g. the current equation between the Finnish allative and illative or between the preterit and present against the background of unpairable cases or verbal categories, according to Steinitz's observations in his path-breaking inquiry into parallelism in Karelian folklore).[15] The interaction between syntactic, morphologic and lexical equivalences and discrepancies, the diverse kinds of semantic contiguities, similarities, synonymies and antonymies, finally the different types of functions of allegedly "isolated lines," all such phenomena call for a systematic analysis indispensable for the comprehension and interpretation of the various grammatical contrivances in poetry. Such a crucial linguistic and poetic problem as parallelism can hardly be mastered by a scrutiny automatically restricted to the external form and excluding any discussion of grammatical and lexical meanings.

In the endless travel songs of the Kola Lapps[16] two juxtaposed persons, performing identical actions, are the uniform topic, impelling an automatic concatenation of verses of such a pattern: "*A* is sitting on the right side of the boat; *B* is sitting on the left side. *A* has a paddle in the right hand; *B* has a paddle in the left hand," etc.

In the Russian sung or narrated folk stories of Foma and Erema (Thomas and Jeremy), both unlucky brothers are used as a comic motivation for a chain of

---

[14] On the present state of international research in parallelistic foundations of written and oral poetry, see: "Grammatical Parallelism and its Russian Facet," *Selected Writings III: Poetry of Grammar and Grammar of Poetry* (The Hague-Paris-New York: Mouton, 1981), 98–135. (In future references this volume is abbreviated as *SW III*).

[15] W. Steinitz, *Der Parallelismus in der finnisch-karelischen Volksdichtung* = *Folklore Fellows Communications*, No. 115 (Helsinki, 1934).

[16] See N. Xaruzin, *Russkie lopari* (= *Izvestija Imp. Ob-a Ljubitelej Estestvoznanija, Antropologii i Ėtnografii, sostojaščego pri Imp. Moskovskom Universitete*, tom LXVI, Moscow, 1890), especially Ch. VI, pp. 342–394.

parallel clauses, parodying the carmen style, typical of Russian folk poetry and presenting quasi-differential characteristics of the two brothers by a juxtaposition of synonymous expressions or closely coincident images: "They uncovered Erema and they found Foma; They beat Erema and they did not pardon Foma; Erema ran away into a birch wood, and Foma into an oak wood," and so on.[17]

In the North-Russian ballad "Vasilij and Sofija"[18] the binary grammatical parallelism becomes the pivot of the plot and carries the whole dramatic development of this beautiful and concise *bylina*. In terms of antithetical parallelism the initial church scene contrasts the pious invocation "Father God!" of the parishioners and Sofia's incestuous call "My brother Vasilij!" The subsequent malicious intervention of the mother introduces a chain of distichs tying together both heroes through a strict correspondence between any line devoted to the brother and its counterpart speaking of his sister. Some of these pairs of parallel members in their stereotyped construction resemble the mentioned clichés of the songs of the Lapps: "Vasilij was buried on the right hand, And Sofija was buried on the left hand." The interlacement of the lovers' fates is reinforced by chiasmic constructions: "Vasilij, drink, but don't give to Sofija, And Sofija, drink, don't give to Vasilij! Yet Vasilij drank and feasted Sofija, yet Sofija drank and feasted Vasilij." The same function is performed by the images of a *kiparis* (cypress) tree, with masculine name, on Sofija's grave, and of a *verba* (willow), with feminine name, on the adjacent grave of Vasilij: "They wove together with their heads,/and they stuck together with their leaves.//" The parallel destruction of both trees by the mother echoes the violent death of both siblings. I doubt that efforts of such scholars as Christine Brooke-Rose[19] to draw a rigorous line of demarcation between tropes and poetic scenery are applicable to this ballad, and in general, the range of poems and poetic trends for which such a boundary actually exists is very limited.

According to one of Hopkins' brightest contributions to poetics, his paper of 1865 "On the Origin of Beauty," such canonical structures as Hebrew poetry "paired off in parallelisms" are well-known, "but the important part played by parallelism of expression in our poetry is not so well-known: I think it will surprise anyone when first pointed out."[20] Notwithstanding some isolated exceptions such as Berry's recent reconnaissance,[21] the role performed by the

[17] See the instructive surveys of these stories: N. Aristov, "Povest' o Fome i Ereme," *Drevnjaja i novaja Rossija*, I, No. 4 (1876), pp. 359–368, and V. Adrianova-Peretc, *Russkaja demokratičeskaja satira XVII v.* (Moscow-Leningrad, 1954), pp. 43–45, as well as their careful examination by P. Bogatyrev, "Improvizacija i normy xudožestvennyx priëmov na materiale povestej XVIII v., nadpisej na lubočnyx kartinkax, skazok i pesen o Ereme i Fome," *To Honor Roman Jakobson* (The Hague-Paris, 1967), I, pp. 318–334.

[18] See particularly its variants published by A. Sobolevskij, *Velikorusskie narodyne pesni*, I (SPb, 1895), Nos. 82–88, and A. Astaxova, *Byliny severa*, II (Moscow-Leningrad, 1951), Nos. 118, 120, 127, 146, 176, and the latter's summarizing notes, pp. 708–711.

[19] See her *Grammar of Metaphor* (London, 1958).

[20] Hopkins, *op. cit.*, p. 106.

[21] F. Berry, *Poets' Grammar: Person, Time and Mood in Poetry* (London, 1958).

"figure of grammar" in world poetry from antiquity up to the present time is still surprising for students of literature a whole century after it was first pointed out by Hopkins. The ancient and medieval theory of poetry had an inkling of poetic grammar and was prone to discriminate between lexical tropes and grammatical figures (*figurae verborum*), but these sound rudiments were later lost.

One may state that in poetry similarity is superimposed on contiguity, and hence "equivalence is promoted to the constitutive device of the sequence."[22] Here any noticeable reiteration of the same grammatical concept becomes an effective poetic device. Any unbiased, attentive, exhaustive, total description of the selection, distribution and interrelation of diverse morphological classes and syntactic constructions in a given poem surprises the examiner himself by unexpected, striking symmetries and antisymmetries, balanced structures, efficient accumulation of equivalent forms and salient contrasts, finally by rigid restrictions in the repertory of morphological and syntactic constituents used in the poem, eliminations which, on the other hand, permit us to follow the masterly interplay of the actualized constituents. Let us insist on the strikingness of these devices; any sensitive reader, as Sapir would say, feels instinctively the poetic effect and the semantic load of these grammatical appliances, "without the slightest attempt at conscious analysis," and in many cases the poet himself in this respect is similar to such a reader. In the same way both the traditional listener and the performer of folk poetry, which is based on a nearly constant parallelism, catches the deviations without, however, being capable of analyzing them, as the Serbian guslars and their audience notice and often condemn any deviation from the syllabic patterns of the epic songs from the regular location of the break but do not know how to define such a slip.

Often contrasts in the grammatical makeup support the metrical division of a poem into strophes and smaller sections, as for instance, in the double trichotomy of the Hussite battle song of the early fifteenth century,[23] or, even, they underlie and build such a stratified composition, as we observe in Marvell's poem "To his Coy Mistress," with its three tripartite paragraphs, grammatically delimited and subdivided.[24]

The juxtaposition of contrasting grammatical concepts may be compared with the so-called "dynamic cutting" in film montage, a type of cutting, which, e.g., in Spottiswoode's definition,[25] uses the juxtaposition of contrasting shots or sequences to generate in the mind of the spectator ideas that these constituent shots or sequences by themselves do not carry.

Among grammatical categories utilized for parallelisms and contrasts we actually find all the parts of speech, both mutable and immutable: numbers,

[22] See "Linguistics and Poetics," *SW III*, 27.
[23] See "Ktož jsú boži bojovníci," *SW III*, 215–231.
[24] Analyzed in a mimeographed supplement to my Warsaw lecture of 1960. [Cf. *Selected Writings VII: Contributions to Comparative Mythology. Studies in Linguistics and Philology, 1972-1982* (Berlin-Amsterdam-New York: Mouton, 1984), 341–348.]
[25] R. Spottiswoode, *Film and Its Technique* (University of California, 1951), p. 417.

genders, cases, grades, tenses, aspects, moods, voices, classes of abstract and concrete words, animates and inanimates, appellatives and proper names, affirmatives and negatives, finite and infinite verbal forms, definite and indefinite pronouns or articles, and diverse syntactic elements and constructions.

The Russian writer Veresaev confessed in his intimate notes that sometimes he felt as if imagery were "a mere counterfeit of genuine poetry."[26] As a rule, in imageless poems it is the "figure of grammar" which dominates and which supplants the tropes. Both the Hussite battle song and such lyrics of Puškin as "*Ja vas ljubil*" are eloquent examples of such a monopoly of grammatical devices. Much more usual, however, is an intensive interplay of both elements, as for instance, in Puškin's stanzas "*Čto v imeni tebe moem*," manifestly contrasting with his cited composition "without images," both written in the same year and probably dedicated to the same addressee, Karolina Sobańska.[27] The imaginative, metaphoric vehicles of a poem may be opposed to its matter-of-fact level by a sharp concomitant contrast of their grammatical constituents, as we observe, for example, in the Polish concise meditations of Cyprian Norwid, one of the greatest world poets of the later nineteenth century.[28]

The obligatory character of the grammatical processes and concepts constrains the poet to reckon with them; either he strives for symmetry and sticks to these simple, repeatable, diaphanous patterns, based on a binary principle, or he may cope with them, when longing for an "organic chaos." I have stated repeatedly that the rhyme technique is "either grammatical or antigrammatical" but never agrammatical, and the same may be applied as well to poets' grammar in general. There is in this respect a remarkable analogy between the role of grammar in poetry and the painter's composition, based on a latent or patent geometrical order or on a revulsion against geometrical arrangements. For the figurative arts geometrical principles represent a "beautiful necessity,"[29] according to the designation taken over by Bragdon from Emerson. It is the same necessity that in language marks out the grammatical meanings.[30] The correspondence between the two fields which already in the thirteenth century was pointed out by Robert Kilwardby[31] and which prompted Spinoza to treat grammar *more geometrico,* has emerged in a linguistic study by Benjamin Lee Whorf, "Language, Mind and Reality" published shortly after his death: Madras, 1942. The author discusses the abstract "designs of sentence structure" as opposed to "individual sentences" and to the vocabulary, which is a "somewhat rudimentary and not

[26] V. Veresaev, "Zapiski dlja sebja," *Novyj mir,* 1960, No. 1, p. 156.
[27] Cf. the comparative scrutiny of these two Puškin poems in the present volume, pp. 47–58.
[28] See "Przeszłość' Cypriana Norwida," in *SW III*, pp. 499–507.
[29] C. Bragdon, *The Beautiful Necessity* (Rochester, New York, 1910).
[30] Cf. R. Jakobson, "Boas' View of Grammatical Meaning," *Selected Writings II: Word and Language* (The Hague-Paris, 1971), pp. 489–496.
[31] See G. Wallerand, *Les oeuvres de Siger de Courtrai* (Louvain, 1913), p. 46.

self-sufficient part" of the linguistic order, and envisages "a 'geometry' of form principles characteristic of each language."[32] A further comparison between grammar and geometry was outlined in Stalin's polemics of 1950 against Marr's linguistic bias: the distinctive property of grammar lies in its abstractive power; "abstracting itself from anything that is particular and concrete in words and sentences, grammar treats only the general patterns, underyling the word changes and the combination of words into sentences, and builds in such a way grammatical rules and laws. In this respect grammar bears a resemblance to geometry, which, when giving its laws, abstracts itself from concrete objects, treats objects as bodies deprived of concreteness and defines their mutual relations not as concrete relations of certain concrete objects but as relations of bodies in general, namely, relations deprived of any concreteness."[33] The abstractive power of human thought, underlying—in the views of the two quoted authors—both geometrical relations and grammar, superimposes simple geometrical and grammatical figures upon the pictorial world of particular objects and upon the concrete lexical "wherewithal" of verbal art, as was shrewdly realized in the thirteenth century by Villard de Honnecourt for graphic arts and by Galfredus for poetry.

The pivotal role performed in the grammatical texture of poetry by diverse kinds of pronouns is due to the fact that pronouns, in contradistinction to all other autonomous words, are purely grammatical, relational units, and besides substantival and adjectival pronouns we must include in this class also adverbial pronouns and the so-called substantive (rather pronominal) verbs such as *to be* and *to have*. The relation of pronouns to non-pronominal words has been repeatedly compared with the relation between geometrical and physical bodies.[34]

Beside common or widespread devices the grammatical texture of poetry offers many salient differential features, typical of a given national literature or of a limited period, a specific trend, an individual poet or even one single work. The thirteenth-century students of arts whose names we have quoted remind us of the extraordinary compositional sense and skill of the Gothic epoch and help us to interpret the impressive structure of the Hussite battle song "Ktož jsú boží bojovníci." We deliberately dwell on this incentive revolutionary poem almost free of tropes, far from decorativeness and mannerism. The grammatical structure of this work reveals a particularly elaborate articulation.

As shown by the analysis of the song,[35] its three strophes in turn display a trinitarian form: they are divided into three smaller strophic units—*membra*. Each of the three strophes exhibits its specific grammatical features which we

---

[32] B. L. Whorf, *Language, Thought and Reality* (New York, 1956), pp. 253, 257.

[33] I. Stalin, *Marksizm i voprosy jazykoznanija* (Moscow, 1950), p. 20. As V. A. Zvegincev brought to my attention, Stalin's confrontation of grammar with geometry was prompted by the views of V. Bogorodickij, an outstanding disciple of the young Baudouin de Courtenay and M. Kruszewski.

[34] See, e.g., A. Zareckij, "O mestoimenii," *Russkij jazyk v škole,* 1960, No. 6. pp. 16–22.

[35] See *SW III,* 215–231, in particular the graphs on 226–231.

labeled "vertical similarities." Each of the three *membra* throughout the three strophes has its particular properties, termed "horizontal similarities" and distinguishing any given *membrum* in the strophe from its two other *membra*. The initial and the final *membra* of the song are linked together with its central *membrum* (the second *membrum* of the second strophe) and differ from the rest of the *membra* by special features, enabling us to connect these three *membra* through a "falling diagonal," in contradistinction to the "rising diagonal" linking the central *membrum* of the song with the final *membrum* of the initial strophe and with the initial *membrum* of the final strophe. Furthermore, noticeable similarities bring together (and separate from the rest of the song) the central *membra* of the first and third strophes with the initial *membrum* of the second strophe, and, on the other hand, the final *membra* of the first and third strophes with the central *membrum* of the second strophe. The former disposition may be labeled "higher upright arc," while the latter will be called "lower upright arc." There appear, moreover, the "inverted arcs," likewise grammatically delimited, a "higher one, uniting the initial *membra* of the first and last strophes with the central *membrum* of the second strophe, and a "lower inverted arc," tying the central *membra* of the first and last strophes with the final *membrum* of the second strophe.

This steadfast "membrification" and congruous geometricity must be viewed against the background of Gothic art and scholasticism, convincingly compared by Erwin Panofsky. In its shape the Czech song of the early fifteenth century approximates the authoritative precepts of the "classic *Summa* with its three requirements of (1) totality (sufficient enumeration), (2) arrangement according to a system of homologous parts and parts of parts (sufficient articulation), and (3) distinctness and deductive cogency (sufficient interrelation)."[36] However immense the difference is between Thomism and the ideology of the anonymous author of *Zisskiana cantio,* the shape of this song totally satisfies the artistic request of Thomas Aquinas: "the senses delight in things duly proportioned as in something akin to them; for, the sense, too, is a kind of reason as is every cognitive power." The grammatical texture of the Hussite chorale corresponds to the compositional principles of Czech contemporaneous painting. In his monograph about the pictorial art of the Hussite epoch,[37] Kropáček analyzes the style of the early fifteenth century and points out a congruous and systematic articulation of the surface, a strict subordination of the individual parts to the total compositional tasks, and a deliberate use of contrasts.

The Czech example helps us to glance into the intricacy of correspondences between the functions of grammar in poetry and of relational geometry in painting. We are faced with the phenomenological problem of an intrinsic kinship between both factors and with a concrete historical search for the convergent development and for the interaction between verbal and

---

[36] E. Panofsky, *Gothic Architecture and Scholasticism* (New York, 1957), p. 31.
[37] Quoted *ibid.,* p. 38.

representational art. Furthermore, in the quest for a delineation of artistic trends and traditions, the analysis of grammatical texture provides us with important clues, and, finally, we approach the vital question of how a poetic work exploits the extant inventory of masterly devices for a new end and re-evaluates them in the light of their novel tasks. Thus, for instance, the masterpiece of Hussite revolutionary poetry has inherited from the opulent Gothic stock both kinds of grammatical parallelism, in Hopkins' parlance "comparison for likeness" and "comparison for unlikeness,"[38] and we have to investigate how the combination of these two, mainly grammatical, ways of proceeding enabled the poet to achieve a coherent, convincing, effective transition from the initial spiritual through the belligerent argumentation of the second strophe to the military orders and battle cries of the finale, or—in other words—how the poetic delight in verbal structures duly proportioned grows into a preceptive power leading to direct action.

[38] Hopkins, *op. cit.,* p. 106.

Two Poems by Puškin

Roman Jakobson

During the late 1930s, while editing Puškin's works in Czech translation, I was struck by the way in which poems that seemed to approximate closely the Russian text, its images and sound structure, often produced the distressing impression of a complete rift with the original because of the inability or impossibility of reproducing their grammatical structure. Gradually, it became clear: in Puškin's poetry the guiding significance of the morphological and syntactic fabric is interwoven with and rivals the artistic role of verbal tropes. Indeed, at times it takes over and becomes the primary, even exclusive, vehicle of the poems' innermost symbolism. Accordingly, in the afterword to the Czech volume of Puškin's lyric poetry, I noted that "in Puškin a striking actualization of grammatical oppositions, especially in verbal and pronominal forms, is connected with a keen regard for meaning. Often contrasts, affinities, and contiguities of tense and number, of verbal aspect and voice, acquire a directly leading role in the composition of particular poems. Emphasized by an opposition of grammatical category, they function like poetic images, and, for instance, a masterful alternation of grammatical categories of person becomes a means of intense dramatization. There can hardly be an example of a more skillful poetic exploitation of morphological possibilities." (Jakobson, 1936: 263; *SW V*: 284.)

In particular, the experience gained during a seminar on Puškin's *The Bronze Horseman* and its translation into other Slavic languages allowed me to characterize an example of a consistent opposition of the imperfective and perfective aspects. In the "Petersburg Tale" it serves as a grammatically expressive projection of the tragic conflict between the limitless and seemingly eternal power of Peter the Great, "ruler of half the world," and the fatal

This chapter is a translation by Stephen Rudy of certain sections of the Russian text of "Poetry of Grammar and Grammar of Poetry" (1961) that were not included in its abridged English version (1968); see Roman Jakobson, *Selected Writings III: Poetry of Grammar and Grammar of Poetry* (The Hague-Paris-New York: Mouton, 1981), 63–64, 72–75, and 78–86.

limitedness of all the actions performed by the characterless clerk Eugene, who dared with his incantatory formula *Užó tebé!* 'That's it for you!' to proclaim the limit of the miracle-working tsar and builder (Jakobson, 1937: 20; *SW V*: 271; 1953: 15–18). Both these experiences convinved me that the question of the interrelations between grammar and poetry demanded a systematic and detailed clarification.

The Russian writer Veresaev confessed in his journal that sometimes he felt as if imagery were "a mere surrogate of genuine poetry" (1960). As a rule, in imageless poetry or "poetry of thought" it is the "figure of grammar," as Hopkins called it (1959: 289), that dominates and supplants the tropes. Such lyrics of Puškin's as *"Ja vas ljubil . . ."* ("I loved you . . .") are graphic examples of a monopoly of grammatical devices. An intensive interplay of both elements can be found in Puškin's quatrains *"Čto v imeni tebe moëm?"* ("What is there for you in my name?", a poem in manifest contrast to the above-mentioned composition "without images," despite the fact that both were written in the same year [(1829)] and were probably dedicated to the same addressee, Karolina Sobańska (Cjavlovskaja, 1958).

Puškin's poem "I loved you" has been cited repeatedly by literary critics as a striking example of imageless poetry. Its vocabulary does not include a single live trope, the one seeming exception, *ljubov' ugasla* 'love has died out', being merely a dead lexicalized metaphor. On the other hand, this eight-line poem is saturated with grammatical figures, even if this essential feature of its texture has not been hitherto accorded proper attention.

1 *Ja vas ljubil: ljubov' ešče, byt' možet,*
2 *V duše moej ugasla ne sovsem;*
3 *No pust' ona vas bol'še ne trevožit;*
4 *Ja ne xoču pečalit' vas ničem.*

5 *Ja vas ljubil bezmolvno, beznadežno,*
6 *To robost'ju, to revnost'ju tomim;*
7 *Ja vas ljubil tak iskrenno, tak nežno,*
8 *Kak daj vam Bog ljubimoj byt' drugim.*

1 *I loved you: love has not yet, it may be,*
2 *Died out completely in my soul;*
3 *But let it not trouble you any more;*
4 *I do not wish to sadden you in any way.*

5 *I loved you silently, hopelessly,*
6 *Tormented now by shyness, now by jealousy;*
7 *I loved you so truly, so tenderly*
8 *As God may grant you to be loved by another.*

The very selection of grammatical forms in the poem is striking. It contains forty-seven words, including a total of twenty-nine inflectional forms. Of the latter, fourteen, i.e., almost half, are pronouns, ten are verbs, and only five are nouns, moreoever, nouns of an abstract, speculative character. In the entire work there is not a single adjective, whereas the number of adverbs is as high as ten. Pronouns—being thoroughly grammatical, purely relational words deprived of a properly lexical, material meaning—are clearly opposed to the remaining inflected parts of speech. All three dramatis personae are designated in the poem exclusively by pronouns: *ja* 'I' *in recto*; *vy* 'you' and *drugoj* 'another' *in obliquo*. The poem consists of two quatrains with alternating rhymes. The first-person pronoun, which always occupies the first syllable of a line, is encountered four times, once in each couplet—in the first and fourth line of the first quatrain, and in the first and third of the second. *Ja* 'I' occurs here only in the nominative case, only as the subject of the proposition, and, moreover, only in combination with the accusative form *vas* 'you'. The second-person pronoun, which occurs exclusively in the accusative and dative (i.e., in the so-called directional cases), figures in the poem six times, once in each line, except for the second line of each quatrain, being, moreover, combined with some other pronoun each time it occurs. The form *vas* 'you', a direct object, is always dependent (directly or indirectly) on a pronominal subject. In four instances that subject is *ja* 'I'; in another it is the anaphoric *ona* 'she', referring to *ljubov'* 'love' on the part of the first-person subject. In contrast, the dative *vam* 'you', which appears in the final, syntactically subordinated, line in place of the direct object *vas*, is coupled with a new pronominal form, *drugim* 'another'. The latter word, in a peripheral case, the "instrumental of the perpetrator of an action,"[1] together with the equally peripheral dative, introduces at the end of the concluding line the third participant in the lyric drama, who is opposed to the nominative *ja* 'I' with which the introductory line began.

The author of this eight-line verse epistle addresses the heroine six times. Three times he repeats the key formula *ja vas ljubil* 'I loved you', which opens first the initial quatrain and then the first and second couplets of the final quatrain, thus introducing into the two-stanza monologue a traditional ternary division: 4 + 2 + 2. The ternary construction unfolds each time in a different way. The first quatrain develops the theme of the *predicate* : an etymological figure replaces the verb *ljubil* 'loved' with the abstract noun *ljubov'* 'love', lending it the appearance of an independent, unconditional being. Despite the orientation toward the past tense, nothing in the development of the lyric theme is shown as being in a state of completion. Here Puškin, an unsurpassed master at utilizing the dramatic collision between verbal aspects, avoids indicative forms of the perfective aspect. The sole exception—$_1$*ljubov' ešče, byt' možet,* $_2$*V duše moej ugasla ne sovsem* 'love has not yet, it may be, Died out completely in my soul'—actually supports the rule, since the surrounding accessory words—*ešče* 'yet', *byt' možet* 'it may be', 'perhaps', *ne sovsem* 'not completely'—bring to naught the fictitious theme of the end. Nothing is completed, but the placing into question of the completion implied by the perfective aspect is answered, on the other hand, after the adversative *no* 'but',

---

[1] [The instrumental, like the dative, is a peripheral case, which further intensifies the ties between the forms *vam* 'you' and *drugim* 'another'.] See Šaxmatov, 1941: §445; Jakobson, 1958: 158.

by a negation of the present tense both in and of itself ($_4$*ja ne xoču* 'I do not want') and in the composition of the descriptive imperative ($_3$*No pust' ona vas bol'še ne trevožit* 'But let it not trouble you any more'). In general, there are no positive turns of phrase with finite present tense forms throughout the poem.

The beginning of the second quatrain repeats the key formula and then goes on to develop the theme of the *subject*. Both the adverbal adverbs and the instrumental forms with accessory passive predicates relating to the same subject "I" extend even into the past the overtly or latently negative terms that in the first quatrain painted the present in a tone of inactive self-denial.

Finally, following the third repetition of the initial formula, the last line of the poem is devoted to its *object*: $_7$*Ja vas ljubil* [. . .] $_8$*Kak daj vam Bog ljubimoj byt' drugim* 'I loved you [. . .] As God may grant you to be loved by another' (with a pronominal polyptoton *vas—vam*). Here for the first time there is a genuine contrast between the two moments of the dramatic development: the two rhyming lines are similar syntactically—each contains a combination of the passive voice with an instrumental ($_6$*revnost'ju tomim* 'tormented by jealousy'—$_8$*ljubimoj byt' drugim* 'to be loved by another')—but the authorial recognition of the 'other' contradicts the earlier tormenting jealousy. The absence of articles in Russian makes it possible not to specify whether it is to a different, vague "other" or to one and the same "other" that the jealousy in the past and the present blessing relate. The two imperative constructions—$_3$*No pust' ona vas bol'še ne trevožit* 'But let it not trouble you any more' and $_8$*Kak daj vam Bog ljubimoj byt' drugim* 'As God may grant you to be loved by another'—complement one another, as it were. In the meantime, the epistle intentionally leaves open the possibility for completely different interpretations of the last verse. On the one hand, it may be understood as an incantatory dénouement to the poem. On the other, the frozen expression *daj vam Bog* 'may God grant you', notwithstanding the imperative, which is whimsically shifted into a subordinate clause (see Slonimskij, 1959: 119), may be interpreted as a kind of "non-real mood," signifying that without supernatural interference the heroine will almost certainly never again encounter another such love. In the latter case the final sentence of the quatrain may be considered a kind of "understood negation," in Jespersen's terms (1924: ch. 24), and becomes yet another of the diverse examples of negation in the poem. Apart from several negative constructions, the entire repertoire of finite forms in the poem is composed of the past tense of the verb *ljubit'* 'to love'.

To repeat, among the inflected words in Puškin's "I loved you," pronouns dominate. There are few nouns, and all of them belong to the speculative sphere characterizing—except for the concluding appeal to God—the psychic world of the first-person speaker. The word in the text that occurs most frequently and that is distributed with the greatest regularity is the pronoun *vy* 'you': it alone appears in the accusative and dative cases and, moreover, exlusively in those cases. Closely linked with it, and second in frequency, is the pronoun *ja* 'I', which is used exclusively as a subject and exclusively at the beginning of a line. The share of the predicates that combine with this subject is allotted to adverbs, whereas the accessory, non-personal verbal forms are accompanied by complements in the instrumental case: *₄pečalit' vas ničem* 'sadden you in any way [lit. with anything]'; *₆To robost'ju, to revnost'ju tomim* 'Tormented now by shyness, now by jealousy'; *₈ljubimoj byt' drugim* 'to be loved by another'. Adjectives, and adnominal forms in general, do not appear in these quatrains. Constructions with prepositions are almost completely absent. The significance of the poetic redistributions of the makeup, frequency, mutual interrelation, and arrangement of the various grammatical categories of the Russian language in this poem is so distinct that it hardly needs a detailed semantic commentary. It is enough to read Julian Tuwim's Polish translation of these verses— *"kochałem panią—i miłości mojej/ Może się jeszcze resztki w duszy tlą"* (1954: 198)—to be immediately convinced that even such a poetic virtuoso, the minute he failed to render the grammatical structure of Puškin's quatrains, could not help but reduce to nil their artistic strength.

The essential literary-critical question of the individuality and comparative characteristics of poems, poets, and poetic schools can and should be posed in the realm of grammar. Despite the common grammatical pattern of Puškin's poetry, each of his poems is unique and unrepeatable in its artistic choice and use of grammatical material. Thus, for example, the quatrains "What is there for you in my name?", though close in time and circumstances to the eight-line poem "I loved you," reveal quite a few distinguishing features.

₁*Čto v imeni tebe moëm?*
₂*Ono umrët, kak šum pečal'nyj*
₃*Volny, plesnuvšej v bereg dal'nyj,*
₄*Kak zvuk nočnoj v lesu gluxom.*

₅*Ono na pamjatnom listke*
₆*Ostavit mërtvyj sled, podobnyj*
₇*Uzoru nadpisi nadgrobnoj*
₈*Na neponjatnom jazyke.*

₉*Čto v nëm? Zabytoe davno*
₁₀*V volnen'jax novyx i mjatežnyx,*
₁₁*Tvoej duše ne dast ono*
₁₂*Vospominanij čistyx, nežnyx.*

₁₃*No v den' pečali, v tišine,*
₁₄*Proiznesi ego toskuja,*
₁₅*Skaži: est' pamjat' obo mne,*
₁₆*Est' v mire serdce, gde živu ja.*

₁What is there for you in my name?
₂It will die, like the sad noise
₃Of a wave that has splashed against a distant shore,
₄Like a nocturnal sound in a dense woods.

₅On the memorial page it
₆Will leave a dead trace akin
₇To the pattern of a tombstone inscription
₈In an incomprehensible language.

₉What is in it? Long forgotten
₁₀In new and stormy agitations,
₁₁It will not give your soul
₁₂Pure, tender memories.

₁₃But on a day of sadness, in silence,
₁₄Pronounce it while languishing,
₁₅Say: there is memory of me,
₁₆There is in the world a heart in which I live.

In this poem, in distinction to the lines of "I loved you," the pronouns, twelve in all, yield in quantity both to nouns (twenty) and adjectives (thirteen), but still continue to play a capital role. They constitute three of the four independent words of the first line: *Čto v imeni tebe moëm?* '*What* is there for *you* in *my* name?' In the authorial speech encompassing all but the last two lines of the poem, all the subjects of the main clauses are purely grammatical, consisting as they do of pronouns: ₁*Čto* 'what', ₂*Ono* 'it', ₅*Ono* 'it', ₉*Čto* 'what'. However, in place of the personal pronouns of "I loved you" interrogative and anaphoric forms predominate here, whereas the second-person pronoun in the first and third quatrain of the poem—whether personal or possessive—occurs exclusively in the dative case, thus remaining merely an addressee, and not the direct theme of the epistle (₁*tebe* 'for [lit. to] you', ₁₁*Tvoej duše* 'to your soul'). Only in the last quatrain does the category of the second person emerge in the verbs, and then it is precisely in the two paired forms of the imperative mood: ₁₄*Proiznesi* 'pronounce', ₁₅*Skaži* 'say'.

Both poems begin and end with pronouns, but in contrast to the eight-line "I loved you," the addresser of this epistle is designated neither by a personal pronoun nor by first-person verbs, but only by a possessive pronoun, which relates exclusively to the author's *name,* and that, moreover, in order to put into doubt any possible meaning the name might have for the poem's addressee: ₁'What is there for you in my name?' True, a first-person pronoun does appear in the penultimate line of the poem, first in an indirect, mediated form: ₁₅*est' pamjat' obo mne* 'there is memory of me'. Finally, in the last, hypercatalectic syllable of the final line, the unexpected first-person subject with a corresponding verbal predicate—so sharply opposed to the preceding inanimate and indirect subjects ('what' and 'it')—appears for the first time: ₁₆*Est' v mire serdce, gde živu ja* 'There is in the world a heart in which live I'. (Note that "I loved you," on the contrary, begins with the pronoun "I".) Yet even this final self-assertion by no means belongs to the author but is thrust upon the addressee by the author: the concluding "I" is spoken by the heroine of the epistle at the author's prompting, while the author himself is conveyed throughout in impersonal terms either of a metonymic (₁*v imeni moëm* 'in my name') or synecdochic nature (₁₆*est' v mire serdce* 'there is in the world a heart'), or in repeated anaphoric references to the discarded metonymy (₅,₁₁*ono* 'it'), or in secondary metonymic reflections (not the name itself but its ₆*mërtvyj sled* ₅*na pamjatnom listke* 'dead trace on the memorial page'), or, finally, in metaphoric replies to metonymic images, developed into complex comparisons (₂*kak . . . ,*

₄*kak...,* ₆*podobnyj* 'like..., like..., akin to...'). In its abundance of tropes this verse epistle essentially differs, to repeat, from the poem "I loved you." If in the latter grammatical figures carry the entire weight, here the artistic roles are divided between poetic grammar and lexicon.

The principle of a proportional section is apparent here, however complex and capricious its embodiment. The text divides into two eight-line units, each with the same introductory question, as if reacting to an invitation to write a name in a guest book or keepsake album (₁'What is there for you in my name?' — ₉'What is in it?'), and with an answer to its own question. The second pair of quatrains changes the embracing rhyme-scheme of the first two in favor of alternating rhymes, giving rise to the unusual collision of two differently rhyming masculine lines at the center of the poem (₈*jazyké* 'language' and ₉*davnó* 'long ago'). Discarding the metaphoric plan of the first two quatrains, the last two transfer the development of the lyrical theme onto the level of literal, direct meanings, and, correspondingly, the negative construction ₁₁*ne dast ono* ₁₂*Vospominanij* 'it will not give... memories' takes the place of the affirmative constructions of a metaphorical order. It is noteworthy that the initial quatrain, which compared the poet's name to the dying "noise of a wave," finds an echo in the third stanza in the related but dead lexical metaphor "new and stormy agitations" [the Russian word for 'agitations', *volnenija,* is derived from *volna* 'wave' — tr.], in which, it would seem, the senseless name is fated to be engulfed.

At the same time, however, the poem as a whole is subject to another sort of division, in its turn of a dichotomous nature: the entire grammatical composition of the terminal quatrain is strikingly opposed to the initial three quatrains. To the indicative mood of the mournful perfective verbs in the non-past tense (semantically, future tense) — ₂*umrët* 'will die', ₆*Ostavit mërtvyj sled* 'will leave a dead trace', ₁₁*ne dast...* ₁₂*Vospominanij* 'will not give... memories' — the final quatrain opposes the imperative of two perfective verbs of speaking (₁₄*Proiznesi* 'pronounce', ₁₅*Skaži* 'say') which enjoin the addressee's direct speech. That speech removes all the imagined losses through a final affirmation of continued life, which counters the authorial tirade directed at the poem's heroine in the first three quatrains by introducing the first verbal form in the imperfective aspect in the poem, ₁₆*živu ja* 'I live'. The entire lexicon of the poem changes accordingly: the heroine is called upon to answer the previous terms *umrët* 'will die', *mërtvyj* 'dead', *nadgrobnaja nadpis'* 'tombstone inscription' with the statement: ₁₆*Est' v mire serdce, gde živu ja* 'There is in the world a heart in which I live', with its hint of the traditional paronomasia *neu*MIR*ájuščij* MIR 'undying world'. The fourth quatrain negates the first three: for you my name is dead, but let it serve you as a sign of my unchanging memory of you. Or, as it is formulated in a later poem by Puškin: *I šleš' otvet/ Tebe ž net otzyva...* 'And you send an answer/ But there is no response to you...' ("Echo," 1831).

The first quatrain had predicted that the poet's name would "die, like the sad noise of a wave," "like a nocturnal sound," and it is precisely to these images that the last stanza returns. There the forgotten name is called upon to resound not at night, vanishing "in a dense woods" (₄*v lesu gluxom*—in the bookish metaphor resuscitated by Puškin), but "on a day of sadness," and not in tune to the "sad noise of a wave" but "in silence" (₁₃*v tišine*). In the last quatrain the replacement of night by day and of noise by silence is clearly symbolic, as is the grammatical shift. It is hardly fortuitous that in place of the adjectives of the first stanza—"sad" and "nocturnal"—nouns figure in the last quatrain—"in a day of sadness," "in silence." In general, in contradistinction to the abundance of attributive adjectives and adverbs characteristic of the first three stanzas (five in each), in the fourth quatrain such forms are entirely lacking, just as they were lacking in the poem "I loved you," where, on the other hand, there are plenty of adverbs, which are almost completely absent in the poem under analysis. The final quatrain of "What is there for you in my name?" breaks with the spectacular, decorative style of the first three stanzas, a style that is entirely alien to the text of "I loved you."

Thus the antithesis of the epistle, its last quatrain, which opens with the adversative *no* 'but', the sole copulative conjunction in the poem, differs essentially in its grammatical makeup from the rest of the poem. Unique to it are the repeated imperative forms, in opposition to the indicative mood used invariably throughout the first three quatrains, and an adverbal gerund, contrasting with the previous nominal participles; in distinction to the preceding part of the text, this quatrain introduces quoted speech, the twice repeated predicate *est'* 'there is', a first-person subject and object, a complete subordinate clause, and, finally, the imperfective aspect of the verb following a string of perfective forms.

Despite the quantitative disproportion of the first, indicative, and the second, imperative parts (twelve initial lines against the final four), both identically form three further degrees of subdivisions into paratactic pairs of independent syntactic groups. The first three-stanza part embraces two syntactically parallel question-answer constructions, once again of unequal length (eight initial lines versus the four lines of the third quatrain). Correspondingly, the second half of the poem, its final quatrain, contains two parallel sentences, which are closely related thematically. The question-answer constructions of the first part both consist of an identical interrogative sentence and of an answer with one and the same anaphoric subject. To this secondary division of the first part there corresponds in the second part the binary character of the second imperative sentence, which includes direct speech and thus breaks down into the introductory demand (*skaži*: 'Say:') and the quote itself (*est'* 'there is'). Finally, the first of the answers breaks down into two parallel sentences of a metephoric stamp and closely related thematically, both with an enjambement in the middle of the stanza (I *Ono umrët, kak šum pečal'nyj* | *Volny . . .*, II *Ono . . . Ostavit mërtvyj sled, podobnyj* | *Uzoru . . .*). This is the last of the three concentric forms of parataxis to be found in the first part of the poem, which is matched in the second part by a division of the quoted speech into parallel, thematically similar sentences (*Est' pamjat'* 'There is memory'; *Est'* . . . *serdce* 'There is a heart').

If the last quatrain includes just as many independent paratactical pairs as do the three preceding quatrains taken together, then—to the contrary—of six dependent groups (three conjunctive circumstantial clauses and three "attributive-predicative adjuncts," as Šaxmatov calls them [1941: §393f.]), three groups belong to the first quatrain, the richest in metaphoric constructions ($_2kak$ . . . 'like', $_3plesnuvšej$ 'splashed against', $_4kak$ 'like'), while in the three remaining quatrains there is but one example of hypotaxis per quatrain (II *podobnyj* 'akin to'; III *Zabytoe* 'forgotten'; IV *gde* 'where').

The most striking fact that emerges from all these delimitations is the sharp and many-sided contrast between the first and last quatrains, i.e., the opening and dénouement of the lyric theme, notwithstanding the simultaneous presence of shared features. Both the contrast and communality find their expression in the sound texture as well. Among the stressed vowels in downbeats, dark (labialized) vowels predominate in the first quatrain, and their number consistently falls in subsequent quatrains, reaching a minimum in the fourth quatrain (I: 8, II: 5, III: 4, IV: 3). Moreover, the maximum number of stressed diffuse (narrow) vowels (*u* and *i*) occur in the two extreme quatrains—the first (6) and fourth (5)—and oppose them to the two internal quatrains (II: 0, III: 2).

Let us briefly recapitulate the movement of the theme from the opening to the dénouement, which is clearly articulated in the treatment of grammatical categories, especially case forms. As the initial quatrains make clear, the poet has been asked to inscribe his name in a keepsake album. An interior dialogue, consisting of alternating questions and answers, serves as a rebuke to this implied proposition.

The name will be heard no more. It will vanish without a trace, "will die," according to the intransitive construction of the first quatrain, where only in the metaphoric image of a "wave that has splashed against a distant shore" does the prepositional accusative give a hint of questing after an object. The second quatrain, replacing the name with its written reflection, introduces a transitive form ("it will leave . . . a trace"), but the epithet "dead" as a direct object returns us to the theme of aimlessness developed in the first quatrain. The metaphoric plan of the second quatrain opens with a dative of comparison ("akin to the pattern") and prepares, as it were, for the appearance of a dative in its basic function: the third quatrain introduces a noun ($_{11}Tvoej\ duše$ 'to your soul') with a dative of advantage (*dativus commodi*), but again the context, in this case the negated "it will not give," reduces the advantage to null.

The sound texture of the last quatrain has something in common with the diffuse vowels of the initial quatrain, and the thematics of the fourth stanza again concentrate on the spoken name of the first quatrain rather than on its written reflection. The lyric plot began with the sound of the name having faded away; it ends with its sound being pronounced "in silence." In the poem's sound texture the muted, neutral diffuse vowels of the two extreme quatrains accordingly echo each other. However, the dénouement changes the role of the name in an essential way. In response to the invitation—clear from the context though not directly specified—to write his name in an album, the poet answers the album's owner with an appeal: $_{14}$*Proiznesi ego toskuja* 'Pronounce it while languishing'. In place of the nominative *ono* 'it', which refers to the "name" in each of the first three quatrains (I$_2$, II$_1$, III$_3$), one finds the accusative of the same anaphoric pronoun (IV$_2$) as the object of a second-person imperative addressed to the heroine, who thus turns at the author's will from an inactive addressee ($_1$*tebe* 'for [lit. to] you') into a persona dramatis or, more accurately, a persona who is called upon to act.

Echoing the triple *ono* of the first three quatrains and the phonic variations on this pronoun in the third quatrain—a fourfold combination of *n* with *o* and with a preceding or following *v*—the fourth quatrain, which eliminates this subject pronoun, opens in a punning way with precisely the same combination:

> *Čto* v NĚ*m? Zabytoe da*vNO
> *V volnen'jax* NOV*yx i mjatežnyx,*
> *Tvoej duše ne dast* oNO
> v*ospominanij čistyx, nežnyx.*
>
> NO v *den' pečali, v tišine . . .*

The name, given throughout the first three quatrains as completely divorced from the insensible surroundings, is ascribed to the heroine in a speech that, though merely emblematic, nevertheless for the first time contains a reference to the possessor of the name: "There is in the world a *heart* . . ." It is noteworthy that the authorial "I" is not named in the poem, and when the last lines of the final quatrain finally have recourse to a first-person pronoun, it enters into the direct speech thrust upon the heroine by the authorial imperatives and designates not the author but the heroine. The loss of memories of "me"-the author is here opposed, in an autonomous framework, to the unshakeable memory of "me"-the forgetful owner of the "memorial page."

The heroine's self-affirmation by means of an appeal to the author's name that is enjoined on her by the author himself is prepared for by the same play on the variations and shifts in the meanings of case forms that the entire poem utilized so intensively. To its numerous case constructions one should apply the searching remarks of Jeremy Bentham (1932: 62) about the close contact and mutual interpenetration of two linguistic spheres—the material and the abstract—which appears, for example, in the vacillation of such prepositions as *v* 'in' between its proper, material, locational meaning, on the one hand, and an incorporeal, abstract meaning, on the other. The conflict between the two functions of combinations of the locative case with the prepositions *v* and *na* 'in' in each of the first three quatrains is given by Puškin in a deliberately sharpened form. In the first quatrain the lines $_1$*Čto v imeni tebe moëm?* 'What is there for you in my name?' and $_3$*Kak zvuk nočnoj v lesu gluxom* 'Like a nocturnal sound in a dense woods' are linked by a grammatical rhyme (the masculine adjectives in the locative *moëm* 'my'—*gluxóm* 'dense'). One and the same preposition is endowed with an abstract meaning in the first case and a concretely localized meaning in the second. The extrinsic preposition *na* 'on, in, at' (opposed in Russian to the embracing preposition *v* 'in, on'), in accordance with the transition from the resounding name to its written form, in turn enters in two parallel lines in the second quatrain, linked by a grammatical rhyme—the first time in a localized sense (*na pamjatnom listké* 'on the memorial page'), the second time in an abstract sense (*na neponjatnom jazyké* 'in an incomprehensible language'). Moreover, the semantic opposition of these two rhyming lines is sharpened by means of a punning paronomasia: *O*NO NA *Pam*JATNOM—NA *ne*PONJATNOM. In the third quatrain the juxtaposition of two phrases with the preposition *v* follows in general outlines the first quatrain, but the elliptical repetition of the question ₉*Čto v něm?* 'What's in it?' allows for a double interpretation along abstract (What does it mean to you?) as well as genuinely localized lines (What does it contain?). In line with this shift the fourth quatrain leans toward the proper meaning of the same preposition (₁₃*v tišine* 'in silence'; ₁₆*Est' v mire* 'There is in the world'). In response to the question posed in the poem's initial line—"What is there for you in my name?"—the heroine is urged to give an answer prompted by the author himself, an answer that contains the embracing preposition *v* three times in its primary, material meaning: *in* the name signed for her and pronounced by her in answer to the poet's appeal, there is contained evidence that there is a person *in* the world *in* whose heart it continues to live. The shift from the nocturnal ₂*Ono umrët* 'It will die' to the diurnal ₁₆*živu ja* 'I live' echoes the gradual replacement of dark vowels by light ones.

Despite their differences, both "I loved you" and "What is there for you in my name?" illustrate essential features of Puškin's poetic grammar, in particular, his sliding between juxtaposed grammatical categories, e.g., different cases or different combinatory meanings of one and the same case, in a word, his continual change of focus. The analysis of such exploitations of grammar hardly eliminates the problem of grammatical parallelism in poetry, but posits it in a new, dynamic dimension.

REFERENCES

BENTHAM, JEREMY, 1932. *Theory of Fictions,* ed. C. K. Ogden (London).

CJAVLOVSKAJA, T., 1958. "Dnevnik A. A. Oleninoj," in *Puškin. Issledovanija i materialy* 11 (Leningrad), 289–292.

HOPKINS, G. M., 1959. *Journals and Papers,* ed. H. House (London).

JAKOBSON, ROMAN, 1936. "Na okraj lyrických básní Puškinových," in: *Vybrané spisy A. S. Puškina,* ed. A. Bem and R. Jakobson, 1 (Prague); see "Marginal Notes on Puškin's Lyric Poetry," in *SW V,* 281–286.

1937 "Socha v symbolice Puškinově," *Slovo a slovesnost* 2; cf. "The Statue in Puškin's Poetic Mythology," in: *SW V,* 237–280.

1953 "The Kernel of Comparative Slavic Literature," *Harvard Slavic Studies* 1; reprinted in: *SW VI,* 1–64.

1958   "Morfologičeskie nabljudenija nad slavjanskim skloneniem," in: *SW II*, 154–183; see "Morphological Observations on Slavic Declension," in: R. Jakobson, *Russian and Slavic Grammar: Studies, 1931–1981* (Berlin-New York: Mouton, 1984), 102–138.

1961   "Poèzija grammatiki i grammatika poèzii," in: *Poetics-Poetyka-Poètika* (Warsaw); reprinted in *SW III*, 63–86.

1968   "Poetry of Grammar and Grammar of Poetry," *Lingua* 21; reprinted in *SW III*, 87–97.

1971   *SW II* = *Selected Writings II: Word and Language* (The Hague-Paris: Mouton).

1979   *SW V* = *Selected Writings V: On Verse, Its Masters and Explorers* (The Hague-Paris-New York: Mouton).

1981   *SW III* = *Selected Writings III: Poetry of Grammar and Grammar of Poetry* (The Hague-Paris-New York: Mouton).

1984   *SW VI* = *Selected Writings VI: Early Slavic Paths and Crossroads* (Berlin-New York: Mouton).

JESPERSEN, O., 1924. *The Philosophy of Grammar* (London-New York).

ŠAXMATOV, A. A., 1941. *Sintaksis russkogo jazyka* (Leningrad).

SLONIMSKIJ, A., 1959. *Masterstvo Puškina* (Moscow).

TUWIM, J., 1954. *Z rosyjskiego* 1 (Warsaw).

VERESAEV, V., 1960. "Zapiski dlja sebja," *Novyj mir* 1.

Subliminal Verbal Patterning in Poetry

Roman Jakobson

> Que le critique d'une part, et que le versificateur d'autre part, le veuille ou non.
>
> Ferdinand de Saussure

Whenever and wherever I discuss the phonological and grammatical texture of poetry, and whatever the language and epoch of the poems examined, one question constantly arises among the readers or listeners: are the designs disclosed by linguistic analysis deliberately and rationally planned in the creative work of the poet and is he really aware of them?

A calculus of probability as well as an accurate comparison of poetic texts with other kinds of verbal messages demonstrates that the striking particularities in the poetic selection, accumulation, juxtaposition, distribution, and exclusion of diverse phonological and grammatical classes cannot be viewed as negligible accidentals governed by the rule of chance. Any significant poetic composition, whether it is an improvisation or the fruit of long and painstaking labor, implies a goal-oriented choice of verbal material.

In particular, when comparing the extant variants of a poem, one realizes the relevance of the phonemic, morphological, and syntactical framework for the author. What the pivots of this network are may and quite frequently does remain outside of his awareness, but even without being able to single out the pertinent expedients, the poet and his receptive reader nevertheless spontaneously apprehend the artistic advantage of a context endowed with those components over a similar one devoid of them.

The poet is more accustomed to abstract those verbal patterns and, especially, those rules of versification which he assumes to be compulsory, whereas a facultative, variational device does not lend itself so easily to a separate interpretation and definition. Obviously, a conscious deliberation may occur and assume a

An earlier version of this chapter was published in *Studies in General and Oriental Linguistics, presented to Shirô Hattori* (Tokyo, 1970); the present version is from *Poetics Today,* Vol. 2, No. 1a (1980): 127–136; and the definitive text is in Roman Jakobson, *Selected Writings III: Poetry of Grammar and Grammar of Poetry* (The Hague-Paris-New York: Mouton, 1981), 136–147.

beneficial role in poetic creation, as Baudelaire emphasized with reference to Edgar Allan Poe. There remains, however, an open question: whether in certain cases intuitive verbal latency does not precede and underlie even such a conscious consideration. The rational account *(prise de conscience)* of the very framework may arise in the author ex post facto or never at all. Schiller's and Goethe's exchange of well-grounded assertions cannot be dogmatically dismissed. According to Schiller's experience *(Erfahrung),* depicted in his letter of March 27, 1801, the poet begins *nur mit dem Bewusstlosen* [merely with the unconscious]. In his reply of April 3, Goethe states that he goes even farther *(ich gehe noch weiter).* He claims that genuine creation of a genuine poet *unbewusst geschehe* [happens unconsciously], while everything done rationally *nach gepflogner Überlegung* [after well-cultivated reasoning] occurs *nur so nebenbei* [only casually]. Goethe does not believe that a poet's supplementary reflection would be capable of amending and improving his work.

Velimir Xlebnikov (1885–1922), the great Russian poet of our century, when recollecting after several years his succinct poem "The Grasshopper," composed around 1908, suddenly realized that throughout its first, crucial sentence — *ot točki do točki* 'between two full stops' — each of the sounds *k, r, l,* and *u* occurs five times "without any wish of the one who wrote this nonsense" *(pomimo želanija napisavšego ètot vzdor),* as he himself confessed in his essays of 1912–1913, and thus joined all those poets who acknowledged that a complex verbal design may be inherent in their work irrespective of their apprehension and volition *(que . . . le versificateur . . . le veuille ou non),* or — to use William Blake's testimony — "without Premeditation and even against my Will." Yet also in his posterior reasonings Xlebnikov failed to recognize the much wider range of those regular phonological recurrences. Actually, all the consonants and vowels which pertain to the trisyllabic stem of the initial, picturesque neologism *krylyškúja,* derived from *krýlyško* 'little wing', display the same "fivefold structuration," so that this sentence, divided by the poet now into three, now into four lines, comprises 5/k/,5 vibrants /r/ and /r'/,5/l/,5 hushing (/ž/,/š/) and 5 hissing continuants (/z/,/s'/), 5/u/, and within each of the two clauses 5/i/ in both different, front and back, contextual variants of the given phoneme:

Krylyškúja zolotopis'môm tončájšix žíl,
Kuznéčik v kúzov púza uložíl
Pribréžnyx mnôgo tráv i vér.

'Winging with the gold script of finest veins,
The grasshopper filled the hollow of his belly
With many offshore weeds and faiths.'

The cited tristich, presenting a continuity of 16 duple, basically trochaic, feet, provides each of its three lines with four stressed syllables. Of the stressed phonemes, five flat (rounded) vowels, 3 /ú/ plus 2 /ó/, are opposed to their five nonflat (unrounded) correlates, 2 /í/ plus 3 /é/; and, on the other hand, these ten noncompact phonemes are divided into five diffuse (high) vowels, 3 /ú/ plus 2 /í/, and their five nondiffuse (middle) correlates, 2 /ó/ plus 3 /é/. The two compact /á/ occupy the same, second from the end position among the stressed vowels of the first and last lines and are both preceded by an /ó/: *pis'mÓm tončÁjšix — mnÓgo trÁv.* The five oxytones of the tristich, all five ending in a closed syllable, complete its pentamerous pattern.

The chain of quintets which dominate the phonological structuration of this passage can be neither fortuitous nor poetically indifferent. Not only the poet himself, originally unaware of the underlying contrivance, but also his responsive readers spontaneously perceive the astonishing integrity of the cited lines without unearthing their foundations.

While discussing examples of "self-contained speech" *(samovitaja reč')* which show a predilection for a "five-ray structure" *(pjatilučevoe stroenie)*, Xlebnikov detected this bent in the capital sentence of his earlier "Grasshopper" (nota bene: written at the same time as Saussure's daring studies on poetic anagrams) but did not pay attention to the guiding role played in this connection by the gerund *Krylyškúja*, the initial neologism of the poem. Only when returning again to the same lines in a later essay (1914), their author was charmed by the anagram hidden in the gerund: according to Xlebnikov, the word *uškúj* ('pirate ship', metonymically 'pirate') sits in the poem "as if in the Trojan horse": *KRYLy-ŠKÚJA* 'winging' *sKRŶL uŠKÚJA derevjánnyj kón'* 'the wooden horse concealed the pirate'. The title hero *KUzNéčIK*, in turn, is paronomastically associated with *uškÚjNIK* 'pirate', and the dialectal designation of the grasshopper, *konjók* 'little horse', must have supported Xlebnikov's analogy with the Trojan horse. The lively ties of cognate words *kuznéčik*, literally 'little smith', *kuznéc* 'smith', *kózni* 'crafty designs', *kovát'*, *kujú* 'to forge', and *kovárnyj* 'crafty' strengthen the imagery, and such a latent mainspring of Xlebnikov's creations as poetic etymology brings together *kuznéčik* with *kúzov* 'basket, hollow', filled with many offshore weeds and faiths or perhaps vaired foreign intruders. The swan evoked in the concluding neology of the same poem, *"Ó lebedívo — Ó ozarí!"*, 'send light!', seems to be a further hint to the Homeric subsoil of its ambiguous imagery: a prayer to the divine swan who begot Helen of Troy. *Lebed-ivo* is modeled upon *ogn-ivo* 'strike-a-light', since the metamorphosis of Zeus into a flaming swan calls to mind the change of flint into fire. The form *ljúbedi* occurring in the primary sketch of "The Grasshopper" was a suggestive blend of *lébedi* 'swans' with the root *ljub-* 'love', a favorite root in Xlebnikov's word coinages. *Krylyškúja*, the keyword of the poem, must have spontaneously, "in pure folly" (*v čistom nerazumii*), inspired and directed its whole composition.

The poet's metalanguage may lag far behind his poetic language, and Xlebnikov proves it not only by the substantial gaps in his observations concerning the quintuple pattern of the discussed tristich, but even more when in the next sentence of the same essay he deplores the lack of such arrangement in his militant quatrain — *Búd'te grózny kak OstrÁnica,||PlÁtov i BaklÁnov,||Pólno vam klÁnjat'sja||Róže basurumÁnov* — and thus surprisingly loses sight of its six quintets: five *a* under stress and downbeat; five flat (rounded) vowels, /ó/, /ú/, and unstressed /u/; five labial, all five initial, stops, /b/, /p/; five velar stops, /g/, /k/; five dental stops, /t/, /t'/; five hissing sibilants, /z/, /s/, /c/. Thus nearly one half of this string of phonemes takes part in the "five-ray" pattern; and, in addition to the cited vowels and obstruents, the lingual sonorants exhibit a chiseled symmetry — /r n r n'||l l n||l n l n'||r r n/ — and all the sonorants of the quatrain are divided evenly into eight liquids and eight nasals.

In the preface of 1919 to his planned Collected Writings, Xlebnikov viewed the short "Grasshopper" as "a minute entrance of the fiery god" (*malyj vyxod boga ognja*). The line between the initial tristich and the terminal prayer, *Pin'-pin' tararáxnul* (originally *Tararapin'pin'knul*) *zinzivér*, astounds one in its combination of the violent, thunderlike stroke *tararax-* with the feeble peep *pin'* and the assignment of the oxymoron to the subject *zinzivér*, which, like other dialectal variants *zenzevér, zenzevél', zenzevéj*, is a loanword cognate with English *ginger* but means 'mallow' in Russian. Incited by Xlebnikov's double reading of *krylyškúja*, one could suspect a similar paronomastic association between *zinzivér* and thunderous *Zevés* 'Zeus': /Z'InZ'IVÉr/ — /Z'IVÉs/.

When the propensity to frequent quintuple sound repetitions in poetry, particularly in its free, supraconscious (*zaumnye*) varieties, was observed and studied by Xlebnikov, this phenomenon prompted his comparisons with the five fingers or toes and with the similar makeup of starfish and honeycombs. How fascinated the late poet and eternal seeker of far-reaching analogies would be to learn that the puzzling question of prevalently fivefold symmetries in flowers and human extremities gave rise to recent scientific discussions, and according to Victor Weisskopf's synthesizing paper — "The Role of Symmetry in Nuclear, Atomic, and Complex Structures" (Contributions to Nobel Symposium 26 August 1968) — "a statistical study of the shape of bubbles in froth has revealed that the polygons that are formed on each bubble by the lines of contact with adjacent bubbles, are mostly pentagons or hexagons. In fact, the average number of corners of these polygons is 5.17. An assembly of cells should have a similar structure and it is suggestive that points of contact may give rise to special growth processes which may reflect the symmetry of the arrangement of these points."

Folklore provides us with particularly eloquent examples of a verbal structure heavily loaded and highly efficient despite its habitual freedom from any control of abstract reasoning. Even such compulsory constituents as the number of syllables in a syllabic line, the constant position of the break or the regular distribution of prosodic features are not educed and recognized per se by a carrier of oral tradition. When he is faced with two versions of a line, one of which disregards the metrical standard, this narrator or listener may qualify the deviating variant as less suitable or totally unacceptable, but he usually shows no capacity for defining the crux of a given deviation.

A few specimens picked up among the short forms of Russian folklore show us tight figures of sound and grammar in close unity with a definitely subliminal method of patterning.

Šlá svin'já iz Pítera,	'A pig was coming from Petersburg,
vsjá spiná istýkana.	[its] back is pierced all over.'

Napjórstok 'thimble' is the answer which is required by this folk riddle and is prompted by perspicuous semantic cues: this article comes to the country from the industrial metropolis and has a rough, pitted surface like the skin of a pig. Strict phonological symmetry closely connects both heptasyllabic lines: the distribution of word boundaries and stresses is exactly alike (-/ʋ-/ʋ-ʋʋ); at least six of the seven successive vowels are identical (/áiáií.a/); apart from the glide /j/ in /sv'in'já/, the number of consonantal phonemes before each of the seven vowels is equal in both sequences (2.2.1.#.2.1.1.) with numerous features shared by the parallel segments: initial preconsonantal continuants /s/ and /v/; two pairs of preconsonantal /s/ (/sv'i/ — /sp'í/ and /sp'i/ — /stí/); two pairs of voiceless stops around /i/ (/p'ít'/ — /tík/); two sonorants, /r/ and /n/, before the final /a/. Grammatical correspondences: feminines *šlá — vsjá*; feminine nouns as subjects, *svin'já — spiná*; preposition and prefix *iz*. The initial clusters of the two alliterating subjects are repeated in the other line: /sp'/ in *spiná* and *iz Pítera* and /sv'/ — /vs'/ in *svin'já* and *vsjá* with a metathesis of consonants and constancy of sharpness (palatalization) in the second, prevocalic consonant.

The answer word is anagrammatized in the text of the riddle. Each hemistich of its second line ends with a syllable similar to the prefix /na-/ of the answer: /sp'iná/ and /istíkana/. The root /p'órst-/ and the last hemistich of the first line of the riddle /isp'ít'ira/ display an equivalent set of consonants with an inverted order: A) 1 2 3 4; B) 3 1 4 2 (the first two phonemes of the set A correspond to the even phonemes of the set B and the last two phonemes of A to the odd phonemes of B). The last hemistich of the riddle /istíkana/ echoes the consonantal sequence contained in the final syllable of the answer /-stak/. Obviously, *Piter* was chosen among the other appropriate city names just for its anagrammatic value. Such anagrams are familiar to folk riddles; cf. *čërnyj kón'||prýgaet v ogón'* 'the black horse jumps into fire': as O. M. Brik pointed out in his historic essay on the sound texture of Russian poetry, all three syllables of the answer *kočergá* 'poker' show up with the due automatic alternations of the stressed varieties /kó/, /čór/, /gá/ and their unstressed counterparts. Furthermore, the prevocalic phonemes of all four stressed syllables of the riddle prompt the four consonantal phonemes of the answer: /čó/ – /kó/ – /rí/ – /gó/.

The dense phonological and grammatical texture of folk riddles is, in general, quite impressive. Two grammatically and prosodically parallel and rhyming trisyllables (- I ʋI-) — *kón' stal'nój,||xvóst l'njanój* 'a horse of steel, a tail of flax' (= a needle with a thread) — each count three identical vowels /óaó/ at least in that preponderant variety of Russian which preserves the pretonic /a/ in such forms as /l'n'anój/; in the other dialects the equivalence of both unstressed vowels is maintained merely on the morphophonemic level. Both lines begin with a voiceless velar. The interval between the two stressed vowels is filled in each line by five identical consonantal phonemes: /n'st.l'n/ (123.45) — /stl'n'.n/ (2341.5). The position of /n'/ makes the only sequential divergence between the two series. A typical syntactic feature frequent in Russian riddles and proverbs is the lack of verbs, a lack which effaces the difference between predicatives with zero copula and attributes.

Another riddle with the same topic and a similar metaphoric contrast of the animal's body and tail displays two pairs of rhyming disyllables — *Zverók s veršók,*|*la xvóst sem' věrst* 'A little beast of some two inches and a tail of seven versts.' These four colons vary a sequence of /v/ or /v'/ plus /o/ or an unstressed /e/ and a postvocalic /r/ after a prevocalic /v'/; under stress this series is concluded with the cluster /st/, while in an unstressed syllable it begins with a hissing continuant: /zv'er/ — /sv'er/ — /vóst/ — /v'órst/.

All these riddles replace the inanimate noun of the answer word by an animate noun of the opposite gender: masc. *napjórstok* 'thimble' by fem. *svin'já* 'pig' and, inversely, fem. *iglá* 'needle' by masc. *kón'* 'horse' or *zverók* 'little beast' and likewise fem. *nít'* 'thread' by masc. *xvóst* 'tail', a synecdoche relating to an animate. Cf., e.g., fem. *grúd'* 'bosom' represented by *lébed'* 'swan', an animate of masculine gender, at the beginning of the riddle — *Bélyj lébed' na bljúde né byl* 'the white swan has not been on a dish' — with a systematic commutation of sharp and plain /b/ and /l/: /b'.l / — /l'.b'.d'/ — /n.bl'.d'./ — /n'.b.l/. In this sentence all twelve occurrences of its four consonantal constituents display a network of symmetrical relations: six (4 + 2) occurrences of two sonorants and six (4 + 2) of two obstruents; three of these four archiphonemes occur each in the same number of sharp (palatalized) and of plain varieties: 2 /l'/ and 2 /l/; 1 /n'/ and 1/n/; 2 /b'/ and 2 /b/, while the acute (dental) stop appears only in its sharp variety — once voiced /d'/ and once with a contextual loss of its morphophonemic voicing (*lébed'*).

No propounder or unriddler of folk enigmas identifies such devices as the presence of all three syllables of the answer in the three initial words of the poker riddle itself (2 1 3) or its binary meter with two border stresses in either line of this distich, its three /ó/ with three subsequent dental nasals (1 2 4), and the prevocalic velar stop in each of the three words concluding the entire puzzle (2 3 4). But everyone would feel that the replacement of *čěrnyj kon'* by the synonymous *vóron kón'* or by *žéléznyj kón'* 'iron horse' could only impair the epigrammatic vigor of this poetic locution. A semblance of prosodic symmetries, sound repetitions, and a verbal substratum — *les mots sous les mots* (J. Starobinski's felicitous expression) — transpire without being supported by some speculative insight into the methods of procedure involved.

Proverbs compete with riddles in their pungent brevity and verbal skill: *Serebró v bórodu, bés v rebró* '[When] silver (a metaphor for grey hair which in turn is a metonymy for old age) [enters] into the beard, a devil (concupiscence) [enters] into the rib (an allusion to the biblical connection between Adam's rib and the emerging woman).' The two nominal pairs form a tenacious grammatical parallelism: corresponding cases in similar syntactical functions. Against this background, contrasting genders become particularly conspicuous: the animate masculine *bés* against the inanimate neuter *serebró* and, in turn, the inanimate neuter *rebró* against the inanimate feminine *bórodu,* and these genders come into a whimsical collision with the virile connotation of *bórodu,* and with the female symbolism of *bés.* The entire terse adage is a paronomastic chain; cf. the rhyme words *serebró - rebró,* the latter encompassed in the former; the entire permutation of similar phonemes which connects the beginning of the proverb *serebró v* with its end *bes v rebró;* within the initial clause the correspondence between the

end of its first and the beginning of its second noun: *serebró – bórodu*. The exquisite prosodic form of the proverb is based on a double contrast between its two clauses: the first one surrounds two contiguous stressed syllables by two pairs of unstressed syllables, whereas the second clause surrounds one single unstressed syllable by two single stressed syllables, and thus exhibits an antisymmetrical submultiple of the former clause. The presence of two accents is the metrical constant of both clauses: ‿ ‿ — — ‿ ‿
— ‿ —

The noted Polish anthropologist K. Moszyński in his *Kultura ludowa Słowian,* II, part 2 (Cracow, 1939), p. 1384, admires "the great formal condensation" of the humorous Russian proverb:

Tabák da bánja,	'Tobacco and bathhouse,
kabák da bába —	pub and female —
odná zabáva.	the only fun.'

(If, however, a stronger accent falls on *odná* or *zabáva* rather than there being equal accents on the two words of the final line, the meaning acquired by this line is 'same fun' in the former case, and 'nothing but fun' in the latter.)

A rigorous cohesion of the entire tristich is achieved through various means. Its persistently uniform rhythmical pattern, $3 \cdot (\cup - | \cup - \cup)$, comprises fifteen pervasive /a/ alternately unstressed and stressed (notice the South Russian vocalism /adná/!). The onset of the three lines differs from all of their following syllables: the last line begins with a vowel, whereas the other 14 vowels of the tristich are preceded by a consonant; both anterior lines begin with voiceless consonants which appear to be the only two unvoiced segments among the 32 phonemes of the proverb (note the regular voicing of /k/ before /d/!). The only two continuants of its 17 consonants occur in the unstressed syllables of the terminal, predicative noun. The restricted grammatical inventory of this opus, its confinement to five nouns and one pronoun, all six in the nominative, and one reiterated conjunction, is a telling example of the elaborate syntactic style proper to proverbs and glimpsed in an observant sketch by P. Glagolevskij — "Sintaksis jazyka russkix poslovic," *Žurnal Ministerstva Narodnogo Prosveščenija* (1871) — but never investigated since. The central line carries the two culminant nouns — first *kabák*, an intrinsic palindrome, and afterwards *bába*, with its doubled syllable /ba/; *kabák* rhymes with the antecedent *tabák*, while *bába* forms an approximate rhyme with the final *zabáva* and shares its /bá/ with all the nouns of the proverb: five /bá/ on the whole. Reiterations and slight variations of the other consonants run jointly with the same vowel throughout the entire tristich:

$_1$/ta/ — /da/ — $_2$/da/ — $_3$/ad/ — /za/; $_1$/ák/ — $_2$/ka/ — /ák/; and $_1$/n'a/ — $_3$/ná/.

All these repetitive, pervasive features tie the four enumerated delights together and frame the chiastic disposition of their two pairs: tools of enjoyment, *tabák* and *bába,* juxtaposed with places of amusement, *kabák* and *bánja.* The metonymic character of these nouns, substituted for direct designations of enjoyments, is set off by the contrastive, intralinear neighborhood of locational and instrumental terms which is, moreover, underscored by the dissimilarity of masculine oxytones and feminine paroxytones.

While being distinct from the short sayings in the choice of devices, folk songs, in turn, reveal a subtle and manifold verbal structure. Two quatrains of a Polish song which belongs to the popular tradition of the countryseat will serve as an appropriate example:

Ty pójdziesz górą	You will go along the hill
a ja doliną,	and I along the valley,
ty zakwitniesz różą	You will blossom as a rose
a ja kaliną.	and I as a squashberry bush.
Ty bedziesz panią	You will be a lady
we wielkim dworze,	in a great court,
a ja zakonnikiem	and I a monk
w ciemnym klasztorze.	in a dark monastery.

Excluding the third, hexasyllabic line of the quatrain, all the lines count five syllables, and the even lines rhyme with each other. Both stanzas reveal a rigorous selection of grammatical categories used. Every line ends with a noun in a marginal case, instrumental or locative, and these are the only nouns of our text. Each of its two only pronouns, one of the second and one of the first person, occurs three times and in contradistinction to the marginal cases and final position of the nouns all these pronouns are in nominative and all of them appear at the beginning of the lines: *ty* 'you' in the first syllable of the odd lines *1–3–5, ja* 'I,' preceded regularly by the adversative conjunction *a,* occupies the second syllable of lines *2–4–7.* The three verbs, all in the second person singular of the perfective present with a futural meaning, follow immediately after the pronoun *ty,* whereas their corresponding first person verbal form after the pronoun *ja* is deleted by ellipsis. In addition to the eight nouns (six in instrumental and two in locative), to the six occurrences of personal pronouns in nominative, to the three finites, and to the thrice repeated conjunction *a,* the text in its second quatrain contains two contextual variants of the preposition 'in' ($_6we$, $_8w$) and two adjective attributes to both locative forms of nouns.

An antithetic parallelism underlies three pairs of clauses: lines *1–2* and *3–4* within the first stanza and the two couplets within the second stanza. These three pairs, in turn, are interconnected by a close formal and semantic parallelism. All three antitheses confront the higher and brighter prospects for the addressee with the gloomier personal expectations of the addresser and employ the symbolic opposition of the hill and the valley first, then a metaphoric contrast between the rose and the squashberry. In the traditional imagery of Western Slavic folklore *kalina* (whose name goes back to Common Slavic *kalŭ* 'mud') is linked ostensibly to marshy lands; cf. the preambles of a Polish folk song: *"Czego, kalino, w dole stoisz?‖Czy ty się letniej suszy boisz?"* 'Why do you, squashberry bush, stand in a valley? Are you afraid of the summer drought?' The cognate Moravian song supplies the same motif with abundant sound figures: *proč, kalino, v STrUZE STOJÍŠ? Snad se TUZE SUcha bOJÍŠ?* 'Why do you, squashberry bush, stand in a stream? Are you greatly afraid of dryness?' The third antithesis predicts high stature for the addressee and a sombre future for the addresser; at the same time, personal nouns of feminine and masculine gender announce the sex of the two characters. The instrumental, used consistently in opposition to the invariable nominatives *ty* and *ja*, presents all these contrasted nouns as mere contingencies which will separate both ill-fated victims until their posthumous talks about the "disjointed love" *(niezłączona miłość)* resting in a joint grave.

The three pairs of antithetic clauses with their concluding instrumentals together form a thorough threefold parallelism of broad and complex grammatical constructions, and against the background of their congruent constituents, the significant functional dissimilarity of the three paired instrumentals becomes prominent. In the first couplet the so-called instrumentals of itinerary — *górą* and *doliną* — assume the function of adverbial adjuncts; in the second couplet the instrumentals of comparison — *różą* and *kaliną* — act as accessory predicatives, whereas in the second quatrain the instrumentals *panią* and *zakonnikiem*, in combination with the copula *będziesz* and with the elliptically omitted *będę*, form actual predicates: The weightiness of this case gradually increases with its transition from the two levels of metaphoric peregrination through a simile comparing both personae with flowers of unlike quality and unlike altitude to the factual placement of the two heroes on two distant steps of the social scale. However, the instrumental in all these three different applications preserves its constant semantic feature of bare marginality and becomes particularly palpable when contrasted with the adduced contextual variations. The medium through which the actor moves is defined as the instrumental of itinerary; the instrumental of comparison confines the validity of the simile to one single display of the subjects, namely, their blossoming in the context quoted. Finally, the predicative instrumental heeds one single, supposedly temporal aspect assumed by the subject; it anticipates the possibility of a further, though here a postmortem change which will draw the severed lovers together. When the last pair of instrumentals deprives this case of any adverbial connotation, both couplets of the second stanza provide the compound predicate with a new adverbial adjunct, namely, two limitative and static locatives of dwelling — *we wielkim dworze* [in a great court] and *w ciemnym klasztorze* [in a dark monastery] — which appear in manifest contradistinction to the dynamic instrumentals of itinerary evoked in the initial couplet.

The close interconnection between the first two of the three parallelisms is marked by the supplementary assonance of lines *1* and *3* (*górą - różą*), faithful to the traditional Polish pattern of partial rhymes, namely rhymes juxtaposing voiced obstruents with sonorants and especially /ż/ with /r/ in view of the latter's alternations with /ż/ < /ř/. The last two parallelisms are begun and concluded by corresponding groups of phonemes: ₃/zakv'itn'eš/ — ₇/zakon'ik'em/, and, with a metathesis: ₄*kaliną* /kal/ — ₈*klasztorze* /kla/ (cf. also the correspondence between ₆*wielkim* /lkim/ and ₈*ciemnym klasztorze* /imkl/).

The lines devoted to the dismal destiny of the first person differ patently from their cheerful counterparts. Under word stress the instrumentals carry a back vowel ($_{1,3}$/u/, $_5$/a/) in the lines concerned with the addressee but show only /i/ in the lines dealing with the apparently disparaged and belittled addresser: *dolinq, kalinq, zakonnikiem.* All four nouns assigned to the maid are disyllabic — *górq, różq, paniq dworze* — in contrast to the lengthy and bulkier nouns of the autobiographic lines — *dolinq, kalinq, zakonnikiem, klasztorze.* Hence, the second person lines possess and the first person lines lack a break before the penult.

Phonology and grammar of oral poetry offer a system of complex and elaborate correspondences which come into being, take effect, and are handed down through generations without anyone's cognizance of the rules governing this intricate network. The immediate and spontaneous grasp of effects without rational elicitation of the processes by which they are produced is not confined to the oral tradition and its transmitters. Intuition may act as the main or, not seldom, even sole designer of the complicated phonological and grammatical structures in the writings of individual poets. Such structures, particularly powerful on the subliminal level, can function without any assistance of logical judgment and patent knowledge both in the poet's creative work and in its perception by the sensitive reader of *Autorenleser* ["author's reader"], according to an apt coinage by that courageous inquirer into the sound shape of poetry, Eduard Sievers.

On Poetic Intentions and Linguistic Devices in Poetry

*A Discussion with Professors and Students
at the University of Cologne*

Roman Jakobson

Kasack: [. . .] You raised the rather difficult question to what extent we, as scholars of literature, may ask ourselves the question whether certain devices deviating from a rule or conforming to a rule — you clarified this very well yesterday — are used consciously or unconsciously. A clue to an answer might be the comparison between different versions, and I am curious whether you have found a conscious employment of prepositions or articles, or other words on this level. The fact that we can find it in the area of rhyme, rhythm or syntax in a wider sense is evident enough. But you have given amazing evidence for the smallest units — hence my question: can a conscious choice be demonstrated through a comparison between different versions in certain writers?

Jakobson: Thank you for this very important question. I should say — I believe I indicated this yesterday — that there are three possibilities — chance, a subconscious activity and a conscious activity. I exclude chance here in this case. It is quite impossible — as any mathematician dealing with probability will tell you — that such an exact distribution of conjunctions and prepositions as we have found in this poem (W. B. Yeats, "The Sorrow of Love," 1925 version) should be quite fortuitous. Some of my students argued with me on this point claiming they would be able to find the same phenomena in *The New York Times*. I offered them a bet of a hundred dollars and they lost so resoundingly that I could

This discussion, chaired by Professor Hansjakob Seiler, Director of the Linguistic Institute of the University of Cologne, was held on 27 May 1975. The discussion was occasioned by Prof. Seiler's course on the theories of Roman Jakobson and by Jakobson's lecture "Poetry as Verbal Art" which used examples from the analysis of Yeats' poem "The Sorrow of Love" (see full study below, 79–107). This translation by Susan Kitron, Tel-Aviv, reproduces (with a few omissions) the transcript published as *Arbeitspapier* No. 32 December 1976 (Institut für Sprachwissenschaft-Universität Köln). The translation previously appeared in *Poetics Today*, Vol. 2, No. 1a (1980): 87–96.

not possibly demand the hundred dollars from them. A short time ago I was even asked the same question in print, by a lecturer at Oxford University, who had published a book, *Structuralist Poetics,* in which a chapter is devoted to my attempts at applying linguistics to poetics. The author made the experiment of taking a few lines out of one of my essays in order to interpret them from the point of view of poetics. The result was really extremely negative. I told him — I had a discussion with him in Oxford quite recently — that if it were a work of poetry, it would be an awfully bad poem.

Now to the most difficult question—subconscious or fully conscious. I must say — and I am sometimes amazed — it is on the whole believed to be subconscious; but then the poet's notes are found, and it becomes apparent that he perceived a great deal quite clearly, nearly theoretically, as it were. Nevertheless, I believe that in most cases we have to do with a subconscious activity. I have written an essay concerning this problem—"Subliminal Verbal Patterning in Poetry." Please permit me to quote an example. We know the Serbian folkloric epic poetry; very often quite illiterate people — shepherds or peasants — are able to recite and sing thousands, even ten thousands of lines from the epic, and it is interesting to note that not only can they memorize all that, but that the role of the art of improvisation is significant. A Prague scholar of Slavic languages and literatures, Professor Murko, came to the singers, wrote down much of their poetry and made friends with some of these *guslars,* as those people call themselves who sing and recite the epic poems. They became friends, and as they were friends they drank wine together on the day of their parting, and one of the guslars, who a short time before had made inquiries about the professor's life (where and how he had spent the years of his childhood and youth, where he had served in the army, etc.), then improvised the story of the scholar's life. In doing so he used the same traditional poetic forms, and then only one of these forms, i.e., the decasyllable with an obligatory break between words after the fourth syllable and a regular distribution of long and short syllables at the end of the line. If these people were asked how many syllables there are in a line, they would be unable to give an answer, since they do not know what a syllable is: "What is this break (caesura) after the fourth syllable?" No idea. Neither do they know anything about quantity. However, at the end of the 19th century a Serbian poet, Nović, who was very interested in the epic tradition, came to one of the shepherds who sang and improvised to learn how to act as a *guslar* and he learnt how to reproduce these poems. He sang, and the peasant, who was very satisfied, told him: "You sing very well, you're doing just fine." Then however, Nović made some slight changes, i.e., he did not place the caesura after the fourth syllable, but after the fifth; and the shepherd said it was bad. "Why bad?" — "Simply bad." Such an intuitive understanding of the norm and its violation is a common occurrence. Once a well-known French scholar of Slavic literature, Vaillant, said to me: "How can you imagine that the forms are really so complicated, if the people do not even realize what these forms are." "Yes," I said, "and what about those Caucasian languages in which there are eighteen grammatical cases?" The natives use these quite accurately, much more so than the scholars, who understand their meaning. At the same time, it is absolutely subliminal. I do believe we cannot exclude the subliminal. There was a magnificent discussion about this between Goethe and Schiller, and this discussion always remains topical. We have to take into account that there are matters which we can now investigate or formulate, but which exist in imaginative literature without our having to assume that the poet is not aware of it — that the poet does not realize it. By the way, Yeats showed great understanding of this problem in his essays, e.g., he wrote an essay about the function of sounds in poetry, in which it can be seen how greatly he appreciated this function. But should one ask him, as in an examination: "Please explain the repetitions of sounds, the repetition of groups, the correspondences between meaning and sound in this or that quatrain," he would perhaps flunk the exam. Yet, I must say that this should be expected. Talking with some of my colleagues after yesterday's lecture I said we were in exactly the same situation as a musicologist investigating a musical composition. There are so many details in a great composition, say one of Mozart, about which we state that the regularities can be determined quite clearly and that they are important for the whole work. However, the audience is enthusiastic, but if I ask them: "Could you define the reason for your enthusiasm?" they will answer: "It is very beautiful." "And what makes it beautiful?" Most people would be in deep water.

*

Well, I have received some questions about the poem (Yeats' "The Sorrow of Love," 1925 version). First some general ones: "Where is the connection between the linguistic analysis of a poem as attempted by you yesterday, and an analysis of its literary substance?"

There are words I am afraid of. One of these words is "substance." A short while ago, when I was asked this question, I asked my friend Seiler what the exact difference was between substance and content [*Gestalt-Inhalt*]. Well, it's difficult to say. They are different words that should be explained differently. But, listen, it's quite a problem. This poem by Yeats — or any other poem — could be translated. Yesterday I read out the translation by Richard Exner, which you have also received. Any such translation may be very nice, but no translation of a work of art can be a real translation. It is a transposition into different media. If the translator is a great poet, his translation is a new and sometimes very beautiful poem. Something of the original may be preserved, but much is lost. It is also very interesting to note that what is preserved is often hardly known to the translator's consciousness. I can quote a nice case, when many years ago I visited Saran, the famous German historian of literature and expert on poetry, pupil of the brilliant Sievers. We spent a pleasant evening talking, and Saran, who did not know a word of Russian, told me he had never heard any Russian poetry and asked me to recite something. Now, I knew that Saran had a poetic hatred. He hated Heine. And I chose a poem by the great Russian Symbolist poet, Aleksandr Blok, a translation from Heine, but I did not say what it was. I read it out to him and he said: "Strange, it's Russian, but it sounds like Heine." You see, something remains, but what? Actually, even in Blok's translation of Heine or of any other German or Italian poet a great deal is lost.

Now we go a step further. There are not only translations, but also transpositions into another art. This poem could be transposed into a painting — perhaps an abstract painting or, on the contrary, a painting in which you can actually see the young girl celebrated by Yeats as well as the heroes of the Iliad and Odyssey who serve as associative links behind the poem. However, something quite different will come out because the semiotic structure is different. It will be an intersemiotic fact. Transposition is permissible. A beautiful picture may even come of it. I consider Blake's illustration of Dante very beautiful; however, it is not Dante, but something quite different. On the other hand, Yeats' poem could also be put to music or could be filmed. All these transpositions show that there is a common element in all these art forms. Something remains. Most of it is gone, though; I would not say it's lost, but it is altogether transformed. Thus, instead of "substance" I would rather speak of "the semiotic factor," something not exactly corresponding to a sign system, but, as it were, expressible in the most varied sign forms. This does exist. What else belongs to the concept of "substance"? Perhaps this: could you tell me, just tell me without bothering about verse, what could be preserved as substance in this poem by Yeats? Hardly anything remains. Tolstoj's famous answer applies here as well. Upon being asked what he had meant to say with *Anna Karenina,* he said one should simply read out *Anna Karenina* from the beginning to the end. The poetic value, as Novalis observed, is to be found in the emphasis on expression — expression in the widest sense of the word. It is the external and internal form of language that makes a poem a poem. I do not exclude the possibility, though, that this poem may be investigated from the aspect of the writer's ideology, his feelings in his younger years, etc. In case of a comparison between this poem and Yeats' memoirs and letters, one could even write an essay — which might be a good class assignment: "The Victorian Erotics in Yeats." I am ready to concede that in this short poem there is enough material for the psychoanalyst, the sociologist, the philosopher, etc. However, I am talking about poetics, and poetics is primarily the inquiry into the sign structure, that is to say the semiotic and, in a narrower sense, the linguistic signs of the work of art. I would like to be even more modest and say: "Please, let the linguists take part in the analysis of the poem as well. They are able to contribute a great deal, all the same." That page with rules, handed out during yesterday's lecture, may make a rather dry impression, but if you see these rules and their interrelations, you will recognize a fairly close connection to the whole construction, to the structure of the poem.

I have answered at such great length because this is the question I am asked most frequently by literary historians and by professors and students of the history of literature in the United States, in Europe or in Japan.

Böckmann: Nevertheless, I would like to ask a complementary question. Insofar as the orientation is according to form, such a microscopic view is certainly very profitable, but if I may refer to your example: Is there a possibility that this typically 'Heinean' quality, which Mr. Saran believed he was able to perceive even through the medium of a translation, may prove to be found in the verbal flow, in gesticulation, in the onset of the utterance itself? After all, this itself ought to be a linguistic phenomenon.

Jakobson: Yes, this question is certainly appropriate. I believe I gave Saran the solution to the puzzle right away. I said: "Yes, you're right; it is a translation of Heine." He was quite taken aback. But what we have here is, I suppose, one of Sievers's brilliant ideas. It is the whole problem of the innate curves, the Becking curves, as he called them. These are physiognomical qualities to be found in rhythm, melody, in the most varied — one might say biological elements of language, of dialogue as well as of poetry. I am unable to understand why no further research in Germany proceeds in this direction. Those were such magnificent hints. At that time they could not find a scientific infrastructure. This was impossible in the ideological climate of that period. In his essays Sievers himself sometimes understood it in a completely mechanical way: "Everything depends on the position of the abdomen," etc. The problem goes much deeper than the position of the abdomen. It is one of the questions on which Sievers assiduously worked in the first quarter of this century. He discovered a great deal, but it was purely by intuition. He himself was like a fakir. When given a typewritten letter — its content does not matter here — the first part of which was written by a woman and the second by a man, Sievers really could determine this and say that there were two persons of different sex who had written the letter. That was really great! Indeed he discovered a lot, though he sometimes exaggerated in some matters. Being a pioneer entails some exaggeration. He exaggerated when giving his opinion of texts written in languages he did not know at all. It's a pity I hurt his feelings when I was still a very young student by writing a review in a paper about his study of a text written in Old Church Slavonic, the so-called Kievan Leaflets. I said that from a few diacritical signs of the manuscript he had drawn conclusions concerning rhyme and melody without noticing that at the end of the printed text there was a note about printing errors and that it was a printing error to which he had fallen a victim. Nevertheless, I believe that even in this case he understood a great deal (though it was a Church Slavonic text and he knew nothing about Old Church Slavonic). It is a pity that when I recognized his discoveries later on, Sievers was already dead. He understood that it was a text written in verse and he understood where the lines ended. That was great, but now I believe that these observations of his could be examined systematically and that much more could be found there. Most important were, I believe, his studies of Germanic verse.

Böckmann: I myself still remember how he once introduced his ideas to us. One had the impression that it was mostly the transposition into rhythmic movements that constituted his starting point, the curves of vibration, which he still fixed for himself with the help of wire figures and on the basis of which he believed he could establish whether a text was appealing or failed to appeal; he was really quite a phenomenon.

Jakobson: He was, indeed, a phenomenon. It was the idea of the connection between what is verbal and gestures, movement, writing, etc. This discovery — I am not exaggerating — could have a great psychological and sociological significance. At that time it was impossible to systematize it, but it was a promising undertaking. I do not only know these matters from Sievers's works, but I had close contact with perhaps the most talented of Sievers's pupils of his last period, and that was Becking. Becking, who had subsequently been much influenced by Prague phonology, as you know from my German essay which has recently been reproduced (*SW II,* 551–553: "Musicology and Linguistics," showed me much about his own experiments and those of his teacher. As far as the problem of "oppositions" is concerned, we are dealing here with a true binary phenomenon — the opposition of types corresponding with each other and types excluding each other; and these are matters of importance for the individual as well as for social life — attraction and repulsion. It is great, but it was premature, as so many brilliant ideas have been, such as the ideas of Baudouin de Courtenay or Saussure, etc., but now it should be thoroughly and quite systematically examined with the help of experiments and on the basis of theoretical considerations.

Drux: Pursuing the former question I would like to ask this: in yesterday's lecture you demonstrated both the existence of various parallelisms on separate levels, i.e., the phonetic and syntactic level, and also the correspondences between the levels; and then you concluded that a significant presence — a multiple representation — of these equivalences constitutes the value of this poem. I would like to ask whether the value, the quality of a poem may be conclusively established through the fact that a great number of parallelisms and equivalences are ascertained.

Jakobson: No, a great poem can never be exhausted through any examination. The most varied equivalences may be discovered there, while others remain undetected in spite of all effort and good will to be accurate and exhaust all possibilities. Yet, we always perceive more and more. I have been dealing with this poem for quite some time, but yesterday, on my journey from Westphalia to Cologne, I suddenly made a new discovery, which I have had no time to refer to. One can never be quite exhaustive, I suppose. You may work on a composition by Mozart, yet your whole analysis does not replace the artistic value of a work of genius. Nevertheless, it is very important, I think, to come as close as possible and to understand what constitutes the poetic or, in another case, the musical essence in all its complexity. The unravelling of these complex problems is important, firstly, because one learns how to comprehend languages not only on the level of the referential function, but also on that of the poetic function. Furthermore, I believe that this work is also important for poets. I have seen this in several cases. I have noticed the impact of the research of the Moscow and

Petersburg circles at the threshhold of the 20th century and, later, of the Prague linguists on poets, on such great Russian poets as Majakovskij or Pasternak, on such great Czech poets as Nezval, Polish poets such as Tuwim, etc. I suppose poets want to see something of the mechanism of their own works, and they learn a great deal in this way. Quite a few poets have testified to this. However, it goes without saying that no research into man creates a new human being. No research into poetry creates a new Yeats.

Habel: Doesn't it lie in the very nature of poetry — since we are speaking about the quality of poets — that poetry should be related to the structure of language and not to content; for it is only the application of the material (the verbal material), but not the content found in it, that constitutes the difference between poetry and prose.

Jakobson: Quite right. I have dealt with this very often. One of the scientific books that have made the deepest impression in my life is the general theory of relativity of Einstein. In spite of the depth of his ideas I have never regarded it as poetry; and I have read letters filled with deep emotions, for instance passionate letters written before suicide; but, for all that, these are no works of art. Novalis said that the poet is an enthusiast for language. He ought to be. But he may be a conscious enthusiast, as Novalis was, or an unconscious one.

X: When, at the end of your next-to-last reply, you mentioned that the theoretical reconstruction of a thing cannot really replace this thing, didn't you thus limit the scope of your method which aims at defining the value of a poem through the establishment of as many such equivalences as possible? One could imagine the case of a person intending to produce levels of a verbal utterance; thus, through the introduction of all kinds of interrelations between those separate levels, he might create a verbal product, which, if possible, possesses as many equivalences and correspondences between these equivalences as the most intricate analysis you have ever made of any poem. Imagine, furthermore, that other people came, whose right to deal with this text cannot be disputed — for you have just said that there is a philosophical, psychological and sociological approach besides the linguistic one—but that these people as well as the producer of this work would eventually say that this is not a work of art. Well, then, there should be some clarification with regard to the limitation of this method.

Jakobson: What you have said about the limitation of the method applies to all sciences in the world. It is always the case that any analysis whatsoever, whether in the field of geology, physics or any other field, has only a temporary value and will subsequently be replaced by a more accurate and more profound one. Besides an accurate method, some poetic intuition is needed for the analysis of a poetic work. Only if one loves poetry (and loves it with understanding), above all, only if one has some empathy, can one do this work. Otherwise, it is the most boring labor in the world. If the above-mentioned method is painstakingly applied to such aspects as the grammatical structure, grammatical parallelisms, the sound structure, I can hardly believe that subjectivity could play a destructive role. In conclusion, I would say: every scientific labor is a synecdoche — it is a part for a whole. Nevertheless, I believe that the number of possible scientific synecdoches is obviously limited.

*

Y: Please, permit me, Professor Jakobson, to ask a perhaps obstinate question concerning the extent to which your method is applicable. I may have phrased this somewhat vaguely, and I'd like to show what I mean on the basis of a concrete example. In your analysis of Brecht's "Lob der Partei" ["In Praise of The Party"] (Jakobson, 1965) you established all the equivalences as well as the poetic function of this poem on the basis of these equivalences. At about the same time a poet in Germany, Heinrich Annacker, wrote a poem operating with quite similar and very strong equivalences and there are students of the German language and literature who have also demonstrated this with the help of your method. For your information, Heinrich Annacker was one of the leading Fascist lyrical poets. I would now like to ask you whether, therefore, there exists a criterion in your analytical method distinguishing between the poet Brecht and the poet Annacker; or whether, after the establishment of the equivalences, both poems are equally good, equally good as poems?

Jakobson: I'd like to answer several quesions at the same time. One is that I do not know the poet Annacker. Therefore it is difficult for me to refer to this concrete case. In Brecht's case a deep paradox emerges from this poem, a quite necessary inner ambiguity. We have here an antinomy that can be established even if nothing were known of the course of his life. This is to be found in the poetic material itself. It is a poem of the sharpest paradoxes. A poet's membership in a party is a subject that may be studied; I don't know whether this is one of the most interesting subjects, but I only deal with what is relevant for poetics; and this question is irrelevant for poetics. I also know that there are poets (and one could quote examples from several languages) who, using the same poetics, were radically Left one year and radically Right the next year, or vice versa. Yet, this makes hardly any difference as far as poetics is concerned. However, if you ask me whether there are trends in poetry corresponding, as it were, to trends in social life, etc., then we touch upon a tempting interdisciplinary problem; in my work in question, however, I would like to remain within the limits of poetics and even within the still narrower limits of linguistic poetics.

I have here still a few questions to which I ought to reply, if only briefly. I distinguish six essential functions of language according to the six elements of every speech act. The question then arises whether, in that case, I am right in referring to the inner logic of linguistic structures on which the hypothesis of the systemic character of languages is based — in view of the heterogeneity of the functions. I am much obliged to Mr. Lehmann for this question. The idea of the uniform system of language seems odd. Whether we assert anything about society or about language, a system is, as it were, a complex and manifold structure. When I examine the linguistic code, I use the adjective "convertible" in English, a term employed for cars (though there is no corresponding technical expression in German). If it is raining, a "convertible" is equipped with a roof and if the weather is fair, the roof can be taken off. This may also, similarly, apply to the linguistic system. Each linguistic function can become the dominant one. For example, the poetic function may appear as the dominant one, and then the utterance becomes imaginative literature. But the same function can operate together with another one that is dominant. When, for instance, an American foundation sent me a questionnaire requesting me to give my opinion of an applicant for a scholarship, the secretary asked me to express "my candid opinion" about the candidate. Most probably, the pun lay below the threshhold of consciousness, and the secretary was not aware of the fact that "candid" and "candidate" are different forms of the same word. Many analogous examples may be quoted. The poetic function plays some part whenever we speak, but it is important whether it is a dominant part or not. And there is no simple accumulation of the six functions. These six functions, interconnected, form a very coherent synthetic whole which should be analyzed in every single case.

*

Now I have two questions here about the concept of teleonomy, and I must say that this is now frequently discussed in biology, not only in Monod's book (1970) but much better and more accurately in works that have recently appeared, for example in the work of the Harvard biologist Ernst Mayr. It is a question whether this concept plays any part in language. It goes without saying that language is geared to expediency. Language is necessarily goal-oriented. However, Mr. van dem Boom asks: "Does this principle also apply to language as a diachronic system?" Yes, I have written quite a lot about this, i.e., about the relationship between the <u>diachronic</u> and the <u>synchronic</u>. I suppose that any changes first arise in the synchronic existence of language and therefore we ought to give a synchronic description of language, to which we should necessarily add the changes that are occurring; these should be described, too. And then we may ask the question: what is the significance of these changes? Very frequently, we can see this significance quite clearly. However, when it is, for instance, a matter of dephonologization and two phonemes coincide, what do we get? First, we then get two varieties, one in which they have not yet coincided, the explicit one, and the second, the elliptical one. <u>Ellipsis</u> plays the principle role in the life of our language, in the microcosm of language as well as in the macrocosm. Language is elliptical from childhood on. Ellipsis is a very important matter. At first I quite naively contrasted an elliptical and an optimal style. In many functions, however, the elliptical style in language proves to be the optimal one. But when someone says: "I'll spend this weekend, that is to say Saturday and Sunday, at home," this is not optimal, but superfluous, redundant. Ellipsis is very often a fight against redundancy. Elliptical factors should be regarded as major, though not the only conditions for linguistic changes, and this situation should be interpreted systematically, which means here, of course, teleonomically or (if you wish to be less circumspect in your use of language) teleologically.

REFERENCES

JAKOBSON, R., 1965. "Der Grammatische Bau des Gedichts von Bertolt Brecht 'Wir sind sie'," in: *SW III,* 660–676.
MAYR, E. 1974. "Teleological and Teleonomic," *Boston Studies in the Philosophy of Sciences* 14, 91–117.
MONOD, J., 1970. *Le hasard et la nécessité* (Paris: Seuil).

Yeats' "Sorrow of Love" through the Years

Roman Jakobson and Stephen Rudy

> Why, what could she have done being what she is?
> Was there another Troy for her to burn?
> "No Second Troy," 1910

1. INTRODUCTION

1.0. Paul Valéry, both a poet and an inquisitive theoretician of poetry as an 'art of language,' recalls the story of the painter Degas, who loved to write poems, yet once complained to Mallarmé that he felt unable to achieve what he wanted in poetry despite being 'full of ideas.' Mallarmé's apt reply was: "Ce n'est point avec des idées, mon cher Degas, que l'on fait des vers. C'est avec des mots" (Valéry, 1945:141). In Valéry's view Mallarmé was right, for the essence of poetry lies precisely in the poetic transformation of verbal material and in the coupling of its phonetic and semantic aspects (cf. 1945:319).

1.1. William Butler Yeats, in a paper written in 1898 in favor of "art that is not mere story-telling," defended the notion that "pattern and rhythm are the road to open symbolism." According to Yeats, "the arts have already become full of pattern and rhythm. Subject pictures no longer interest us [. . .]." In this context he refers precisely to Degas, in Yeats' opinion an artist whose excessive and obstinate desire to 'picture' life — "and life at its most vivid and vigorous" — had harmed his work (1973:283f.). The poet's emphasis on pattern reminds one of Benjamin Lee Whorf, the penetrating linguist who realized that "the 'patternment' aspect of language always overrides and controls the 'lexation' or name-giving aspect" (1956: 258), and an inquiry into the role of "pattern" in Yeats' own poetry becomes particularly attractive, especially when one is confronted with his constant and careful modifications of his own works.

This chapter appeared as a separate publication (Lisse: Peter de Ridder Press, 1977) with a limited distribution, was then published in *Poetics Today,* Vol. 2, No. 1a (1980): 97–125, and was reprinted in Roman Jakobson, *Selected Writings III: Poetry of Grammar and Grammar of Poetry* (The Hague-Paris-New York: Mouton, 1981), 600–638.

2. TEXT AND VARIANTS

2.0. As early as 1899 Yeats stated that he "revised, and, to a great extent, re-wrote [. . .] certain lyrics" (1957:846). His epigraph to *Collected Works in Verse and Prose* (Stratford-on-Avon, 1908) reads:

> The friends that have it I do wrong
> When ever I remake a song,
> Should know what issue is at stake:
> It is myself that I remake (1957:778).

And in January, 1927 he mentions "new revisions on which my heart is greatly set" and adds, characteristically, "one is always cutting out the dead wood" (1957: 848). For the 1925 edition of his *Early Poems and Stories* he "altered considerably" several of his poems, among them "The Sorrow of Love," "till they are altogether new poems. Whatever changes I have made are but an attempt to express better what I thought and felt when I was a very young man" (1957: 842).

2.1. "The Sorrow of Love," which we will henceforth refer to as *SL,* is preserved in the poet's manuscript of October 1891 (*SL 1891*), then in two variants of 1892 differing slightly from each other, one published in the volume *The Countess Kathleen and Various Legends and Lyrics* (*SL 1892*) and the other in the weekly *The Independent* of October 20, 1892 (*SL 1892 Ind*). Later single changes appeared in Yeats' *Poems* (1895) and in their revised edition (1899). The radically reshaped text appeared first in Yeats' *Early Poems and Stories* (*SL 1925*), the notes to which, expressly mentioning *SL,* were quoted above. For an exhaustive survey of the text's history see Yeats (1957: 119–120), G. Monteiro (1966: 367–8), and R. Ellmann (1954: 122 and 317 note).

2.2. The poet's "Sorrow of Love," which may be traced in its textual changes through over three decades, proved to be fruitful material for investigation. The comparative reproduction of *SL 1925* and the first version included in one of Yeats' volumes, *SL 1892*, with all other relevant textual variants, follows:

The Sorrow of Love
(Final version, 1925)

I
$_1$The brawling of a sparrow in the eaves,
$_2$The brilliant moon and all the milky sky,
$_3$And all that famous harmony of leaves,
$_4$Had blotted out man's image and his cry.

II
$_1$A girl arose that had red mournful lips
$_2$And seemed the greatness of the world in tears,
$_3$Doomed like Odysseus and the labouring ships
$_4$And proud as Priam murdered with his peers;

$_1$Arose, and on the instant clamorous eaves,
$_2$A climbing moon upon an empty sky,
III $_3$And all that lamentation of the leaves,
$_4$Could but compose man's image and his cry.

The Sorrow of Love ^{a}
(First book version, 1892)

$_1$The quarrel ^{b} of the sparrows in the eaves,
I $_2$The full round moon and the star-laden sky,
$_3$And the loud song of the ever-singing leaves ^{c}
$_4$Had hid ^{d} away earth's old and weary ^{e} cry.

$_1$And then you came with those red mournful lips,
II $_2$And with you came the whole of the world's tears,
$_3$And all the sorrows ^{f} of her labouring ships
$_4$And all the burden ^{g} of her myriad ^{h} years.

$_1$And now the sparrows warring ^{i} in the eaves,
III $_2$The crumbling ^{j} moon, the white ^{k} stars in the sky,
$_3$And the loud chanting of the unquiet leaves, ^{l}
$_4$Are shaken with earth's old and weary ^{e} cry.

2.3. Actually, the poem offers two profoundly different texts, the early version of 1892, with a series of variants from the manuscript of 1891 to the final retouchings of 1895, and, on the other hand, the last, radically revised version of 1925. The final revision was so extensive that the vocabulary of the two versions has in common only: 1) the rhyme-words — in a few cases with their antecedent auxiliary words (I $_1$*in the eaves*, $_2$*and* [. . .] *the* [. . .] *sky*, $_3$*of* [. . .] *leaves*, $_4$*and* [. . .] *cry*; III $_3$*of the* [. . .] *leaves*, $_4$*and* [. . .] *cry*) and with the exception of one substitution (*1925:II* $_4$*peers* for *1892: years*) — or with their attributes in the inner quatrain (II $_1$*red mournful*, $_3$*labouring*); 2) seven initial accessory monosyllables (five *and*, two *the*, one *had*); 3) one noun inside the second line of each quatrain (I $_2$*moon*, II $_2$*world*, III $_2$*moon*).

3. COMPOSITION

3.0. The poem consists of three quatrains which in their structure display two patent binary oppositions: the two outer quatrains (I and III) exhibit common properties distinct from those of the inner quatrain (II), while at the same time they differ essentially in their internal structure from each other.

---

^{a} *1892 Ind:* the World ^{b} *1892 Ind:* quarreling ^{c} *1895.* leaves, ^{d} *1891:* hushed ^{e} *1892 Ind:* bitter ^{f} *1892 Ind:* sorrow; *1895:* trouble ^{g} *1895:* trouble ^{h} *1891:* million ^{i} *1891:* angry sparrows; *1892 Ind:* warring sparrows ^{j} *1891* and *1892 Ind:* withered; *1895:* curd-pale ^{k} *1892 Ind:* pale ^{l} *1891:* The wearisome loud chaunting of the leaves,

3.1. Both in the early and final version the poem confronts two opposite levels of subject matter, the upper and lower respectively. Six lines are devoted to each of them. The upper sphere, which may be labeled the 'overground' level, is treated in the first three lines of each outer quatrain. The lower level is focused upon in the four lines of the inner quatrain and in the fourth line of each outer quatrain. The last line of these two quatrains (I_4 and III_4) designates its topic as *earth* in the early version of the poem and as *man* in the late version, and the lower level may thus be defined as 'terrestrial' in respect to *SL 1892* and as specifically 'human' in *SL 1925*.

3.20. Only the outer quatrains expressly designate the two different levels and bring them into conflict. In both versions of the poem the initial quatrain portrays the outcome of this combat as a victory, and the final quatrain — as a defeat, of the overground level. Yet the extent of these outcomes varies significantly in the two versions of the poem. In the early version (*SL 1892*) the two rival levels continue to coexist, and only their hierarchy undergoes a change: at the beginning the overground I_4*Had hid away earth's old and weary cry*, but at the end it is the characters of the overground who III_4*Are shaken with earth's* [. . .] *cry*. To this preserved contiguity of the adversary spheres the late version of the poem (*SL 1925*) replies first by the obliteration of the human level (the overground I_4*Had blotted out man's image and his cry*) and then, conversely, by the dissolution of the overground in the human level (the characters of the upper level III_4*Could but compose man's image and his cry*). (In the parlance of the French translator Yves Bonnefoy, "Ne purent être qu'à l'image de l'homme et son cri d'angoisse," and in R. Exner's German translation, "Verdichten sich zu Menschenruf und Menschenbild." As indicated by *A Concordance to the Poems of W. B. Yeats*, the verb *compose* appears in Yeats' poetry but once, in the final line of *SL 1925* [Parrish, 1963:159].)

3.21. The mere contiguity, definable in metonymic terms, which characterized the two spheres in the outer quatrains of *SL 1892*, in *SL 1925* turns into a mutual metamorphosis of two contrastive sets of givens. The alternation of auditory and visual phenomena which delineate the upper sphere remains valid in both versions (the noise of the sparrow, the celestial view, the sound of leaves). In the early version, however, the lower sphere is merely audible, whereas in *SL 1925* it incorporates the visual dimension as well (*image* and *cry*) and thus corresponds in its deployment to the overground level.

3.3. In the inner quatrain of *SL 1925*, the heroine who suddenly emerges (II_1*A girl arose*) is identified — through a chain of similes (II_2 *seemed,* $_3$*like,* $_4$*as*) — with the tragic and heroic human world. The system of metaphors underlying the inner quatrain of *SL 1925* differs patently from the whimsical metathetic confrontation of the two sociative prepositions *with* (II_1*And then you came with* [. . . .], $_2$*And with you came* [. . .]) in *SL 1892* and from the series of summarizing totalizers (II $_2$*the whole of* [. . .], $_3$*And all the* [. . .] *of* [. . .], $_4$*And all the* [. . .] *of*

[. . .]) in the early version. The first of these totalizers (II $_2$*the whole of the world's tears*) was transformed in *SL 1925* into II $_2$*the greatness of the world in tears*, which is in rough semantic contrast with I $_2$*The brawling of a sparrow in the eaves*, while at the same time demonstrating an expressive formal parallelism that further emphasizes the irreconcilable divergences between the two levels.

3.4. To the simultaneous concord and discord between the parts of each of the integral poems, Yeats' creed as poet and creative visionary adds a different fusion of stability and variability, namely his view of development as "a temporal image of that which remains in itself," to quote Hegel as cited by the poet (1956: 249). The two kinds of continual conflict between being and its opposite encompass both 'coexistence' and 'succession' according to Yeats, and in the case under discussion this applies to the dramatic tension both between the inner and outer or initial and final stanzas within one version of the poem and between the poem in its two different versions, the latter of which is seen by the author on the one hand as an "altogether new" poem (1957:842) and on the other hand as still belonging "to the time when [it was] first written" (1957:855). Like the individual stanzas of *SL 1892* or *1925,* which find their antithesis within the given version, these two versions in turn stand next to each other in an antithetical struggle and harmonious complementarity.

3.5. In the "Dedication" to his *Early Poems and Stories* (1925) Yeats concludes his comments on the new versions of some poems "written before his seven-and-twentieth year" with the conviction: "I have found a more appropriate simplicity" (1957:855). Critics, with rare exceptions (see R. Cowell, 1969:144), have repudiated the alteration of *SL* with such statements as: "the new version as a whole is both ill-digested and obscure" (MacNeice, 1941:71); "the poem has been emptied of its vital content" (Hone, 1943:126); the earlier versions of *SL* "were inherently more logical and less pretentious and hence more charming" (Saul, 1957:56). It seems necessary to replace such unsubstantiated polemical replies to the poet's own view by a detailed and objective comparison of Yeats' poem in its two phases.

4. GRAMMAR
4.0. It is against the background of the manifest grammatical symmetry underlying and uniting the three quatrains — and this symmetry is indeed supreme in *SL 1925* — that the significant individuality of each stanza in the dramatic composition of the entire poem gains a particular potency and eloquence. The distinct and thematically related features which differentiate single quatrains, their distichs, and single lines are achieved either through appreciable deviations from the predominant morphological and syntactic matrices or through the filling of these matrices with semantically divergent lexical and phraseological constituents. Robert Frost's metaphor, a favorite of I. A. Richards, on poets' preference for playing tennis with a net is valid not only for meter and rhyme but for the grammatical pattern of a poem as well.

5. $-ING-$FORMS

1925

5.0. Before focusing on the two basic grammatical opposites — noun and verb — let us mention the intermediate morphological entity which is, according to Strang (1968:175), "best labeled non-committally the *-ing-form*." Such forms appear once in every stanza of *SL 1925*, each time introducing the motif of movement into the nominal part of the three sentences: the first, in a substantival function, I $_1$ *The brawling*, and the other two in an adjectival use, II $_3$ *the labouring ships* and III $_2$ *A climbing moon*.

1891 – 1892

5.1. Like *SL 1925*, the manuscript of 1891 contained one *-ing*-form in each quatrain, two of the three in adjectival and one in substantival function (I $_3$ *eversinging*, II $_3$ *labouring*, III $_3$ *the* [. . .] *chaunting*). Their salient pattern in *SL 1891* was their location in the third line of each quatrain. *SL 1892* displays a greater tendency toward dynamism in the third quatrain, in which, besides the already-mentioned substantival III $_3$ *the* [. . .] *chaunting*, one finds the two attributes, $_1$ *warring* and $_2$ *crumbling*.

6. NOUNS

1925

6.0. The poem contains twenty-seven (3^3) nouns, nine (3^2) in each quatrain, of which three in each quatrain occur with prepositions:

I $_1$ (of) *sparrow*, (in) *eaves*; $_2$ *moon, sky*; $_3$ *harmony*, (of) *leaves*; $_4$ *man's image, cry*.

II $_1$ *girl, lips*; $_2$ *greatness*, (of) *world*, (in) *tears*; $_3$ *Odysseus, ships*; $_4$ *Priam*, (with) *peers*.

III $_1$ (on) *instant, eaves*; $_2$ *moon*, (upon) *sky*; $_3$ *lamentation*, (of) *leaves*; $_4$ *man's, image, cry*.

6.1. One even line of each quatrain has three nouns (I $_4$, II $_2$, III $_4$), and any other line — two nouns. This rule can be further specified. In the outer (odd) quatrains the even line of the even distich contains an odd number of nouns (3), whereas in the inner (even) quatrains this odd number of nouns (3) is found in the even line of the odd distich. Any other line of the poem contains an even number of nouns (2).

6.2. Each quatrain has only one abstract noun, each of more than one syllable and each followed by the same preposition: I $_3$ *harmony* (of); II $_2$ *greatness* (of); III $_3$ *lamentation* (of).

6.3. The poem contains six personal (human, i.e., belonging to the *who*-gender) nouns, of which two common (II $_1$ *girl*, $_4$ *peers*) and two proper names ($_3$ *Odysseus*,

₄*Priam*) appear in the inner quatrain, whereas each of the outer quatrains has only one personal noun, the possessive *man's* in I₄ and III₄. Of these six personal nouns only one (II ₁*girl*) belongs to the feminine (*she-*) gender, while the other five are of the masculine (*he-*) gender.

6.40. Only nouns function as rhyme-fellows, and the plural occurs solely in rhymes: eight of the twelve rhyme-fellows are plural nouns. Might not this propensity of the rhyming line-ends for the plural perhaps underscore a contrast between the frame of the lines and their inside? Is not the inside of the line the actual arena in which the individual actors of the drama perform, such as 'the brawling sparrow' and 'the brilliant moon,' 'a girl' and 'man,' 'Odysseus' and 'Priam'?

6.41. The distinctness of the rhymes is highlighted not only by their grammatical peculiarities, but also by the consistent use of monosyllabic words in all the rhymes of the poem and by the common vocalic properties that all of them share: the rhymes of the first quatrain, all repeated in the third, are built on the phoneme /i/ alone or as the asyllabic end of the diphthong /ai/, while all four lines of the second quatrain use /I/, the lax (short) opposite of the tense /i/.

6.42. The two constituents of each of the six rhymes are morphologically homogeneous but syntactically heterogeneous. In each quatrain one line ends in a grammatical subject (I ₂*sky*, II ₃*ships*, III ₁*eaves*), one in a direct object (I ₄*cry*, II ₁*lips*, III ₄*cry*), and two in prepositional constructions (I ₁*in the eaves,* ₃*of leaves*; II ₂*in tears,* ₄*with his peers*; III ₂*upon an empty sky,* ₃*of the leaves*).

6.43. The variety in the syntactic use of the rhyming nouns achieved in *SL 1925* is lacking in the early version, where ten of the rhyme-fellows belong to prepositional constructions. The only exception in *SL 1892* is the rhyming of the subject I ₂*sky* with the direct object I ₄*cry*, which grammatically underlines the striking opposition of the overground and terrestrial levels (cf. 3.2ff. above).

1892

6.5. The distribution of nouns is here less symmetrical than in the final version. There is a total of 25 nouns in *SL 1892*, the number per quatrain oscillating between nine (I) and eight (II and III). One line of each quatrain contains three nouns; two lines — two nouns each; and one line — two or one.

6.6. All three abstract nouns of *SL 1925* are innovations of the final version; the early version is completely devoid of abstracts. There are no properly personal nouns, but *SL 1892* contains three possessive forms, each in an even line of a different quatrain and each pertaining to a noun which exhibits, in Jespersen's terms (1924:237), "some approach to personification": II ₂*the world's tears* and I ₄, III₄ *earth's cry*, the latter in positional correspondence to the possessive form of the properly personal noun in *SL 1925*, I₄, III ₄*man's*. (As regards the personalization of the possessives of *SL 1892*, cf. such lines in Yeats' works as "The wandering earth *herself* [. . .]" [1957:65, line 18] or "before earth took him to *her* stony care" [1957:126, line 4]). It is noteworthy that in both versions the possessive always falls on the metrical upbeat (cf. 17.30ff.). The increase of personalization among the nouns of *SL 1925* is also witnessed by the replacement of the personal pronoun *you* in II $_{1-2}$ of *SL 1892* by the noun II $_1$*girl* cf. 19.7.).

6.7 The number of plurals in the rhyme-fellows remains constant in both versions, but *SL 1892* has, in addition, four plural nouns *inside* the line, one in quatrains I and II, and two in quatrain III; I $_1$*sparrows*; II $_3$*sorrows*, III $_1$*sparrows*, $_2$*stars*. All four interior plurals are framed by hissing sibilants, an initial /s/ and a final /z/, and have a stressed vowel followed by /r/. Thus the grammatical differentiation between the inside and the end of the lines achieved in *SL 1925* by the restriction of plural nouns to the latter (cf. 6.40.) is missing in *SL 1892*.

6.8. The word *sorrows* of II $_3$ was apparently discarded in the final version to avoid the repetition of the words of the title within the text, as in a similar way the tentative title of *SL 1892 Ind*, "The Sorrow of the World" was cancelled because *world*, not *love*, occurs in the text. The pun-like confrontation of II $_3$*sorrows* and I$_1$,III $_1$*sparrows* became confined in *SL 1925* to the title and opening line, where *sparrows* imitate the singular form of *Sorrow*. This change from plural to singular, effective not only in grammatical meaning but also in sound (cf. 16.2. below) — I $_1$*The brawling of a sparrow* [. . .] — met with the objections of the critic Parkinson (1951:168), for whom "*brawling* is not perfectly right; can one sparrow brawl?". Cf., however, such usages of this word in Yeats' poetry as "big brawling lout" (1957:301, line 9) of "I took you for a brawling ghost" (1957:304, variant to line 41).

7. PRENOMINAL ATTRIBUTES

1925

7.0. The phrases built of nouns and prenominal attributes (adjectives proper and -*ing*-forms) in the three quatrains of *SL 1925* display a remarkably symmetrical patterning:

	LINE:	1.	2.	3.	4.	TOTAL
	I:	—	2	1	— =	3
QUATRAIN	II:	2	—	1	— =	3
	III:	1	2	—	— =	3
						$\overline{\overline{9}}$

7.1. Each quatrain contains two lines with and two lines without prenominal attributes. There are no prenominal attributes in the fourth line of any quatrain. Of the first three lines in each quatrain, one line contains two, one line — one, and one line — no prenominal attributes. The third line contains no more than one prenominal attribute (I $_3$ *famous*, II $_3$ *labouring*, III$_3$———). If one of the first three lines contains no prenominal attributes, a neighboring line will have two of them: I $_1$———, $_2$*brilliant, milky*; II $_1$*red, mournful*, $_2$———; III $_2$*climbing, empty*, $_3$———). In contradistinction to the outer quatrains, with prenominal attributes in contiguous lines, the inner quatrain has such attributes in its odd lines only. The line without prenominal attributes advances from one quatrain to the next, so that its distribution forms a descending curve. The distribution of prenominal attributes in the first three lines of the final quatrain displays a mirror symmetry to that of the initial quatrain $(1,2, - \longleftrightarrow - ,2,1)$.

1892

7.2. The early version of *SL* is almost twice as rich in prenominal attributes with an epithetical function (total $17-18$) and has a higher number of such attributes in the outer as opposed to the inner quatrains: seven in I ($_2$*full round*, $_2$*star-laden*, $_3$*loud*, $_3$*ever-singing*, $_4$*old and weary*) and seven in the earliest two versions of III (*1891* and *1892 Ind.*), whereas the number in *SL 1892* is reduced to six — $_2$*crumbling*, $_2$*white*, $_3$*loud*, $_3$*unquiet*, $_4$*old and weary* — by the replacement of the prenominal attribute *1891: angry* (*1892 Ind: warring*) *sparrows* by III $_1$*sparrows warring*. On the other hand, II contains only four prenominal attributes: $_1$*red mournful*, $_3$*labouring*, $_4$*myriad*.

7.3. One could say that the changes found in *SL 1925* are in line with such slogans as Marianne Moore's warning against the use of too many adjectives and adverbs, which is based upon the notion that "poetry is all nouns and verbs" (*New York Times*, March 22, 1961, p. 31). As Parkinson states, the revised text of the poem "reduces the number and sensuous reference of epithets" (1951:172). Yeats himself acknowledges a tendency toward the exfoliation of his style (1965: 291).

8. POSTPOSITIVE ATTRIBUTES

8.0. *SL 1925* contains postpositive (semi-predicative) attributes only in the second distich of the inner quatrain (cf. 15.0.). Of the three occurrences, two are past passive participles (II $_3$*Doomed*, $_4$*murdered*) and one is an adjective (II $_4$*proud*). The only postpositive attribute in *SL 1892* (II $_1$*sparrows WARRING in the eaves*) was absent in the two earliest variants (*1891, 1892 Ind.*).

9. PRONOUNS

1925

9.0. Only three pronouns occur in the poem. All three are attributive, and each of them — *his, that, all* — is repeated three times, giving a sum total of nine. *His* occupies the penultimate syllable of the last line in each quatrain and refers expressly to a masculine noun: I $_4$*his cry*, II $_4$*his peers*, III $_4$*his cry* (*man's* in I$_4$ and III$_4$; *Priam* in II$_4$). *That* appears in one odd line of each quatrain, as a demonstrative pronoun referring, in a rather high-flown manner, to abstracts in the outer quatrains (I $_3$*that* [. . .] *harmony*, III $_3$*that lamentation*) and as a relative pronoun referring to a feminine noun in the inner quatrain (II $_1$*a girl* [. . .] *that*) — in accordance with the subordinative structure of this stanza (cf.

14.1.). *All* occurs only in the outer quatrains, two times in contiguous lines of the first and once in the third, in the combinations *and all the* (I_2), *And all that* (I_3, III_3), and refers to singular nouns of the overground level, I $_2$*sky*, I $_3$*harmony of leaves*, III $_3$*lamentation of the leaves*.

1892

9.1. The outer quatrains of *SL 1892* are devoid of pronouns, whereas the inner quatrain contains seven. In *SL 1925* Yeats "dropped the stimulation of the structure of address" (Parkinson, 1951:168), while all the early versions of *SL* twice make use of the personal pronoun *you* in the first distich, with reference to the female addressee of the poem, and then of *her* in the second distich, with reference to the *world*, which merges with the addressee: II $_1$*you came with* [. . .] $_2$*And with you came the whole of the world's tears*. All the lines of the inner quatrain are dominated by the *she*-gender, which is directly expressed in both lines of the second distich and clearly alluded to in the *you* and *world* of the first distich (cf. 6.6. above). In *SL 1925* the feminine pronoun of the first distich (the relative *that* of II $_1$) gives way to the masculine pronoun of the second distich (II $_4$*his*), and the division into two distichs contrasted in gender is supported by the distribution of feminine and masculine nouns (II $_1$*girl* and $_2$*world* vs. $_3$*Odysseus*, $_4$*Priam, peers*). Twice, in turn, the pronoun *all* opens the contiguous lines of the second distich in the inner quatrain of *SL 1892* (II $_{3,4}$*And all the* [. . .]), where it refers to nouns of the terrestrial level (II $_3$*sorrows*, $_4$*burdens*); in *SL 1925* this pronoun is found, on the contrary, in the *outer* quatrains (I_3, III $_3$*And all that* [. . .]), where it refers to the *overground* level (cf. 9.0. above). Finally, II $_1$*those*, in the context *you came with those red mournful lips*, reinforces the odic manner of direct address in the early version and makes the roles of both the addresser and the addressee more prominent (cf. 19.7.).

10. ADVERBS

10.0. Two adverbs, II $_1$*then* and III $_1$*now*, each preceded by the initial conjunction *And*, open the two sentences of the second and third quatrains of *SL 1892* (note also a third adverbial form in the first quatrain which is part of the complex adjective I $_3$*And* [. . .] *ever-singing*). All three disappear in *SL 1925* (cf. 18.71. below).

11. ARTICLES

1925

11.0. The nine occurrences of *the* in the three quatrains form an arithmetical regression: 4—3—2. In the first half of the poem, three lines contain two definite articles each, and three — none, whereas the second half has three lines with one definite article in each, and three without any. In each quatrain of the poem, there are two lines with, and two without, definite articles.

	LINE: 1.	2.	3.	4.	TOTAL
QUATRAIN: I:	2 *the*	2 *the*	—	—	4
II:	—	2 *the*	1 *the*	—	3
III:	1 *the*	—	1 *the*	—	2
					9

Only one line in each quatrain, and in each case a different line, contains both the definite article and prenominal attributes: I_2, II_3, III_1. Each quatrain has one line with the indefinite article *a* and/or *an*, which may be compared to the equal distribution of lines with the definite article (2 lines per quatrain). The final line of each quatrain is completely devoid of articles.

11.1. The distribution of the articles is limited to the first two lines in the first quatrain and forms a rectangle. In the second and third quatrains the articles extend over the first three lines of each and form the figure of an oblique-angled quadrangle:

I:
The	*a*	the
The		the

II:
A		
the		the
		the

III:
The		
A		an
		the

1892

11.2. Of the articles, *a* is totally absent from *SL 1892*, whereas the distribution of the definite articles — 18 in the entire poem: seven in each of the outer quatrains and four in the inner one — corresponds strikingly to the identical pattern of prenominal attributes in the two earliest variants of the poem (cf. 7.2. above). It should be noted, finally, that in each quatrain of *SL 1892* only one line lacks the definite article: the final line of the outer quatrains, and the initial line of the inner quatrain.

12. CONNECTIVES

1925

12.0. The poem contains two equational conjunctions, both confined to the inner quatrain (II_3*like*, $_4$*as*), against nine copulative conjunctions, three instances of *and* in each quatrain. The other class of connectives, namely the prepositions (which here include *of, in, with, on,* and *upon*), like copulative conjunctions, numbers nine *in toto*, three per quatrain. The latter two classes of connectives taken together are attested nine times in each half of the poem ($I_1 - II_2$ and $II_3 - III_4$).

12.1. The distribution of these two categories (copulative conjunctions and prepositions) forms an identical chiasmus in the two distichs of each quatrain:

	CONJ.	+	PREP.	=	TOTAL
FIRST DISTICH:	1	chiasmus	2	=	3
SECOND DISTICH:	2		1	=	3
QUATRAIN	3		3	=	6

Thus in the transition from the first distich to the second each quatrain displays one and the same movement from government performed by the prepositions to grammatical agreement carried by the copulative conjunction *and*. This rule of transition from superposition to alignment may be juxtaposed to the consistent absence of masculine personal nouns in the first distichs of all three quatrains and the presence of such nouns in the final distich of each quatrain (cf. 6.3.).

1892

12.2. Unlike *SL 1925*, the early version completely lacks equational conjunctions (cf. 3.3. above). As regards the copulative conjunctions and prepositions, their distribution in the two distichs of the first quatrain coincides with that of *SL 1925*. The tendency toward a higher number of prepositions in the first distich as opposed to the second is observable also in the other two quatrains of *SL 1892*, but the distribution is less regular than that of *SL 1925*, where the pattern established by the first quatrain was generalized throughout the poem. Thus, the distribution by distich exhibits the following pattern in *SL 1892* taken as a whole:

	CONJ.	+	PREP.	=	TOTAL
FIRST DISTICHS:	4		7	=	11
SECOND DISTICHS:	6		5	=	11
QUATRAINS:	10		12	=	22

In other words, the total number of all connectives throughout the early version of the poem is the same for its odd and even distichs. This equality is strengthened in *SL 1925* by the equal number of copulative conjunctions and prepositions in the poem as a whole and in each of its quatrains, and by the total number of such forms in each distich of the entire text (cf. 12.1. above).

13. FINITE VERBS

1925

13.0. In the first half of the poem three lines without finites (I_{1-3}) are followed by three lines each containing one or more finites ($I_4 - II_2$); in the second half of the poem the last line of each three-line group ($II_3 - III_1$, III_{2-4}) contains a finite.

13.1. The number of finites is limited to six active forms referring to the third person. Three of these forms (1 + 2) appear in the outer quatrains, and three — in the first distich of the inner quatrain. The ratio of verbs to nouns is 1 : 3 in the inner and 1 : 8 in the two outer quatrains.

13.2. All three semantic types of verbs outlined by Jespersen (1924:86) — verbs of action, of process, and of state — occur, each twice, among the six finite forms of *SL 1925*. The verbs of action are represented by two compound forms bound to the first hemistich of the last line in the outer quatrains (I $_4$*Had blotted out*, III $_4$*Could but compose*). The verbs of state are restricted to the first distich of the inner quatrain (II $_1$*had*, $_2$*And seemed*). The repeated verb of process occurs in the initial hemistich of the inner and last quatrains (II $_1$*arose*, III $_1$*Arose*). In *SL 1925* the verbs of action in their compound form each consist of four syllables, the verbs of process — two, and the verbs of state — of only one syllable.

13.3. The finites of the three quatrains exhibit a pervasive interplay. The initial and final predicates of the poem (I $_4$*Had blotted out*, III $_4$*Could but compose*), its only compound verbal forms and its only verbs of action, are dramatically played against one another. The auxiliary (I $_4$*Had* [. . .]) yields patently to the independent appearance of the same verb (II $_1$*had* [. . .] *lips*), which then pairs with the only other verb of status, II $_2$*And seemed* [. . .]. The only verb of process, *arose*, which heads the whole sentence of the inner quatrain (II $_1$*A girl arose* [. . .]), is repeated to introduce the third quatrain (III $_1$*Arose, and* [. . .]) and, finally, forms an internal rhyme with the last verb of the poem, III $_4$[. . .] *compose*.

1892

13.4. *SL 1925* contains a higher number of finites and, at the same time, exhibits a greater grammatical uniformity in their use than does the early version. The repertory of verbs in *SL 1892* is limited to four finites, two in the first distich of the inner quatrain and two in the last lines of the outer quatrains. The ratio of verbs to nouns is here 1 : 4 in the inner quatrain and 1 : 8 in the outer quatrain. The inner quatrain twice uses the same preterit, *came*, first in reference to the second person (II $_1$*you came with* [. . .]) and then in reference to the third person (II $_2$*with you came the whole* [. . .]). The compound finite forms of the outer quatrains, the sole verbs of action, differ in tense and voice (I $_4$*Had hid away*, III $_4$*Are shaken*).

13.5. In contradistinction to *SL 1925*, the early version lacks verbs of state. The verbs of action in the two versions are bound to the last line of the outer quatrains, whereas the first distich of the inner quatrain contains the verbs of process in *SL 1892* and the verbs of state in *SL 1925*. The verb of process occurs twice in both the early and final version, but in the former refers to different persons (second and third respectively) and in the latter qualifies as a genuine repetition (referring in both instances to II $_1$*A girl*). In *SL 1925* this verb of process pertains to the initial hemistich of the inner and final quatrains, while in *SL 1892* it is attached to the initial hemistich of the first and second line of the inner quatrain.

13.6. Despite these variations, the different semantic types of verbs follow the same mirror symmetry in both versions:

	1925	1892
Action	*Had blotted out*	*Had hid away*
Process	*arose*	*came*
State	*had*	

State	*seemed*	
Process	*Arose*	*came*
Action	*Could but compose*	*Are shaken*

14. COORDINATION AND SUBORDINATION OF CLAUSES

1925

14.0. The substantial difference between the inner quatrain and the two outer ones lies in their syntactic organization. The first and third quatrains are built on a coordination of four elliptical clauses: I a) $_1$*The brawling* [. . .] (*Had blotted out* [. . .]); b) $_2$*The brilliant moon* (*Had blotted out* [. . .]); c) $_2$*and all the milky sky* (*Had blotted out* [. . .]); d) $_3$*And* [. . .] *that harmony* [. . .] $_4$*Had blotted out man's image and his cry;* III a) (*a girl*) $_1$*Arose;* b) $_1$*and* [. . .] *eaves (Could but compose* [. . .]); c) $_2$*A* [. . .] *moon* [. . .] *(Could but compose* [. . .]); d) $_3$*And* [. . .] *that lamentation* [. . .] $_4$*Could but compose man's image and his cry.*

14.1. In the inner stanza, on the contrary, the syntactic division into four parts is based on grammatical subordination: II a) $_1$*A girl arose*; b) $_1$*that had* [. . .] $_2$*And seemed* [. . .]; c) $_3$*Doomed* [. . .] $_4$*And proud* [. . .]; d) $_4$*murdered* [. . .] (cf. 15.0.). Each of the two inner parts of this quatrain —b) and c) — is in turn divided into two coordinate sections, each of which is bound together by the conjunction *and*.

1892

14.2. Each of the outer quatrains forms a sentence of four coordinated subjects bound elliptically with one and the same predicate: I a) $_1$*The quarrel* [. . .] (*Had hid away* [. . .]; b) $_2$*The* [. . .] *moon (Had hid away* [. . .]); c) $_2$*and* [. . .] *the* [. . .] *sky (Had hid away* [. . .]); d) $_3$*And the* [. . .] *song* [. . .] $_4$*Had hid away earth's old and weary cry;* III a) $_1$*And now the sparrows* [. . .]; b) $_2$*The* [. . .] *moon* [. . .]; c) $_2$*the* [. . .] *stars* [. . .]; d) $_3$*And the* [. . .] *chaunting* [. . .] $_4$*Are shaken with earth's old and weary cry.* In contradistinction to *SL 1925*, in the early version the inner quatrain also forms a coordinate sentence, which consists of a complete initial clause — a) II $_1$*And then you came* [. . .] — followed by an elliptical combination of one predicate with three consequent subjects — b) $_2$*And with you came the whole* [. . .]; c) $_3$*And (with you came) all the sorrows* [. . .]; d) $_4$*(with you came) all the burden* [. . .].

14.3. Thus in *SL 1892* coordination remains the constructive principle within each of the three quatrains, whereas *SL 1925* opposes the outer, coordinate quatrains to the inner quatrain, which is built on the principle of subordination (cf. 19.5.).

15. PREDICATION

1925

15.0. In the outer quatrain of both the early and final version, all the nominal subjects of the first three lines await their predicate in the fourth line. In the inner quatrain of *SL 1925* the main clause — II ₁*A girl arose* — takes up the initial hemistich of the first line, but the rest of the first distich is occupied by two collaterally subordinated clauses whose different predicates relate to the same antecedent subject, whereas in the outer quatrains different coordinated subjects relate to one and the same final predicate. In the final distich of this inner quatrain the two lines begin with semi-predicates of contracted collateral clauses (II ₃*Doomed* — ₄*And proud*) which are subordinated to an antecedent headword and followed in the final hemistich by a participial clause of lower syntactic rank (II ₄*murdered with his peers*).

1892

15.1. The basic structural difference between the inner quatrain of *SL 1892* and its outer quatrains lies in the progressive direction of the latter as opposed to the regressive orientation of the former (on these terms cf. Halliday, 1963; and Yngve, 1961). Although the inner quatrain is composed, like the outer quatrains, of coordinated subjects with a joint predicate, there is an essential difference in the order of the primaries: in the outer quatrains the predicate is placed after the subject, whereas in the inner it appears before them (II ₂[. . .] *came the whole* [. . .] ₃*And all the sorrows* [. . .] ₄*And all the burden*). In the terms of *A Vision*, "these pairs of opposites [subject and predicate] whirl in contrary directions" (1956:74). The same may be said of the distinctive criterion for the opposition of inner versus outer quatrains in *SL 1925*, i.e., the principle of subordination as opposed to that of coordination (cf. 14.3, above).

15.2. Each of the two versions of *SL* contains one deviation from the opposition between the inner and outer quatrains established by the expression of subject and predicate. In *SL 1892* the first clause of the inner quatrain is the only one in the stanza which places the predicate after the subject (II ₁*And then you came* [. . .]). In *SL 1925* the initial, elliptical clause of the third quatrain, III ₁*Arose*, referring to the subject II ₁*A girl*, is the only one among the elliptic clauses of the stanza which omits the subject rather than the predicate. It is significant that in both versions of *SL* the deviation occurs in regard to the only verb which is twice repeated and which signals the appearance of the heroine.

16. SOUNDS

16.0. According to Yeats' meditation of 1900, "all sounds, all colours, all forms, either because of their preordained energies or because of long association, evoke indefinable and yet precise emotions, or, as I prefer to think, call down among us certain disembodied powers, whose footsteps over our hearts we call emotions" ("The Symbolism of Poetry," in 1968:156f.).

16.1. The phonological association established in the early version of *SL* between the title of the lyric and the auditory imagery of its first quatrain is maintained in *SL 1925*: *Sorrow* — I $_1$*sparrow*, and *Love* — I $_3$*leaves*. Within the twelve lines of the poem the interplay of words allied in sound creates an affinity and contrast either between the components of the same line or between diverse lines within the same quatrain, and even within the same distichs, or, conversely, between correlative lines of two different quatrains. The appearance of expressive consonantal clusters through the use of tightly-knit word groups and of vocalic syncope furthers and widens the application of this poetic device.

16.2. Among other reasons for the textual changes in the final version of the outer quatrains (cf. 19.10. below), a pertinent role belongs to the paronomastic link established in these two stanzas between the auditory performance reported in their first lines and the visual phenomena referred to in their second lines. Moreover, especially in the first quatrain, a distinct alliteration binds these two vocables of the first distich, oriented respectively toward hearing and sight, with the predicate of the fourth line: I $_1$*brawling* /br. l/ — $_2$*brilliant* /br. l/ — $_4$*Had blotted* /bl/, and III $_1$*clamorous* /kl.m/ — $_2$*climbing* /kl.m/ — $_2$*empty* /mp/ — $_3$*lamentation* /l.m/ — $_4$*Could but compose* /k.mp/. The junctural cluster /db/ is common to both final predicates of the outer quatrains (I $_4$*Had blotted out* — III $_4$*Could but*). Note also the similar juncture /tk/ of III $_1$*instant clamorous* — III $_4$*but compose*. It is worth mentioning that none of the quoted words occurred in the early version.

16.3. *Moon*, the significant verbal image which in all variants of *SL* heads the second line of the two outer stanzas (cf. 19.21.f. below), finds no further support for its initial /m/ all through the first quatrain of the early version, and the only complementary instance of /m/ in the third quatrain — III $_2$*crumbling moon* of *SL 1892* — was replaced in all editions from 1895 to 1924 by the nasal-less epithet *curd-pale*. Yet the latter form maintains the /k/, /r/, /l/ of its antecedent (which must have had an influence even on the sound shape and suffix of the corresponding attribute *climbing* in *SL 1925*). The chromatic and paronomastic correspondence to III $_2$*The curd-pale* /rd. . .l/ *lips* or *crumbling* /r.m.l/ *moon* was enclosed in the II $_1$*red mournful* /r.dm. . .l/ *lips* of the inner quatrain with three further enhancing occurrences of /m/: II$_1$, $_2$*came and* $_4$*myriad* (cf. 16.8. and 19.30.). The focal innovation of *SL 1925* in its outer quatrains was the providing of $_2$*moon* with its vocalic, grammatical (*he*-gender), and semantic counterpart in the other even line of the same stanzas — I$_4$ and III $_4$*man's* (cf. 19.11.).

16.4. In the outer quatrains of *SL 1925* the abstracts of the third, intermediate line — I $_3$*harmony* /m.n/ and III $_3$*lamentation* /m.n/ — throw a paronomastic bridge between I, III $_2$*moon* and $_4$*man's*; at the same time they intensify the antithetic relation between the inner and outer stanzas, whereas in *SL 1892* the final distichs of the outer quatrains repeatedly confront I $_3$*the loud* /l.d/ *song* (or III ₃*chaunting*) *of the* [...] *leaves* with I₄ and III ₄*earth's old* /l.d/ *and weary cry.*

16.5. In *SL 1925* the even lines of the outer quatrains, in contradistinction to the odd lines, possess a clear-cut masculine break after the second downbeat of the iambic pentameter. In the outer quatrains the first hemistich of the second line finishes with *moon,* and the second hemistich of the fourth line begins with *man's.* The initial /m/ of the two alternants is symmetrically reinforced by the phonemic environment. In contradistinction to the only couple of grave (labial) nasals in *SL 1895* and subsequent editions before 1925 (I ₂ and III ₂*moon*), the outer quatrains of *SL 1925* number fourteen instances of this phoneme: within the initial quatrain /m/ appears twice in each of its even lines and in the intermediate line (I ₂*moon* [...] *milky sky,* ₄*man's image,* ₃*famous harmony*); the final quatrain has one /m/ in each odd line and three in each even line (III ₁*clamorous,* ₂*climbing moon* [...]*empty sky,* ₃*lamentation,* ₄*compose man's image*). The double chain of the /m.n/ responses is most telling: I *moon—harmony—man's*; III *moon — lamentation — man's.* It is also significant that precisely the final picture of the lonesome lunar wanderer contains the greatest accumulation of nasals: III ₂*A climbing moon upon an empty sky* (with seven nasals: three labial, three dental and one velar).

16.6 In the initial simile of the inner quatrain the sounds of the 'tenor', II ₁*girl* /g.rl/, show twofold ties with the 'vehicle', II ₂*greatness* /gr/ *of the world* /rl/. Let us mention in this connection that Marjorie Perloff was right in pointing out the 'trilled r's' in the poet's recorded readings of his own poems (1970:29); the r-colored vowels of English include a postvocalic /r/ in Yeats' sound pattern, so that the vowel of *girl* and *world* is here really followed by a pair of liquid phonemes /rl/. The seven occurrences of a tautosyllabic /r/ distinctly detach the inner quatrain of *SL 1925* from the outer quatrains, where /r/, with one exception (I ₃*harmony*), regularly occupies a prevocalic position.

16.7. The only internal noun common to both versions of the second stanza — II₂*world* — is in both of them supplied with an antecedent analogous in its sonorant cluster /rl/: in *SL 1925* the preceding line of the same quatrain opens with the noun II ₁*girl,* whereas in *SL 1892* the corresponding line of the initial quatrain has two complex epithets each containing a cluster of these liquids — I ₂*full round* /lr/ [...] *star-laden* /rl/ — echoed by /rl/ in II ₃*her lab(ou)ring* [...].

16.8. In the inner quatrain of *SL 1925*, two subordinate constructions, the first and last not only in this stanza but also in the poem as a whole, are bound together by their melancholy mood and form a complex paronomasia: II ₁*had red mournful* [...] — ₄*murdered* /dr.dm,r — m.rd.rd/. It is curious that Parkinson (1951:169) scorned the latter "major word" as prosaic, unordered, and unable to "participate in the alliterative pattern": II ₄*proud*/pr/ — *Priam* /pr/

— *peers* /p.r/. An alliterative pattern concludes each outer quatrain in *SL 1892* (I $_3$*harmony* — $_4$*Had* — $_4$*his*, III $_4$*Could* — *compose* — *cry*), along with a triple vocalic 'anlaut': I $_4$*away earth's old* and III $_4$*Are shaken with earth's old* [. . .]. Furthermore, one observes that although it does not take part in the alliteration of the initial consonants, II $_4$*murdered* in *SL 1925* is nevertheless tied to the words of the antecedent hemistich: *proud* /pr.d/ — /rd.rd/ and *Priam* /pr.m/ — /m.r/. The two marginal lines of the inner quatrain inspired Yeats from *SL 1892* on to seek a paronomastic bond in their somber imagery: II $_1$*mournful* /m.r/ *lips* — $_4$*myriad* /m.r/ *years*. In *SL 1925* both of these lines are patently framed in their sound shape by the imagery of the surrounding distichs: I $_3$*harmony of leaves* /rm.n...l/ — II $_1$*red mournful lips* /r.dm.rn..l/ — II $_4$*murdered* /m.rd.rd/ — III $_1$*clam(o)rous eaves* /l.mr/.

16.9. The only epithets taken over from the early version of the poem by *SL 1925* are those attached to the rhyme-words of the odd lines in the inner quatrain: II $_1$*red mournful lips* and $_3$*lab(ou)ring ships*. The latter attribute shared its sounds /l.br/ with II $_4$*burden* /b.r/ of *SL 1892* and II $_{3,4}$*trouble* /r.b.l/ of *SL 1895*. In *SL 1925* the inward antithesis (*a sparrow* — *the world*) of the outwardly similar lines I $_1$ and II $_2$ (*the* [. . .] *of* [. . .] *in* [. . .]; cf. 3.3, above) bursts into the utmost semantic contrast between the chirp of a single little bird and the heavy scend of Odysseus' ships: I $_1$*brawling* — II $_3$*lab(ou)ring*, tied together by the common suffix *-ing* and by their identical but differently ordered root consonants /br.l/ — /l.br/. The same lines of these two quatrains were juxtaposed in *SL 1892* by the pun-like paronomasia I $_1$*of the sparrows* — II $_3$*the sorrows of* (cf. 6.8.).

17. VERSE PATTERN

17.0. A detailed structural analysis of the masculine iambic pentameter in which *SL* is written would obviously require a careful examination of the poet's and his contemporaries' output in the same and cognate meters. Except for a few preliminary sketches by Dougherty (1973) and Bailey (1975), a systematic, linguistically-based inquiry into modern English versification has scarcely even begun, as compared to at least six decades of Slavic, especially Russian, investigation in the domain of metrics, with its historically and methodologically fruitful results in such questions as the rhythmical relevance of word boundaries and of higher syntactic units of varying rank.

17.1. For the main topic of our study — the comprehensive investigation of the basic oppositions which determine the relation, on the one hand, between the different parts of the poem in each version and, on the other, between *SL 1892* and *SL 1925* — the most illuminating aspect of the verse is the various patterning of the two fundamental prosodic types of words which fulfill the downbeats of the binary meter. These two types have been clearly distinguished both in the Russian tradition of metrical studies and in the most recent papers devoted to English versification. Thus P. Kiparsky singles out (1975:581), on the one hand, "members of lexical categories — nouns (including members of compounds), adjectives, verbs, and adverbs" and, on the other hand, "members of non-lexical categories (such as *his, the, and, with*)" which are in construction with the lexical members. (Russian tradition terms these two classes of units as 'lexical' and 'formal' respectively.) In *SL 1925,* for example, there is a significant difference between downbeats carrying the primary or only stress in the separate lexical constituents, e.g., I $_2$*milky sky,* with two primary stresses, as opposed to I $_3$*har-mony,* with the primary stress on the first syllable, or I $_1$*in the eaves,* with the primary stress on the third.

17.20. In *SL 1925* the outer quatrains display a clear regressive undulatory curve in the treatment of the downbeats: the three odd downbeats carry a greater percentage of primary stresses — and may thus be designated as 'heavy' down-beats — than do the two even ('light') downbeats (see Figure 1). In these two outer quatrains, as in all stanzas of *SL* irrespective of its version, the final down-beat of all lines is consistently allotted a primary stress. In the initial quatrain of *SL 1925* all three of the odd (heavy) downbeats receive a primary stress in all the lines, whereas the fourth and second downbeats carry a primary stress only in 1 and 2 lines respectively.

17.21. In the final quatrain the numerical superiority of primary stresses on odd downbeats over the even downbeats remains valid, but is reduced throughout, thus slightly flattening out the undulatory curve exhibited in the initial quatrain: the first and third downbeats each carry three primary stresses, and the second and fourth — two.

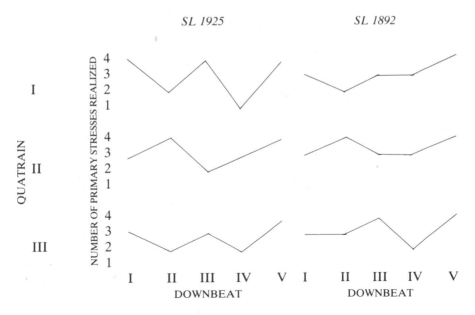

Fig. 1. *Frequency of primary stresses on the downbeats in the two versions.*

17.22. In opposition to the outer quatrains, with their sequence descent/ascent
$(4-2-4$ and $3-2-3)$, the inner quatrain displays the reverse sequence $(3-4-2)$,
followed by a gradual ascent $(3-4)$, so that it once again differs strikingly from
the two outer quatrains (cf. particularly 18.30.ff. below).

17.23. In *SL 1892*, as mentioned, the final downbeat of any line always carries a
primary stress, but in the other four downbeats the undulatory curve is much less
pronounced than in *SL 1925*: besides a sequence of descent and ascent, two
neighboring downbeats may display an equal number of primary stresses. Thus
there appears a mirror symmetry between the initial and final quatrain: descent —
ascent — equality, and equality — ascent — descent, respectively (see Figure
1). The sequence equality — ascent $(3-3-4)$, which concludes the order of
downbeats in the initial and inner quatrains, opens the final quatrain. In terms
of this relation, the inner quatrain of *SL 1892* occupies an intermediary place
between the two outer quatrains.

17.30. Within the line, monosyllabic lexical words occur on upbeats and are
followed by downbeats under primary stress 10 times in *SL 1892*, four times in
each outer quatrain (with a consistent lexical symmetry between I and III: *moon
— star — loud — earth's*), and two times in the inner quatrain: I $_2$*full round
moon*, $_2$*star-laden*, $_3$*loud song*, $_4$*earth's old*; II $_1$*red mournful*, $_2$*world's tears*;
III $_2$*curd-pale moon*, $_2$*white stars*, $_3$*loud chaunting*, $_4$*earth's old*.

17.31. Each quatrain of the final version preserves only one instance of the same
phenomenon, literally repeating II $_1$*red mournful*, and replacing the possessive
earth's by I $_4$ and III $_4$*man's*. The avoidance of filling inner upbeats with stressed
monosyllabic words approaches a rule.

17.4. Only *SL 1925* contains instances of the standard use of stressed monosyllables in the initial upbeat (anacrusis): II $_3$*Doomed like Odysseus*, III $_4$*Could but
compose*.

18. CONSTRUCTIVE PRINCIPLES

1925

18.00. *SL 1925* displays an astounding symmetry in the distribution of the major
grammatical categories among the three quatrains, a symmetry which is either
lacking or muted in the early version. It may indeed be considered a persuasive
example of the 'geometrical symbolism' (1956:80) which was so vital a force both
in the poet's subliminal imagery and in his abstract thought. The operative
principle regulating the poem's symmetries is here the number 3 and its
exponents $(3^2, 3^3)$. When reflecting on the 'Great Wheel' as the 'principal symbol'
of the universe, Yeats insisted that "each set of 3 is itself a wheel" (1956:82f.). In
his description of the 28 phases Yeats qualifies the first phase as "not being
human" (1956:105), so that three to the third power (3^3) in fact exhausts the
entire human realm.

18.01. There are 27 nouns *in toto* (3^3), 9 per quatrain (3^2), which include 3
abstracts and 3 nouns with prepositions, each distributed one per quatrain (cf.

6.0., 6.2.). A total of three *-ing*-forms are present, one per quatrain (cf. 5.0.). Prenominal attributes and pronouns each total 9 (3^2), the former distributed symmetrically (3 per quatrain; cf. 7.1.), the latter displaying only partial symmetry (three different pronouns, two of which appear once in each quatrain; cf. 9.0.). The occurrences of the definite article also total 9 (cf. 11.0.). The connectives total 18, of which 9 (3^2) are copulative conjunctions and 9 (3^2) — prepositions, each appearing 3 times per quatrain (cf. 12.0.). Only in the distribution of verbs does the principle of three find expression in a dichotomy of inner vs. outer stanzas rather than in their symmetrical equivalence (cf. 13.1.).

1892

18.02. The impressive symmetrical identity established between the quatrains of *SL 1925* by the distribution of grammatical categories is almost entirely lacking in *SL 1892*. Of the major categories, only the possessives are equally apportioned, one per stanza (cf. 6.6.). Instead of the equivalence symmetry of *SL 1925*, one finds in *SL 1892* a dissimilatory use of grammatical means to distinguish the inner from the two outer quatrains.

18.10. In *SL 1892* the contrast between the three quatrains is conveyed either by the presence of certain grammatical categories in the inner quatrain, coupled with their absence in I and III, or by an equal distribution of certain categories in the two outer quatrains as opposed to their lower frequency in the inner, and here it is the number 7, rather than 3, which serves as the operative principle.
18.11. Thus, on the one hand, there are 7 pronouns in the inner quatrain, while the outer quatrains of *SL 1892* are completely devoid of this category (cf. 9.1.). On the other hand, the inner quatrain has a lower number (4) of both prenominal attributes (cf. 7.2.) and definite articles (cf. 11.2.) than the outer quatrains, which each contain 7 such entities (but cf. 7.2.).
18.12. The inner quatrain of *SL 1892* also differs from the outer ones by the repetitive character of the initial part of the two lines within each distich (and their pronounced use of oxytones — cf. 19.41.) and by the presence of redoubled grammatical words (the pronouns II $_{1,2}$*you*, $_{3,4}$*all*, $_{3,4}$*her* and the sociative prepositions $_{1,2}$*with*), which are lacking in the outer quatrains but are here strictly distributed by distich: II $_1$*And then YOU came WITH* [. . .] — $_2$*And WITH YOU came* [. . .]; $_{3,4}$*And ALL the (*$_3$*sorrows,* $_4$*burden) of HER* [. . .]. (In *SL 1895* and subsequent editions before 1925 the parallelism of the line-beginnings in the second distich was complete: II $_{3,4}$*And all the trouble of her* [. . .].) The inner quatrain, moreover, is clearly dominated by the *she*-gender (cf. 9.1.), which is merely hinted at in the last lines of the two outer quatrains (cf. 6.6.).
18.13. Finally, the inner quatrain of *SL 1892*, although it follows the principle of coordination displayed by the two outer quatrains, is differentiated from them in terms of predication. Whereas the two outer quatrains are built on a progressive principle of four coordinated subjects bound elliptically to one and the same final verb, the inner quatrain opens with one complete 'subject-predicate' clause, but then in the second line reverses the order of primaries into a sequence 'predicate-subject' (see 14.2.).

18.2. It is worth noting that the two versions in several instances employ identical grammatical categories for opposite purposes. Generally, as is the case with prenominal attributes, articles and pronouns, the categories denoting equivalence of the quatrains in *SL 1925* designate contrast in *SL 1892*. The opposite case also holds: possessives, used in the early version as one of the sole means of establishing equivalence between quatrains, are, on the contrary, one of the sole means of contrasting the inner and outer quatrains in the late version.

1925

18.3. Despite the overwhelming preference of the final version for symmetries of equivalence rather than of contrast, the inner quatrain of *SL 1925* differs just as dramatically from the two outer quatrains as does that of *SL 1892*. In consecutive order each line of this quatrain breaks off manifestly from the pattern of the first stanza, which constitutes a separate sentence, detached in the final version from the rest of the text by the only full stop within the poem. As opposed to the outer quatrains, which are built entirely on the principle of coordination, it is based on subordination (see 14.0.) and contains the only two verbs of state to be found in the poem (13.5.). The initial line of the inner quatrain is the only line in which one finds two finites; moreover, of these, one belongs to the main clause (II $_1$*arose*) and the other — to the first subordinate clause in the text (II $_1$*had*). The second line of this quatrain inaugurates a mirror-image sequence of diversified verbal types echoing the verbs of action, process and state which have appeared so far, but in reverse order. It also opens the set of three similes, which mark the metaphoric constitution of this quatrain as opposed to the metonymic structure of the two outer ones.

18.4. At the border between the two halves of the poem, the third line of the inner quatrain in *SL 1925* opens the distich II$_{3-4}$, the grammatical makeup of which diverges strikingly from all the other lines of the poem. This distich is the only to possess: 1) three personal nouns of the *he*-gender, namely two proper names (II $_3$*Odysseus,* $_4$*Priam*) and the appellative $_4$*peers*; 2) three postpositive semi-predicative attributes (II $_3$*Doomed,* $_4$*proud,* and *murdered*); 3) the only two equational conjunctions ($_3$*like,* $_4$*as*); and 4) the only sociative preposition in *SL 1925* ($_4$*with*). In contradistinction to this distich, the first distich of the same quatrain has three finites (II $_1$*arose, had,* $_2$*seemed*) and two nouns of the *she*-gender ($_1$*girl,* $_2$*world* — cf. 6.6.). Thus a clear-cut set of features marks the borderline between the two halves of the poem.

18.5. The division of the poem into two halves of six lines each, further subdivided into two triplets, is also suggested by the distribution of certain grammatical categories. In the first half of the poem, three lines devoid of verbs are followed by three lines each containing at least one verb; in the second half, each of the two triplets has a verb in its last line. The definite article also displays a symmetrical distribution by halves and triplets: in the first half, a triplet containing two definite articles per line is followed by a triplet devoid of them; in the second half, a triplet containing one *the* per line alternates with a triplet again devoid of definite articles. Furthermore, the 18 copulative conjunctions and prepositions evenly divide into two sets of 9, one in each half of the poem.

18.60. Another division into two groups of six lines each is clearly suggested by the subject matter. As mentioned above (3.1.), in both versions six lines are devoted to the 'overground' and six lines to the 'terrestrial' (*SL 1892*) or 'human' (*SL 1925*) level. This division is supported by the distribution of personal and non-personal nouns and pronouns: the personals are bound exclusively to the six 'terrestrial' or 'human' lines. The two versions differ, however, in the gender characterization of the personal nouns and pronouns of the terrestrial level. In *SL 1892* the four lines of the inner quatrain and the last line of each outer quatrain refer exclusively to the feminine gender. In *SL 1925*, however, the 'human' lines are divided according to gender: those which belong to the second distichs of the quatrains are characterized as masculine (I_4, II_{3-4}, III_4); the others as feminine (II_{1-2}). The grammatical differentiation of the distichs finds consistent expression also in the relative distribution of copulative conjunctions and prepositions (12.1.). The division of the quatrains into distichs is furthered by the alternating rhyme scheme (ABAB).

18.61. It is significant that verbs appear in both versions only in the six lines referring to the terrestrial or human level. The only exception to this rule is the bare repetitive transfer from the inner quatrain, III $_1$*Arose*, in *SL 1925* (cf. 15.2.).

18.70. The external (marginal) and internal segments of the individual lines are mutually opposed by grammatical means. The line-ends in both versions are delimited by the fact that the rhyme-words are monosyllabic nouns and by the fact that plural nouns are proper in *SL 1925* only, and in *SL 1892* preponderantly, to the rhymes (cf. 6.40. and 6.7.). In *SL 1925* any internal concrete noun enters into a metonymical relation with the following rhyme-word, which in most instances specifies its framework: I $_1$*a sparrow in the eaves*, $_2$*The* [. . .] *moon and all the milky sky*; II $_2$*A girl* [. . .] *that had red mournful lips*, $_3$*Odysseus and the labouring ships*, $_4$*Priam murdered with his peers;* III $_2$*A* [. . .] *moon upon an empty sky.*

18.71. In *SL 1925* the final line of each quatrain is signaled grammatically by the presence of a noun of masculine human gender (I $_4$*man's*, II $_4$*Priam*, III $_4$*man's*) and of a corresponding possessive *his*, referring to these nouns and elsewhere absent, and by the lack of either articles (cf. 11.0.) or prenominal attributes (cf. 7.1.).

18.72. The transition from one phase to another signaled in *SL 1892* by the pairs of adverbs, II $_1$*then* and III $_1$*now*, is obliterated in *SL 1925*. There, in agreement with *A Vision* (Yeats, 1956:136), "every image is separate from every other, for if image were linked to image, the soul would awake from its immovable trance." The focus upon time in *SL 1892* and its exclusion in *SL 1925* become particularly palpable when one opposes the six temporal indications of the early version —

I $_3$*ever-* [. . .], $_4$*old*; II $_1$*then,* $_4$*myriad years*; III $_1$*now,* $_4$*old* — to the total lack of such indications in the final version.

18.8. In both versions the properties common to the two outer quatrains are evident, whatever their relation (equivalence or contrast) to the inner. The equivalence of the two is semantically underlined, especially in *SL 1925*, where the first three lines in each portray a metonymic contiguity of overground images, visual in the even line, auditory in the odd lines, and thus correspond to the alternation of *man's* visible *image and his* audible *cry* in I $_4$, III $_4$. In *SL 1892* the terrestrial level referred to in the last line of each outer quatrain is described solely in auditory images (I $_4$, III $_4$*earth's old and weary cry*).

18.90. The contrariety of the two outer quatrains finds a sharper grammatical expression in the early version, viz. the differences of tense and voice in the verbs through the emergence of the present and passive — III $_4$*Are shaken* (cf. 13.4.) and the confinement of preposition-less rhyme-words to the first quatrain (cf. 6.43.), whereas *SL 1925* has recourse chiefly to lexical means for contrasting the two outer quatrains. For example, an ironical turn inverts the syntactic hierarchy of the first two rhyme-words: in I $_2$*sky* is a subject and I $_1$*eaves* an adverbial of place, while in the third quatrain the role of subject is assigned to III $_1$*eaves,* and $_2$*sky* is declassed to an adverbial of place (see further 19.0.ff., below).

18.91. The compound preterit forms of the predicate in the two outer quatrains of *SL 1925* are semantically opposed to each other: the initial one destructive and turned to the past, the final one constructive and prospective.

19. SEMANTIC CORRESPONDENCES

19.0. In the epithets of the manuscript version (*SL 1891*) there may be observed what the poet terms "an enforced attraction between Opposites" (1956:93); III $_3$ *The wearisome* [!] *loud chaunting of the leaves* suddenly reappears III $_4$*shaken with earth's old and weary* [!] *cry*.

19.10. In comparison with *SL 1892*, the final version achieves a greater contrast between the two outer quatrains by impoverishing the image of the overground level in the third quatrain, and thus effectively pushes into the foreground the relation between the two opposite spheres. The characters that filled the overground lines of the first quatrain in *SL 1892* and *SL 1925* gradually diminish in number and their epithets become more subdued: I $_1$*a sparrow*, substituted in *SL 1925* for I $_1$ and III $_1$ *the sparrows* of *SL 1892*, disappears behind the metonymy III $_1$*clamorous eaves* in the last stanza of the final version; the *famous harmony of leaves* which adorned I $_3$ gives way in III $_3$ to their plain *lamentation*; I $_2$*the star-laden sky* and *the milky sky*, the grammatical subjects of the two versions, change in the final quatrain of *SL 1925* into a mere circumstantial modifier of place with a meager epithet, III $_2$*upon an empty sky*.

19.11. At the end of the two outer quatrains, the possessive *earth's* in *SL 1892* and *man's* in *SL 1925* designate the chief entity of the lower sphere (cf. 3.1.). In the early version, I$_2$ and III $_2$*sky* stood in direct opposition to the *earth's* [. . .] *cry* in the next even line of the same quatrains, whereas in the final version an analogous opposition embraces the initial nouns of the equivalent lines I$_2$ and III $_2$*moon* in respect to I$_4$ and III $_4$*man's* (cf. 16.3.).

19.20. The threshold of the nineties was for Yeats marked by a "continual discovery of mystic truths" (1973:30); the creation of *SL 1891* belongs to the period of his growing inclination toward esoteric research, with a faith in the correspondence between the human soul and body and the planets from Saturn to the Moon (1973:23).

19.21. The lunar body, as the main symbol in the poet's mythology, was promoted by Yeats with particular persistence in the first draft of his treatise *A Vision* (1925), which was prepared by the poet at the same time and with as much zeal as the final version of "The Sorrow of Love" (included by the author in another book of the same year, his *Early Poem and Stories*). In his note of 1925 to the latter collection (1957:842) Yeats testifies that he is "now once more in *A Vision* busy with that thought, the antitheses of day and night and of moon and of sun"; he immediately turns to the cycle *The Rose* and relates that "upon reading these poems for the first time for several years" he realizes that their heroine has been imagined "as suffering with man and not as something pursued and seen from afar."

19.22. Already in the early version of *SL* the contrasting images of I $_2$*The full round moon* and III $_2$*The crumbling* (*1891: withered*) *moon* were apparently related to the author's gradually maturing mystical doctrine later systematized in *A Vision*. This "philosophy of life and death" found its poetic embodiment in the *phantasmagoria* "The Phases of the Moon," first printed in 1919 (1957:821) and later included in the first edition of *A Vision*. This poem evokes the stage "When the moon's full" (1957:375, line 75ff.), immediately followed by "the crumbling of the moon" (ibid., line 87ff.) and focuses on the diverse effects of these phases "Upon the body and upon the soul" (1957:376, line 93). It is significant that from 1895 on, *crumbling* was replaced in *SL* by the trope *curd-pale,* and that in the final version of the poem these two telling epithets were supplanted by more remote allusions: I $_2$*The brilliant moon* and III $_2$*A climbing moon*, the latter ambiguous (climbing toward the zenith or rather toward the next phase?) and the former, *brilliant,* according to the author's own acknowledgement, for its "numbness and dullness," so "that all might seem, as it were, remembered with indifference, except some one vivid image" (1965:291). That "one vivid image" must have been the dominant noun *moon* itself, the central visual motif common to the two pictures of the overground level in *SL 1925* (cf. 16.3.).

19.23. "The full moon is Phase 15," Yeats writes, and "as we approach Phase 15, personal beauty increases and at Phase 14 and Phase 16 the greatest human beauty becomes possible" (1956:78, 131). While the inner quatrain of *SL* alludes to Phase 15, the two outer quatrains reflect its adjacent Phases.

> Under the frenzy of the fourteenth moon,
> The soul begins to tremble into stillness,
> To die into the labyrinth of itself!

> (1957:374, lines 53–55)

"Man's image and his cry," blotted out according to the initial quatrain of *SL 1925*, corresponds to the song of Robartes in "The Phases of the Moon" and to its further lines announcing the full moon:

> All thought becomes an image and the soul
> Becomes a body [. . .]

> (1957:374, lines 58f.)

— or in the terms of *SL 1925*, II ₁*A girl arose.*

> And after that the crumbling of the moon.
> The soul remembering its loneliness
> Shudders in many cradles; all is changed.

> (1957:375, lines 87–89)

As explained in *A Vision* (1956:137f.), "there is always an element of frenzy," but "Phase 16 is in contrast to Phase 14, in spite of their resemblance of extreme subjectivity [. . .]. It has found its antithesis, and therefore self-knowledge and self-mastery." Briefly, it is the phase in which all the physical illusions of Phase 14 *Could but compose man's image and his cry.*

19.30. The inner quatrain lacks such pairs of opposites as *sky* and *earth* of *SL 1892* or *moon* and *man* of *SL 1925*. Yet at the same time, the *moon* of the two outer stanzas displays a particular correspondence to the heroine of the adjacent inner quatrain. In *SL 1892* the juxtaposed portrayals of I ₂*The full round moon* and II ₁*those red mournful lips* exhibit a multiple correspondence in the morphological and phonological make-up of the two phrases: *full* — [. . .] *ful* and /r.ndm.n/ — /r.dm.rn/.

19.31. "My love sorrow [!]," says Yeats, "was my obsession, never leaving by day or night" (1973:74), and a passage in the first draft of Yeats' *Autobiography*, with a more than free paraphrase of Leonardo da Vinci's *Notebooks*, throws light on the image of the III ₂*climbing moon* and its counterpart, the "arising" II ₂*girl* [. . .] *that had red mournful lips* of *SL 1925*: "At last she came to me in I think January of my thirtieth year [. . .]. I could not give her the love that was her beauty's right. [. . .] All our lives long, as da Vinci says, we long, thinking it is but the moon that we long [for], for our destruction, and how, when we meet [it] in the shape of a most fair woman, can we do less than leave all others for her? Do we not seek our dissolution upon her lips?" (1973:88). These lines may be confronted with an earlier paragraph of the same *Memoirs* (p. 72), the poet's confession of his twenty-seventh (3³) year: "I think my love seemed almost hopeless [. . .]. I had never since childhood kissed a woman's lips."

19.32. The outline of Phase 15 in *A Vision* (1956:136) adds that "now contemplation and desire, united into one, inhabit a world where every beloved image has

bodily form, and every bodily form is loved. This love knows nothing of desire, for desire implies effort [. . .]. As all effort has ceased, all thought has become image, because no thought could exist if it were not carried to its own extinction."
19.33. The motto to the poet's reflections on the Fifteenth Phase of the Moon reads: "No description except that this is a phase of complete beauty" (1956:135). In *SL 1892* the inner quatrain, centered around this particular phase, strikingly differs from the outer stanzas grammatically and compositionally (cf. 18.10.ff.). Each of the two distichs is built on a widely pleonastic scheme. The first two lines display a pun-like juxtaposition of two identical sociative prepositions, one synecdochic (II $_1$*you came with those* [. . .] *lips*) and the other purely metonymic (II $_2$*with you came the whole of the world's tears*). In *SL 1895* the second distich achieved a heptasyllabic tautology, II $_{3,4}$*And all the trouble of her* [. . .], with a salient sound figure, /r.b.l/ — /l.b.r/ *(labouring)* — /r.b.l/.

19.40. The relative isolation of the second stanza with respect to the other quatrains of *SL 1892* is to a certain extent counterbalanced by the equivalent correspondences between the early version of this inner quatrain and a few of the surrounding poems of the cycle entitled *The Rose*. Writing on the birth of "those women who are most touching in their beauty," Yeats states in *A Vision* that Helen was of Phase 14 (1956:132). The reference to Troy, later openly disclosed in *SL 1925*, remains rather obscure in the early version, but is clearly revealed in a poem which neighbors on *SL* in *The Rose* cycle, "The Rose of the World":

> Who dreamed that beauty passes like a dream?
> For *these red lips, with all their mournful pride,*
> *Mournful* that no new wonder may betide,
> *Troy passed away* in one high funeral gleam,
> And Usna's children died.
>
> (1957:111)

19.41. Not only phraseological but also versificational features reveal the affinity between the inner quatrain of *SL 1892* and the other lyrics of the same cycle. The repeated *arose* in II $_1$ and III $_1$ of *SL 1925* prompts one critic, John Unterecker, to see a double vision of "a girl arose" and "a girl, a rose" (1959:159). The line II $_1$ is the only one in the poem with all the first three downbeats followed by a word boundary — *A girl/ arose/ that had/ red* [. . .] (cf. in *SL 1892* the corresponding line — II $_1$*And then/ you came/ with those/ red* [. . .], and in *SL 1925* such initial oxytones in the same quatrain as II $_2$*And seemed/*, $_4$*And proud/*); it is interesting to note that the poem "The Rose" (1892) which opens the cycle of the same name (1893, 1957:100f.) has the identical rhythm in its first line — *"Red Rose,/ proud Rose,/ sad Rose/* [. . .]" — literally repeated at the end of the poem (line 24), as well as in the initial line of the second twelve-line stanza — $_{13}$*"Come near,/ come near,/ come near/* [. . .]."
19.42. We are looking for correspondences between "The Sorrow of Love" and the adjacent poems of *The Rose*, but there is another tempting question, that of key words, abundant in the surrounding verses, which were passed over in

silence in *SL*. Together with *SL* the poem "When You Are Old" is addressed to Maud Gonne (cf. Bradford, 1961:454) and is the only other text of *The Rose* cycle composed in three quatrains of iambic pentameter. It is hardly by chance that in this poem, which is placed in the edition of 1892 just before, and in editions from 1895 on immediately after, "The Sorrow of Love," the vocable *love,* confined to the title of *SL,* occurs six times, four times as a verb in the second quatrain (II ₁*How many loved* [. . .], ₂*And loved your beauty,* ₃*But one man loved* [. . .], ₄*And loved the sorrows* [. . .]) and twice as a substantive (II ₂*with love false or true,* III ₂[. . .] *how Love fled*). In *SL* both love and Helen remain unnamed.

19.5. As to Helen's fate, "is it not because she desires so little, gives so little that men will die and murder in her service?" (1956:133). According to the inner quatrain of *SL 1892,* she is accompanied by *the whole of the world's tears,* while in the ultimate version of this stanza, it is *the world in tears,* the second dramatis persona, which emerges as one of her metaphoric incarnations. Her further embodiments, the men who "die and murder" within the scene of the following distich, complete the list of personal nouns, and their subordinative pyramid pointedly distinguishes the inner stanza of *SL 1925* from the surrounding constructs (cf. 14.1.), a dissimilarity further enhanced by the fact that the third central downbeat, which is the heaviest in the two outer quatrains, is the lightest downbeat in the inner stanza (cf. 17.20.).

19.6. *The world,* incidentally, is the general character assigned in *A Vision* to the Phases 14, 15, 16 of the Great Wheel, with the subsequent inference *Sorrow* (1956:102), and it was under the title "The Sorrow of the World" that *SL 1892 Ind* appeared (cf. 6.8.).

19.7. While the similarity association guides the patterning of the inner quatrain of *SL 1925,* in the early version of the poem the leading role belongs to relations of contiguity. The complete lack of human nouns (vs. four in the same stanza of *SL 1925*), the surplus of pronouns (seven vs. two in the final version), and especially the reiterated *you* of *SL 1892,* corresponding to *A girl* of *SL 1925,* all testify to the deictic function which underlies the inner quatrain of the early version. Quantifiers, as II ₂*the whole of the world's tears* and II ₄*myriad years,* are akin to the vocabulary of external relationship. The stanza devoted to Phase Fifteen either indicates (*SL 1892*) or names (*SL 1925*), but in either case restrains 'description' (cf. 19.33.).

19.8. The critics may argue about which of the two versions is more 'defective' and which of them requires more 'indulgence.' Nevertheless, the exacting selection and arrangement of verbal symbols summoned in "The Sorrow of Love" to build a harmonious system of rich semantic correlations and, in Yeats' own terms, "too much woven into the fabric of [his] work for [him] to give a detailed account of them one by one" (1957:843) indeed warrant the poet's assertion: *And words obey my call.*

REFERENCES

ALLT, G.D.P., 1944–5. "Yeats and the Revision of His Early Work," in *Hermathena* LXIV, 90–101; LXV, 40–57.

BAILEY, JAMES, 1975. "Linguistic Givens and Their Metrical Realization in a Poem by Yeats," *Language and Style* VIII, 1, 21–33.

BONNEFOY, Y., 1973. "Le Chagrin de l'Amour," (trans.), *Argile* 1, 65.

BRADFORD, C., 1961–2. "Yeats and Maud Gonne," *Texas Studies in Language and Literature* 3, 452–474.

COWELL, R., 1969. *W. B. Yeats* (New York).

DOUGHERTY, A., 1973. *A Study of Rhythmic Structure in the Verse of William Butler Yeats* (The Hague-Paris).

ELLMANN, R., 1954. *The Identity of Yeats* (London-New York).

EXNER, R., 1960. "Trübsal der Liebe," in W.B. Yeats (trans.), *Werke* I, ed. by W. Vordtriede (Neuwied).

HALLIDAY, M.A.K., 1963. "Class in Relation to the Axes of Chain and Choice in Language," *Linguistics* 2, 5–15.

HENN, T.R., 1965. *The Lonely Tower: Studies in the Poetry of W.B. Yeats* (London).

HONE, J., 1943. *W.B. Yeats* (New York).

JESPERSEN, OTTO, 1924. *The Philosophy of Grammar* (London).

KIPARSKY, P., 1975. "Stress, Syntax, and Meter," *Language* LI, 576–617.

MACNEICE, LOUIS, 1941. *The Poetry of W.B. Yeats* (London).

MONTEIRO, GEORGE, 1966. "Unrecorded Variants in Two Yeats Poems," *Papers of the Bibliographical Society of America* LX, 367f.

PARKINSON, T., 1951. *W.B. Yeats Self-Critic* (Berkeley-Los Angeles).

PARRISH, S.M., 1963. *A Concordance to the Poems of W.B. Yeats* (Cornell, N.Y.).

PERLOFF, MARJORIE, 1970. *Rhyme and Meaning in the Poetry of Yeats* (The Hague-Paris).

SAUL, G. B., 1957. *Prolegomena to the Study of Yeats' Poems* (Philadelphia).

STALLWORTHY, J., 1963. *Between the Lines: Yeats's Poetry in the Making* (Oxford).

STAMM, R., 1948. "The Sorrow of Love. A Poem by William Butler Yeats Revised by Himself," *English Studies* XXIX, 79–87.

STRANG, B., 1968. *The Structure of English Grammar* (London).

UNTERECKER, JOHN, 1959. *A Reader's Guide to William Butler Yeats* (New York).

VALERY, PAUL, 1945. "Poésie et Pensée Abstraite," in his *Variété*, V (Paris).

WHORF, B. L., 1956. *Language, Thought, and Reality* (Cambridge, Mass.).

YEATS, WILLIAM BUTLER, 1892. *The Countess Kathleen and Various Legends and Lyrics* (London).

1925   *Early Poems and Stories* (London).

1956 (1925) *A Vision* (New York).

1957   *The Variorum Edition of the Poems*, ed. by P. Allt and R. K. Alspach (New York).

1965   *Autobiography* (New York).

1968   *Essays and Introductions* (New York).

1973   *Memoirs: Autobiography — First Draft, Journal*, ed. by D. Donoghue (New York).

YNGVE, V.H., 1961. "The Depth Hypothesis," *Proceedings of Symposia in Applied Mathematics* XII, 130–138.

Poetry and Life

On a Generation that Squandered Its Poets

Roman Jakobson

> Killed; —
> Little matter
> Whether I or he
> Killed them.

Majakovskij's poetry—his imagery—his lyrical composition—I have written about these things and published some of my remarks. The idea of writing a monograph has never left me. Majakovskij's poetry is qualitatively different from everything in Russian verse before him, however intent one may be on establishing genetic links. This is what makes the subject particularly intriguing. The structure of his poetry is profoundly original and revolutionary. But how is it possible to write about Majakovskij's poetry now, when the paramount subject is not the rhythm, but the death of the poet, when (if I may resort to Majakovskij's own poetic phrase) "sudden grief" is not yet ready to give in to "a clearly realized pain"?

During one of our meetings, Majakovskij, as was his custom, read me his latest poems. Considering his creative potential I could not help comparing them with what he might have produced. "Very good," I said, "but not as good as Majakovskij." Yet now the creative powers are canceled out, the inimitable stanzas can no longer be compared to anything else, the words "Majakovskij's last poems" have suddenly taken on a tragic meaning. Sheer grief at his absence has overshadowed the absent one. Now it is more painful, but still easier, to write not about the one we have lost but rather about our own loss and those of us who have suffered it.

It is our generation that has suffered the loss. Roughly, those of us who are now between thirty and forty-five years old. Those who, already fully matured, entered into the years of the Revolution not as unmolded clay, but still not

This translation by Edward J. Brown first appeared in his *Major Soviet Writers* (New York: Oxford University Press, 1973).

111

hardened, still capable of adapting to experience and change, still capable of taking a dynamic rather than a static view of our lives.

It has been said more than once that the first poetic love of our generation was Aleksandr Blok. Velimir Xlebnikov gave us a new epos, the first genuinely epic creations after many decades of drought. Even his briefer verses create the impression of epic fragments, and Xlebnikov easily combined them into narrative poems. Xlebnikov is epic in spite of our anti-epic times, and therein lies one of the reasons he is somewhat alien to the average reader. Other poets brought his poetry closer to the reader; they drew upon Xlebnikov, pouring out his "word ocean" into many lyrical streamlets. In contrast to Xlebnikov, Majakovskij embodied the lyrical urges of this generation. "The broad epic canvas" is deeply alien to him and unacceptable. Even when he attempts "a bloody Iliad of the Revolution," or "an Odyssey of the famine years," what appears is not an epic but a heroic lyric on a grand scale, offered "at the top of his voice." There was a point when symbolist poetry was in its decline and it was still not clear which of the two new mutually antagonistic trends, Acmeism or Futurism, would prevail. Xlebnikov and Majakovskij gave to contemporary literary art its leitmotif. The name Gumilev marks a collateral branch of modern Russian poetry—its characteristic overtone. For Xlebnikov and for Majakovskij "the homeland of creative poetry is the future"; in contrast, Esenin is a lyrical glance backward. His verse expresses the weariness of a generation.

Modern Russian poetry after 1910 is largely defined by these names. The verse of Aseev and Selvinskij is bright indeed, but it is a reflected light. They do not announce but reflect the spirit of the times. Their magnitude is a derivative quantity. Pasternak's books and perhaps those of Mandel'štam are remarkable, but theirs is chamber verse:[1] new creation will not be kindled by it. The heart of a generation cannot take fire with such verses because they do not shatter the boundaries of the present.

Gumilev (1886–1921) was shot; after prolonged mental agony and in great pain, Blok (1880–1921) died; amid cruel privations and under circumstances of inhuman suffering, Xlebnikov (1885–1922) passed away; after careful planning Esenin (1895–1925) and Majakovskij (1894–1930) killed themselves. And so it happened that during the third decade of this century, those who inspired a generation perished between the ages of thirty and forty, each of them sharing a sense of doom so vivid and sustained that it became unbearable.

This is true not only of those who were killed or killed themselves; Blok and Xlebnikov, when they took to their beds with disease, had also perished. Zamjatin wrote in his reminiscences: "We are all to blame for this.... I remember that I could not stand it and I phoned Gorkij: Blok is dead. We can't be forgiven for that." Šklovskij wrote in a tribute to Xlebnikov:

---

[1] When we say "chamber" [*kamernaja*] we certainly do not intend to detract from the value of their work as poetic craftsmanship. The poetry of Evgenij Baratynskij or of Innokentij Annenskij, for instance, might be called thus.

Forgive us for yourself and for others whom we will kill. The state is not responsible for the destruction of people. When Christ lived and spoke the state did not understand his Aramaic, and it has never understood simple human speech. The Roman soldiers who pierced Christ's hands are no more to blame than the nails. Nevertheless, it is very painful for those whom they crucify.[2]

Blok the poet fell silent and died long before the man, but his younger contemporaries snatched verses even from death. ("Wherever I die I'll die singing," wrote Majakovskij.) Xlebnikov knew he was dying. His body decomposed while he lived. He asked for flowers in his room so that the stench would not be noticed, and he kept writing to the end. A day before his suicide Esenin wrote a masterful poem about his impending death. Majakovskij's farewell letter is full of poetry: we find the professional writer in every line of that document. He wrote it two nights before his death and in the interval there were to be conversations and conferences about the everyday business of literature; but in that letter we read: "Please don't gossip. The deceased hated gossip." We remember that Majakovskij's long-standing demand upon himself was that the poet must "hurry time forward." And here he is, already looking at his suicide note through the eyes of someone reading it the day after tomorrow. The letter, with its several literary motifs and with Majakovskij's own death in it, is so closely interrelated with his poetry that it can be understood only in the context of that poetry.

The poetry of Majakovskij from his first verses, in "A Slap in the Face of Public Taste," to his last lines is one and indivisible. It represents the dialectical development of a single theme. It is an extraordinarily unified symbolic system. A symbol once thrown out only as a kind of hint will later be developed and presented in a totally new perspective. He himself underlines these links in his verse by alluding to earlier works. In the poem "About That" [*Pro èto*], for instance, he recalls certain lines from the poem "Man" [*Čelovek*], written several years earlier, and in the latter poem he refers to lyrics of an even earlier period. An image at first offered humorously may later and in a different context lose its comic effect, or conversely, a motif developed solemnly may be repeated in a parodistic vein. Yet this does not mean that the beliefs of yesterday are necessarily held up to scorn; rather, we have here two levels, the tragic and the comic, of a single symbolic system, as in the medieval theater. A single clear purpose directs the system of symbols. "We shall thunder out a new myth upon the world."

A mythology of Majakovskij?

His first collection of poems was entitled *I*. Vladimir Majakovskij is not only the hero of his first play, but his name is the title of that tragedy, as well as of his last collection of poems. The author dedicates his verse "to his beloved self."

---

[2] Xlebnikov himself describes his own death using suicide imagery: "What? Zangezi's dead!/ Not only that, he slit his own throat./ What a sad piece of news!/ What sorrowful news!// He left a short note:/ 'Razor, have my throat!'/ The wide iron sedge/ Slit the waters of his life, he's no more . . ."

When Majakovskij was working on the poem "Man" he said, "I want to depict simply man, man in general, not an abstraction, à la Andreev, but a genuine 'Ivan' who waves his arms, eats cabbage soup, and can be directly felt." But Majakovskij could directly feel only himself. This is said very well in Trotsky's article on him (an intelligent article, the poet said): "In order to raise man he elevates him to the level of Majakovskij. The Greeks were anthropomorphists, naïvely likening the forces of nature to themselves; our poet is a Majakomorphist, and he populates the squares, the streets, and the fields of the Revolution only with himself." Even when the hero of Majakovskij's poem appears as the 150,000,000-member collective, realized in one Ivan—a fantastic epic hero—the latter in turn assumes the familiar features of the poet's "ego." This ego asserts itself even more frankly in the rough drafts of the poem.[3]

Empirical reality neither exhausts nor fully takes in the various shapes of the poet's ego. Majakovskij passes before us in one of his "innumerable souls." "The unbending spirit of eternal rebellion" has poured itself into the poet's muscles, the irresponsible spirit without name or patronymic, "from future days, just a man." "And I feel that I am too small for myself. Someone obstinately bursts out of me." Weariness with fixed and narrow confines, the urge to transcend static boundaries—such is Majakovskij's infinitely varied theme. No lair in the world can contain the poet and the unruly horde of his desires. "Driven into the earthly pen I drag a daily yoke." "The accursed earth has me chained." The grief of Peter the Great is that of a "prisoner, held in chains in his own city." Hulks of districts wriggle out of the "zones marked off by the governor." The cage of the blockade in Majakovskij's verses turns into the world prison destroyed by a cosmic gust directed "beyond the radiant slits of sunsets." The poet's revolutionary call is directed at all of those "for whom life is cramped and unbearable," "who cry out because the nooses of noon are too tight." The ego of the poet is a battering ram, thudding into a forbidden Future; it is a mighty will "hurled over the last limit" toward the incarnation of the Future, toward an absolute fullness of being: "one must rip joy from the days yet to come."

Opposed to this creative urge toward a transformed future is the stabilizing force of an immutable present, overlaid, as this present is, by a stagnating slime, which stifles life in its tight, hard mold. The Russian name for this element is *byt*. It is curious that this word and its derivatives should have such a prominent place in the Russian language (from which it spread even to the Komi), while West European languages have no word that corresponds to it. Perhaps the reason is that in the European collective consciousness there is no concept of such a force as might oppose and break down the established norms of life. The revolt of the individual against the fixed forms of social convention presupposes the existence of such a force. The real antithesis of *byt* is a slippage of social norms that is immediately sensed by those involved in social life. In Russia this

[3] "New name,/ tear off!/ fly/ into the space of the world dwelling/ thousand-year-old/ low sky,/ vanish, you blue-ass!/ It is I./ I, I/ I/ I/ I/ I/ the inspired sewage-disposal man of the earth . . ."

sense of an unstable foundation has been present for a very long time, and not just as a historical generalization, but as a direct experience. We recall that in the early nineteenth century, during the time of Čaadaev, there was the sense of a "dead and stagnant life," but at the same time a feeling of instability and uncertainty: "Everything is slipping away, everything is passing," wrote Čaadaev. "In our own homes we are as it were in temporary quarters. In our family life we seem foreigners. In our cities we look like nomads." And as Majakovskij put it:

> . . . laws/concepts/faiths
> The granite blocks of cities
> And even the very sun's reliable glow—
> Everything had become as it were fluid,
> Seemed to be sliding a little—
> A little bit thinned and watered down.

But all these shifts, all this "leaking of the poet's room," are only a "hardly audible draft, which is probably only felt by the very tip of the soul." Inertia continues to reign. It is the poet's primordial enemy, and he never tires of returning to this theme. "Motionless *byt*." "Everything stands as it has been for ages. *Byt* is like a horse that can't be spurred and stands still." "Slits of *byt* are filled with fat and coagulate, quiet and wide." "The swamp of *byt* is covered over with slime and weeds." "Old little *byt* is moldy." "The giant *byt* crawls everywhere through the holes." "Force booming *byt* to sing!" "Put the question of *byt* on the agenda." "In fall,/ winter,/ spring,/ summer/ During the day/ during sleep/ I don't accept/ I hate this/ all. /All/ that in us/ is hammered in by past slavishness/ all/ that like the swarm of trifles/ was covering/ and covered with *byt*/ even our red-flagged ranks." Only in the poem "About That" is the poet's desperate struggle with *byt* fully laid bare. There it is not personified as it is elsewhere in his work. On the contrary, the poet hammers his verbal attack directly into that moribund *byt* which he despises. And *byt* reacts by executing the rebel "with all rifles and batteries, from every Mauser and Browning." Elsewhere in Majakovskij this phenomenon is, as we have said, personified— not however as a living person, but rather, in the poet's own phrase, as an animated tendency. In "Man" the poet's enemy is very broadly generalized as "Ruler of all, my rival, my invincible enemy." But it is also possible to localize this enemy and give him a particular shape. One may call him "Wilson," domicile him in Chicago, and, in the language of fairy-tale hyperbole, outline his every portrait (as in "150,000,000"). But then the poet offers a "little footnote": "Those who draw the Wilsons, Lloyd Georges, and Clemenceaus sometimes show their mugs with moustaches, sometimes not; but that's beside the point since they're all one and the same thing." The enemy is a universal image. The forces of nature, people, metaphysical substances, are only its incidental aspects and disguises: "The same old bald fellow directs us unseen, the master of the earthly cancan. Sometimes in the shape of an idea, sometimes a kind of devil, or then again he glows as God, hidden behind a cloud." If we should try to translate the Majakovskian mythology into the language of speculative philosophy, the exact equivalent for this enmity would be the antimony "I" versus "not-I." A better designation for Majakovskij's enemy could hardly be found.

Just as the creative ego of the poet is not coextensive with his actually existing self, so conversely the latter does not take in all of the former. In the faceless regiment of his acquaintances, all tangled in the "apartment-house spider web,"

> One of them/I recognized
> As like as a twin
> Myself/my very own self.

This terrible "double" of the poet is his conventional and commonplace "self," the purchaser and owner whom Xlebnikov once contrasted with the inventor and discoverer. That self has an emotional attachment to a securely selfish and stable life, to "*my* little place, and a household that's *mine*, with *my* little picture on the wall."

The poet is oppressed by the specter of an unchangeable world order, a universal apartment-house *byt*: "No sound, the universe is asleep".

> Revolutions shake up violently the bodies of kingdoms,
> The human herd changes its herdsmen.
> But you/uncrowned ruler of our hearts
> No rebellion ever touches.

Against this unbearable might of *byt* an uprising as yet unheard of and nameless must be contrived. The terms used in speaking of the class struggle are only conventional figures, only approximate symbols, only one of the levels: the *part for the whole*. Majakovskij, who has witnessed "the sudden reversals of fortune in battles not yet fought," must give new meaning to the habitual terminology. In the rough draft of the poem "150,000,000" we find the following definitions:

> To be a bourgeois does not mean to own capital or squander gold. It means to be the heel of a corpse on the throat of the young. It means a mouth stopped up with fat. To be a proletarian doesn't mean to have a dirty face and work in a factory; it means to be in love with the future that's going to explode the filth of the cellars—believe me.

The basic fusion of Majakovskij's poetry with the theme of the revolution has often been pointed out. But another indissoluble combination of motifs in the poet's work has not so far been noticed: revolution and the destruction of the poet. This idea is suggested even as early as the *Tragedy* [1913], and later this fact that the linkage of the two is not accidental becomes "clear to the point of hallucination." No mercy will be shown to the army of zealots, or to the doomed volunteers in the struggle. The poet himself is an expiatory offering in the name of that universal and real resurrection that is to come; that was the theme of the poem "War and the Universe" [*Vojna i mir*]. And in the poem "A Cloud in Trousers" [*Oblako v štanax*] the poet promises that when a certain year comes "in the thorny crown" of revolutions, "For you/I will tear out my soul/and trample on it till it spreads out,/and I'll give it to you,/a bloody banner." In the poems written after the revolution the same idea is there, but in the past tense. The poet, mobilized by the revolution, has "stamped on the throat of his own song." (This line occurs in the last poem he published, an address to his "comrade-descendants" of the future, written in clear awareness of the coming end.) In the poem "About That" the poet is destroyed by *byt*. "The bloodletting is over. . . . Only high above the Kremlin the tatters of the poet shine in the wind—a little red flag." This image is plainly an echo of "A Cloud in Trousers."

The poet's hungry ear captures the music of the future, but he is not destined to enter the Promised Land. A vision of the future is present in all the most essential pages of Majakovskij's work. "And such a day dawned—Andersen's fairy tales crawled about like little pups at his feet"; "You can't tell whether it's air, or a flower, or a bird. It sings, and it's fragrant, and it's brightly colored all at once"; "Call us Cain or call us Abel, it doesn't matter. The future is here." For Majakovskij the future is a dialectical synthesis. The removal of all contradictions finds its expression in the facetious image of Christ playing checkers with Cain, in the myth of the universe permeated by love, and in the proposition "The commune is a place where bureaucrats will disappear and there will be many poems and songs." The present disharmony, the contradiction between poetry and building, "the delicate business of the poet's place in the working ranks," is one of Majakovskij's most acute problems. "Why," he asked, "should literature occupy its own special little corner? Either it should appear in every newspaper, every day, on every page, or else it's totally useless. The kind of literature that's dished out as dessert can go to hell" (from the *Reminiscences* of D. Lebedev).

Majakovskij always regarded ironically talk of the insignificance and death of poetry (really nonsense, he would say, but useful for the purpose of revolutionizing art). He planned to pose the question of the future of art in the "Fifth International" [*Pjatyj internacional*], a poem that he worked on long and carefully but never finished. According to the outline of the work, the first stage of the revolution, a worldwide social transformation, has been completed, but humanity is bored. *Byt* still survives. So a new revolutionary act of world-shaking proportions is required: "A revolution of the spirit" in the name of a new organization of life, a new art, and a new science. The published introduction to the poem is an order to abolish the beauties of verse and to introduce into poetry the brevity and accuracy of mathematical formulas. He offers an example of a poetic structure built on the model of a logical problem. When I reacted skeptically to this poetic program—the exhortation in verse against verse—Majakovskij smiled: "But didn't you notice that the solution of my logical problem is a transrational solution?"

The remarkable poem "Homeward!" [*Domoj!*] is devoted to the contradiction between the rational and the irrational. It is a dream about the fusion of the two elements, a kind of rationalization of the irrational:

> I feel/like a Soviet factory
> Manufacturing happiness.
> I don't want/to be plucked
> Like a flower/after the day's work
> . . . .
> I want/the heart to be paid
> Its wage of love/at the specialist's rate
> I want/the factory committee
> To put a lock on my lips
> When the work is done
> I want/the pen to be equal to the bayonet
> And I want Stalin/to report in the name of the Politburo
> About the production of verse
> As he does about pig iron and steel.
> Thus, and so it is/we've reached
> The topmost level/up from the workers' hovels
> In the Union/of Republics
> The appreciation of verse/has exceeded the prewar level.

The idea of the acceptance of the irrational appears in Majakovskij's work in various guises, and each of the images he uses for this purpose tends to reappear in his poetry. The stars ("You know, if they light up the stars,/that means, somebody needs them!"). The madness of spring ("Everyting is clear concerning bread/and concerning peace./But the prime question,/the question of spring/must be/elucidated.") And the heart that changes winter to spring and water to wine ("It's that I'm/going to raise my heart like a flag,/a marvelous twentieth-century miracle"). And that hostile answer of the enemy in the poem "Man": "If the heart is everything/then why,/why have I been gathering you, my dear money!/How do they dare to sing?/Who gave them the right?/Who said the days could blossom into July?/Lock the heavens in wires!/Twist the earth into streets!"

But Majakovskij's central irrational theme is the theme of love. It is a theme that cruelly punishes those who dare to forget it, whose storms toss us about violently and push everything else out of our ken. And like poetry itself this theme is both inseparable from and in disharmony with our present life; it is "closely mingled with our jobs, our incomes, and all the rest." And love is crushed by *byt*:

> Omnipotent one
> You thought up a pair of hands
> Fixed it
> So that everyone has a head.
> Why couldn't you fix it
> So that without torment
> We could just kiss and kiss and kiss?

Eliminate the irrational? Majakovskij draws a bitterly satirical picture. On the one hand, the heavy boredom of certain rational revelations: the usefulness of the cooperative, the danger of liquor, political education, and on the other hand, an unashamed hooligan of planetary dimensions (in the poem "A Type" [*Tip*]). Here we have a satirical sharpening of the dialectical contradiction.

Majakovskij says "yes" to the rationalization of production, technology, and the planned economy if as a result of all this "the partially opened eye of the future sparkles with real earthly love." But he rejects it all if it means only a selfish clutching at the present. If that's the case then grandiose technology becomes only a "highly perfected apparatus of parochialism and gossip on the worldwide scale" (from an essay "My Discovery of America"). Just such a planetary narrowness and parochialism permeates life in the year 1970, as shown in Majakovskij's play about the future, *The Bedbug* [*Klop*], where we see a rational organization without emotion, with no superfluous expenditure of energy, without dreams. A worldwide social revolution has been achieved, but the revolution of the spirit is still in the future. The play is a quiet protest against the spiritual inheritors of those languid judges who, in his early satirical poem "without knowing just why or wherefore, attacked Peru." Some of the characters in *The Bedbug* have a close affinity with the world of Zamjatin's *We*, although Majakovskij bitterly ridicules not only the rational utopian community but the rebellion against it in the name of alcohol, the irrational and unregulated individual happiness. Zamjatin, however, idealizes that rebellion.

Majakovskij has an unshakable faith that, beyond the mountain of suffering, beyond each rising plateau of revolutions, there does exist the "real heaven on earth," the only possible resolution of all contradictions. *Byt* is only a surrogate for the coming synthesis; it doesn't remove contradictions but only conceals them. The poet is unwilling to compromise with the dialectic; he rejects any mechanical softening of the contraditions. The objects of Majakovskij's unsparing sarcasm are the "compromisers" (as in the play *Mystery-Bouffe*). Among the gallery of "bureaucrat-compromisers" portrayed in his agitational pieces, we have in *The Bathhouse* [*Banja*] the *Glavnačpups* Pobedonosikov, whose very title is an acronym for "Chief Administrator for the Organizing of Compromises." Obstacles in the road to the future—such is the true nature of these "artificial people." The time machine will surely spew them out.

It seemed to him a criminal illusion to suppose that the essential and vital problem of building a worldwide "wonderful life" could be put aside for the sake of devising some kind of personal happiness. "It's early to rejoice," he wrote. The opening scenes of *The Bedbug* develop the idea that people are tired of a life full of struggle, tired of front-line equality, tired of military metaphors. "This is not 1919. People want to live." They build family nests for themselves: "Roses will bloom and be fragrant at the present juncture of time." "Such is the elegant fulfillment of our comrade's life of struggle." Oleg Bajan, the servant of beauty in *The Bedbug,* formulates this sentiment in the following words: "We have managed to compromise and control class and other contradictions, and in this a person armed with a Marxist eye, so to speak, can't help seeing, as in a single drop of water, the future happiness of mankind, which the common people call socialism." (In an earlier, lyrical context the same idea took this form: "There he is in a soft bed, fruit beside him and wine on the night table.") Majakovskij's sharply chiseled lines express unlimited contempt for all those who seek comfort and rest. All such people receive their answer from the mechanic in *The Bedbug*: "We'll never crawl out of our trenches with a white flag in our hands." And the poem "About That" develops the same theme in the form of an intimate personal experience. In that work Majakovskij begs for the advent of love, his savior: "Confiscate my pain—take it away!" And Majakovskij answers himself:

> Leave off./Don't/not a word/no requests,
> What's the point/that you/alone/should succeed?
> I'll wait/and together with the whole unloved earth
> With the whole/human mass/we'll win it.
> Seven years I stood/and I'll stand two hundred
> Nailed here/waiting for it.
> On the bridge of years/derided/scorned
> A redeemer of earthly love/I must stand
> Stand for all/for everyone I'll atone
> For everyone I'll weep.

But Majakovskij knows very well that even if his youth should be renewed four times and he should four times grow old again, that would only mean a fourfold increase of his torment, a four times multiplied horror at the senseless daily grind and at premature celebrations of victory. In any case, he will never live to see the revelation all over the world of an absolute fullness of life, and the final count still stands: "I've not lived out my earthly lot; I've not lived through my earthly love." His destiny is to be an expiatory victim who never knew joy:

> A bullet for the rest
> For some a knife.
> But what about me?
> And when?

Majakovskij has now given us the final answer to that question.

The Russian Futurists believed in cutting themselves loose from the "classic generals," and yet they are vitally tied to the Russian literary tradition. It is interesting to note that famous line of Majakovskij's, so full of bravado (and at the same time a tactical slogan): "But why don't we attack Puškin?" It was followed not long after by those mournful lines addressed to the same Puškin: "You know I too will soon be dead and mute./And after my death/we two will be quite close together." Majakovskij's dreams of the future that repeat the utopian visions of Dostoevskij's Versilov in *A Raw Youth,* the poet's frequent hymns to the "man-god," the "thirteenth apostle's" fight against God, the ethical rejection of Him—all this is much closer to Russian literature of an earlier day than it is to official and regimented Soviet "godlessness." And Majakovskij's belief in personal immortality has nothing to do with the official catechism of Jaroslavskij's "godless" movement. The poet's vision of the coming resurrection of the dead is vitally linked with the materialistic mysticism of the Russian philosopher Fedorov.

When in the spring of 1920 I returned to Moscow, which was tightly blockaded, I brought with me recent books and information about scientific developments in the West. Majakovskij made me repeat several times my somewhat confused remarks on the general theory of relativity, and about the growing interest in that concept in Western Europe. The idea of the liberation of energy, the problem of the time dimension, and the idea that movement at the speed of light may actually be a reverse movement in time—all these things fascinated Majakovskij. I'd seldom seen him so interested and attentive. "Don't you think," he suddenly asked, "that we'll at last achieve immortality?" I was astonished, and I mumbled a skeptical comment. He thrust his jaw forward with that hypnotic insistence so familiar to anyone who knew Majakovskij well: "I'm absolutely convinced," he said, "that one day there will be no more death. And the dead will be resurrected. I've got to find some scientist who'll give me a precise account of what's in Einstein's books. It's out of the question that I shouldn't understand it. I'll see to it that this scientist receives an academician's ration." At that point I became aware of a Majakovskij that I'd never known before. The demand for victory over death had taken hold of him. He told me later that he was writing a poem called "The Fourth International" (he afterward changed it to "The Fifth International") that would deal with such things. "Einstein will be a member of that International. The poem will be much more important than '150,000,000.' " Majakovskij was at the time obsessed with the idea of sending Einstein a congratulatory telegram "from the art of the future to the science of the future." We never again returned to this matter in our conversations, and he never finished "The Fifth International." But in the epilogue to "About That" we find the lines: "I see it, I see it clearly to the last sharp detail. . . . On the bright eminence of time, impervious to rot or destruction, the workshop of human resurrection."

The epilogue to "About That" carries the following heading: "A request addressed to . . . (Please, comrade chemist, fill in the name yourself)." I haven't the slightest doubt that for Majakovskij this was not just a literary device but a genuine and seriously offered request to some "quiet chemist with a domed forehead" living in the thirtieth century:

Resurrect me!
Even if only because I was a poet
And waited for you,
And put behind me prosaic nonsense.
Resurrect me—
Just for that!
Do resurrect me—
I want to live it all out.

The very same "Institute for Human Resurrections" reappears in the play *The Bedbug* but in a comic context. It is the insistent theme of Majakovskij's last writings. Consider the situation in *The Bathhouse*: "A phosphorescent woman out of the future, empowered to select the best people for the future age appears in the time machine: At the first signal we blast off, and smash through old decrepit time. . . . Winged time will sweep away and cut loose the ballast, heavy with rubbish and ruined by lack of faith." Once again we see that the pledge of resurrection is faith. Moreover, the people of the future must transform not only their own future, but also the past: "The fence of time/our feet will trample. . . . As it has been written by us,/so will the world be/on Wednesday,/in the past/and now/and tomorrow/and forever" (from "150,000,000"). The poem written in memory of Lenin offers the same idea, yet in disguised form:

> Death will never dare
> To touch him.
> He stands
> In the total sum of what's to be!
> The young attend
> to these verses on his death
> But their hearts know
> That he's deathless.

In Majakovskij's earliest writings personal immortality is achieved in spite of science. "You students," he says, "all the stuff we know and study is rubbish. Physics, astronomy, and chemistry are all nonsense" (from the poem "Man"). At that time he regarded science as an idle occupation involving only the extraction of square roots or a kind of inhuman collection of fossilized fragments of the summer before last. His satirical "Hymn to the Scholar" became a genuine and fervent hymn only when he thought he had found the miraculous instrument of human resurrection in Einstein's "futuristic brain" and in the physics and chemistry of the future. "Like logs thrown into a boom we are thrown at birth into the Volga of human time; we toss about as we float downstream. But from now on that great river shall be submissive to us. I'll make time stand still, move in another direction and at a new rate of speed. People will be able to get out of the day like passengers getting out of a bus."

Whatever the means of achieving immortality, the vision of it in Majakovskij's verse is unchangeable: there can be no resurrection of the spirit without the body, without the flesh itself. Immortality has nothing to do with any other world; it is indissolubly tied to this one. "I'm all for the heart," he wrote in "Man," "but how can bodiless beings have a heart?/ . . . My eyes fixed earthward. . . /This herd of the bodiless,/how they/bore me!" "We want to live here on earth—/no higher and no lower" (*Mystery-Bouffe*). "With the last measure of my heart/I believe/in this life,/in this world,/in all of it" ("About That"). Majakovskij's dream is of an everlasting earth, and this earth is placed in sharp opposition to all superterrestrial, fleshless abstractions. In his poetry and in Xlebnikov's the theme of earthly life is presented in a coarse, physical incarnation (they even talk about the "flesh" rather than the body). An extreme expression of this is the cult of tender feeling for the beast with his beastly wisdom.

"They will arise from the mounds of graves/and their buried bones will grow flesh" ("War and the Universe"), wrote Majakovskij. And those lines are not just present simply as a poetic device that motivates the whimsical interweaving of two separate narrative levels. On the contrary—that vision is Majakovskij's most cherished poetic myth.

This constant infatuation with a wonderful future is linked in Majakovskij with a pronounced dislike of children, a fact that would seem at first sight to be hardly consonant with his fanatical belief in tomorrow. But just as we find in Dostoevsky an obtrusive and neurotic "father hatred" linked with great veneration for ancestors and reverence for tradition, so in Majakovskij's spiritual world an abstract faith in the coming transformation of the world is joined quite properly with hatred for the evil continuum of specific tomorrows that only prolong today ("the calendar is nothing but the calendar!") and with undying hostility to that "brood-hen" love that serves only to reproduce the present way of life. Majakovskij was indeed capable of giving full due to the creative mission of those "kids of the collective" in their unending quarrel with the old world, but at the same time he bristled whenever an actual "kid" ran into the room. Majakovskij never recognized his own myth of the future in any concrete child; these he regarded simply as new offshoots of the hydraheaded enemy. That is why we find in the marvelous movie scenario *How Are You?* [*Kak poživaete?*] childlike grotesques, which are the legitimate offspring of the Manilov pair Aristide and Themistocles in Gogol's *Dead Souls*. We recall that his youthful poem "A Few Words about Myself" [*Neskol'ko slov obo mne samom*] begins with the line "I love to watch children dying." And in the same poem child-murder is elevated to a cosmic theme: "Sun!/My father!/At least you have pity and torment me not!/That's my blood you shed flowing along this low road." And surrounded by that very aura of sunshine, the same "child complex" appears as both an immemorial and personal motif in the poem "War and the Universe":

> Listen—
> The sun just shed his first rays
> not yet knowing
> where he'll go when he's done his day's work;
> and that's me
> Majakovskij,
> Bringing as sacrifice to the idol's pedestal
> a beheaded infant.

There's no doubt that in Majakovskij the theme of child-murder and suicide are closely linked: these are simply two different ways of depriving the present of its immediate succession, of "tearing through decrepit time."

Majakovskij's conception of the poet's role is clearly bound up with his belief in the possibility of conquering time and breaking its steady, slow step. He did not regard poetry as a mechanical superstructure added to the ready-made base of existence (it is no accident that he was so close to the Formalist literary critics). A genuine poet is not one "who feeds in the calm pastures of everyday life; his mug is not pointed at the ground." "The weak ones simply beat time and wait for something to happen that they can echo; but the powerful rush far enough ahead so as to drag time along behind them!" Majakovskij's recurrent image of the poet is one who overtakes time, and we may say that this is the actual likeness of Majakovskij himself. Xlebnikov and Majakovskij accurately forecast the Revolution (including the date); that is only a detail, but a rather important one. It would seem that never until our day has the writer's fate been laid bare with such pitiless candor in his own words. Impatient to know life, he recognizes it in his own story. The "God-seeker" Blok and the Marxist Majakovskij both understood clearly that verses are dictated to the poet by some primordial, mysterious force. "We know not whence comes the basic beat of rhythm." We don't even know where this rhythm is located: "outside of me or within me? But most likely within me." The poet himself senses the necessity of his own verse, and his contemporaries feel that the poet's destiny is no accident. Is there any one of us who doesn't share the impression that the poet's volumes are a kind of scenario in which he plays out the story of his life? The poet is the principal character, and subordinate parts are also included; but the performers for these later roles are recruited as the action develops and to the extent that the plot requires them. The plot has been laid out ahead of time right down to the details of the dénouement.

The motif of suicide, so alien to the thematics of the Futurist and "Left Front" groups, continually recurs in the work of Majakovskij, from his earliest writings, where madmen hang themselves in an unequal struggle with *byt* (the director, the "man with two kisses" in the *Tragedy*), to the scenario *How Are You?*, in which a newspaper article about a girl's suicide induces horror in the poet. And when he tells about a young communist who committed suicide he adds, "How like me that is. Horrors!" He tries on, so to speak, all possible varieties of suicide: "Rejoice now! He'll execute himself. . . . The locomotive's wheel will embrace my neck". "I'll run to the canal and there stick my head in the water's grinning mug. . . ." "The heart bursts for a bullet, the throat raves for a razor. . . . Beckons to the water, leads to the roof's slope. . . . Druggist, give me the means to send my soul without any pain into the spacious beyond."

A simple résumé of Majakovskij's poetic autobiography would be the following: the poet nurtured in his heart the unparalleled anguish of the present generation. That is why his verse is charged with hatred for the strongholds of the established order, and in his own work he finds "the alphabet of coming ages." Majakovskij's earliest and most characteristic image is one in which he "goes out through the city leaving his soul on the spears of houses, shred by shred." The hopelessness of his lonely struggle with the daily routine became clearer to him at every turn. The brand of martyrdom is burned into him. There's no way to win an early victory. The poet is the doomed "outcast of the present."

> Mama!
> Tell my sisters, Ljuda and Olja,
> That there's no way out.

Gradually the idea that "there's no way out" lost its purely literary character. From the poetic passage it found its way into prose, and "there's no way out" turned up as an author's remark in the margin of the manuscript for "About That." And from that prose context the same idea made its way into the poet's life: in his suicide note he said: "Mama, sisters, comrades, forgive me. This is not a good method (I don't recommend it to others), but for me there's no other way out."

The act was long in preparation. Fifteen years earlier in a prologue to a collection of poems, he wrote:

Often I think
Hadn't I better just
Let a bullet mark the period of my sentence.
Anyway, today
I'm giving my farewell concert.

As time went on the theme of suicide became more and more pressing. Majakovskij's most intense poems, "Man" (1916) and "About That" (1923), are dedicated to it. Each of these works is an ominous song of the victory of *byt* over the poet; their leitmotif is "Love's boat has smashed against the daily grind" (a line from his suicide note). The first poem is a detailed depiction of Majakovskij's suicide. In the second there is already a clear sense that the suicide theme transcends literature and is in the realm of "literature of fact." Once again—but even more disturbingly—the images of the first poem file past, the keenly observed stages of existence: the "half-death" in the vortex of the horrifyingly trivial, then the "final death"—"The lead in my heart! Not even a shudder!" This theme of suicide had become so real that it was out of the question to sketch the scene anymore. It had to be exorcised. Propaganda pieces were necessary in order to slow down the inexorable movement of that theme. "About That" already initiates this long cycle of exorcism. "I won't give them the satisfaction of seeing me dead of a bullet." "I want to live on and on, moving through the years." The lines to Sergej Esenin are the high point of this cycle. According to Majakovskij, the salubrious aim of the lines addressed to Esenin was to neutralize the impact of Esenin's death poem. But when you read them now, they sound even more sepulchral than Esenin's last lines. Esenin's lines equate life and death, but Majakovskij in his poem can only say about life that it's harder than death. This is the same sort of doubtful propaganda for life found in Majakovskij's earlier lines to the effect that only disquiet about the afterlife is a restraint upon the bullet. Such, too, are the farewell words in his suicide letter: "Stay happy here."

In spite of all this the obituary writers vie with one another: "One could expect anything of Majakovskij, but not that he would kill himself" (E. Adamovič). And Lunačarskij: "The idea of suicide is simply incompatible with our image of the poet." And Malkin: "His death cannot be reconciled with his whole life, which was that of a poet completely dedicated to the Revolution." And the newspaper *Pravda*: "His death is just as inconsistent with the life he led, as it is unmotivated by his poetry." And A. Xalatov: "Such a death was hardly proper for the Majakovskij we knew." Or Kol'csov: "It is not right for him. Can it be that none of us knew Majakovskij?" Petr Pil'skij: "He did not, of course, reveal any reason for us to expect such an end." And finally, the poet Demjan Bednyj: "Incredible! What could he have lacked?"

Could these men of letters have forgotten or so misunderstood *All That Majakovskij Composed*? Or was there a general conviction that all of it was only "composed," only invented? Sound literary criticism rejects any direct or immediate conclusions about the biography of a poet when these are based merely on the evidence of his works, but it does not at all follow from this that there is no connection whatsoever between the artist's biography and his art. Such an "antibiographical" position would be the equivalent, in reverse, of the simplistic biographical approach. Have we forgotten Majakovskij's admiration for the "genuine heroism and martyrdom" of Xlebnikov, his teacher? "His life," wrote Majakovskij, "matched his brilliant verbal constructs. That life is an example for poets and a reproach to poetizers." And it was Majakovskij who wrote that even a poet's style of dress, even his intimate conversations with his wife should be determined by the whole of his poetic production. He understood very well the close connection between poetry and life.

After Esenin's suicide poem, said Majakovskij, his death became a literary fact. "It was clear at once that those powerful verses, just those verses, would bring to the bullet or the noose many who had been hesitating." And when he approached the writing of his own autobiography, Majakovskij remarked that the facts of a poet's life are interesting "only if they became fixed in the word." Who would dare assert that Majakovskij's suicide was not fixed in the word? "Don't gossip!" Majakovskij adjured us just before his death. Yet those who stubbornly mark out a strict boundary between the "purely personal" fate of the poet and his literary biography create an atmosphere of low-grade, highly personal gossip by means of those significant silences.

It is a historical fact that the people around Majakovskij simply did not believe in his lyrical monologues. "They listened, all smiling, to the eminent clown." They took his various masquerades for the true face of the man: first the pose of the fop ("It's good when the soul is shielded from inspection by a yellow blouse"); then the performance of an overeager journalist and agitator: "It's good, when you're in the teeth of the gallows, to cry out: 'Drink Van Houten's cocoa' " ("A Cloud in Trousers"). But then when he carried out that slogan in practice in his advertising jingles ("Use the tea with the gold label!" "If you want good luck and good fortune buy a government lottery ticket!") his audience saw the rhymed advertisement but missed the teeth of the gallows. As it turns out, it was easier to believe in the benefits of a lottery loan or the excellent quality of the pacifiers sold in the state stores than it was to believe that the poet had reached an extreme of despair, that he was in a state of misery and near-death. "About That" is a long and hopeless cry to the ages, but Moscow doesn't believe in tears. They stamped and whistled at this routine Majakovskian artistic stunt, the latest of his "magnificent absurdities," but when the theatrical cranberry juice of the puppet show became real, genuine, thick blood, they were taken aback: Incredible! Inconsistent!

Majakovskij, as an act of self-preservation, often helped to spread illusions about himself. The record of a conversation we had in 1927 demonstrates this. I said, "The total sum of possible experience has been measured out to us. We might have predicted the early decline of our generation. But the symptoms of this are rapidly increasing in number. Take Aseev's line 'What about us, what about us, can it be we've lost our youth?' And consider Šklovskij's memorial service to himself." Majakovskij answered: "Utter nonsense. Everything is ahead of me. If I ever thought that the best of me was in the past that would be the end for me." I reminded him of a recent poem of his in which the following lines occurred:

I was born/increased in size
fed from the bottle—
I lived/worked/grew oldish
And life will pass
As the Azores Islands
Once passed into the distance.

"That's nothing," he said, "just a formal ending. An image only. I can make as many of them as you like. My poem 'Homeward' in the first version ended with the lines:

I want my country to understand me
But if not—so what:
I'll just pass my country by
Like a slanting rain in summer.

But you know, Brik told me to strike those lines out because they didn't go with the tone of the whole poem. So I struck them out."

The simplistic Formalist literary credo professed by the Russian Futurists inevitably propelled their poetry toward the antithesis of Formalism—toward the cultivation of the heart's "raw cry" and uninhibited frankness. Formalist literary theory placed the lyrical monologue in quotes and disguised the "ego" of the lyric poet under a pseudonym. But what unbounded horror results when suddenly you see through the pseudonym, and the phantoms of art invade reality, just as in Majakovskij's scenario *Bound in Film* a girl is kidnapped from a movie set by a mad artist and lands in "real life."

Toward the end of his life the satire and the laudatory ode had completely overshadowed his elegiac verse, which, by the way, he identified with the lyric in general. In the West the existence of this basic core in Majakovskij's poetry was not even suspected. The West knew only the "drummer of the October Revolution." There are many explanations for this victory of the "agit-prop." In 1923 Majakovskij had reached the end of the road as far as the elegiac mode was concerned. In an artistic sense "About That" was a "repetition of the past," intensified and raised to perfection. His journalistic verse was a search for something new; it was an experiment in the production of new materials and in untested genres. To my skeptical comments about these poems Majakovskij replied: "Later on you'll understand them." And when *The Bedbug* and *The Bathhouse* appeared it became clear that his most recent poems had been a huge laboratory experiment in language and theme, a labor masterfully exploited in his first efforts in the area of prose drama and offering a rich potential for future growth.

Finally, in connection with its social setting, the journalistic verse of Majakovskij represented a shift from an unrestrained frontal attack in the direction of an exhausting trench warfare. *Byt,* with its swarm of heartbreaking trivia, is still with him. And it is no longer "rubbish with its own proper face," but "petty, small, vulgar rubbish." You cannot resist the pressure of such rubbish by grandiloquent pronouncements "in general and in toto," or by theses on communism, or by pure poetic devices. "Now you have to see the enemy and take aim at him." You have to smash the "swarm of trivia" offered by *byt* "in a small way" and not grieve that the battle has been reduced to many minor engagements. The invention of strategies for describing "trifles that may also prove a sure step into the future"—this is how Majakovskij understood the immediate task of the poet.

Just as one must not reduce Majakovskij the propagandist to a single dimension, so, too, one-sided interpretations of the poet's death are shallow and opaque. "The preliminary investigation indicates that his act was prompted by motives of a purely personal character." But the poet had already provided an answer to that in the subtitle of "About That": "From personal motives, but about the general way of life."

Bela Kun preached to the late poet not to "subordinate the great cause to our own petty personal feelings." Majakovskij had entered his objection in good time:

> With this petty/and personal theme
> That's been sung so many times
> I've trod the poetical treadmill
> And I'm going to tread it again.
> This theme/right now
> Is a prayer to Buddha
> And sharpens a black man's knife for his master.
> If there's life on Mars/and on it just one
> Human-hearted creature
> Then he too is writing now
> About that same thing.

The journalist Kol'cov hastened to explain: "Majakovskij himself was wholly absorbed in the business affairs of various literary groups and in political matters. Someone else fired that shot, some outsider who happened to be in control of a revolutionary poet's mind and will. It was the result of the temporary pressure of circumstances." And once again we recall the rebuke Majakovskij delivered long before the fact:

> Dreams are a harm
> And it's useless to fantasize.
> You've got to bear the burden of service.
> But sometimes—
> Life appears to you in a new light
> And through the mess of trifles
> You catch sight of something great and good.

"We condemn this senseless, unforgivable act. It was a stupid and cowardly death. We cannot but protest most vigorously against his departure from life, against his incongruous end." (Such was the pronouncement of the Moscow Soviet and others.) But Majakovskij had already parodied these very funeral speeches in *The Bedbug*: "Zoja Berezkin's shot herself—Aha! She'll catch it for that at her party-section meeting." Says a doctor in the future world commune: "What is suicide? . . . You shot at yourself? . . . Was it an accident?" "No, it was from love." "Nonsense. . . . Love makes you want to build bridges and have children. . . . But you. . . . Yes, yes, yes!"

In general life has been imitating Majakovskij's satirical lines with horrifying regularity. Pobedonosikov, the comic figure in *The Bathhouse*, who has many features that remind us of Lunačarskij, brags that "I have no time for boat rides. . . . Such petty entertainments are for various secretaries: 'Float on, gondola mine!' I have no gondola but a ship of state." And now Lunačarskij himself faithfully echoes his comic double. At a meeting called in memory of the poet the minister hastens to explain that the former's farewell lines about a "love-boat smashed on daily grind" have a pathetic sound: "We know very well that it was not on any love-boat that he sailed our stormy seas. He was the captain of a mighty ship of state." These efforts to forget the "purely personal" tragedy of Majakovskij sometimes take the form of conscious parody. A group of writers in a provincial town published a resolution in which they assure Soviet society that they will take very seriously the advice of the late poet not to follow his example.

It is very strange that on this occasion such terms as "accidental," "personal" and so forth are used precisely by those who have always preached a strict social determinism. But how can one speak of a private episode when the law of large numbers is at work, in view of the fact that in a few years' time the whole bloom of Russian poetry has been swept away?

In one of Majakovskij's longer poems each of the world's countries brings its best gift to the man of the future; Russia brings him poetry. "The power of their voices is most resoundingly woven into song." Western Europe is enraptured with Russian art; the medieval icon and the modern film, the classical ballet and the latest theatrical experiment, yesterday's novel and the latest music. And yet that art which is probably Russia's greatest achievement, her poetry, has never really been an export item. It is intimately Russian and closely linked to the Russian language and would probably not survive the misfortunes of translation. Russian poetry has witnessed two periods of high flowering: the beginning of the nineteenth century and the present century. And the earlier period as well as the later had as its epilogue the untimely death of very many great poets. If you can imagine how slight the contributions of Schiller, Hoffmann, Heine, and especially Goethe would have been if they had all disappeared in their thirties, then you will understand the significance of the following Russian statistics: Ryleev was executed when he was thirty-one. Batjuškov went mad when he was thirty. Venevitinov died at the age of twenty-two, Del'vig at thirty-two. Griboedov was killed when he was thirty-four, Puškin when he was thirty-seven, Lermontov when he was twenty-six. Their fate has more than once been characterized as a form of suicide. Majakovskij himself compared his duel with *byt* to the fatal duels of Puškin and Lermontov. There is much in common in the reactions of society in both periods to these untimely losses. Once again, a feeling of sudden and profound emptiness overwhelms one, an oppressive sense of an evil destiny lying heavily on Russian intellectual life. But now as then other notes are louder and more insistent.

The Western mind can hardly comprehend the stupid, unrestrained abuse of the dead poets. A certain Kikin expressed great disappointment that Martynov, the killer of that "cowardly scoundrel Lermontov," had been arrested. And Czar Nicholas I's final words on the same poet were: "He was a dog and he died a dog's death." And in the same spirit the emigré newspaper *The Rudder* (*Rul'*) carried no obituary on the occasion of Majakovskij's death, but instead a cluster of abusive remarks leading up to the following conclusion: "Majakovskij's whole life gave off a bad smell. Is it possible that his tragic end could set all that right?" (Ofrosimov). But what of Kikins and Ofrosimovs? They're but illiterate zeros who will be mentioned in the history of Russian culture, if at all, only for having defecated on the fresh graves of poets. It is incomparably more distressing to see slops of slander and lies poured on the dead poet by Xodasevič, who is privy to poetry. He certainly knows the value of things; he knows he is slanderously smearing one of the greatest Russian poets. When he caustically remarks that only some fifteen active years were allotted to Majakovskij—"the lifetime of a horse"—it is self-abuse, gallows humor, mockery of the tragic balance sheet of his own generation. If Majakovskij's final balance sheet was "life and I are quits," then Xodasevič's shabby little fate is "the most terrible of amortizations, the amortization of heart and soul."

The latter was written about émigré philistines. But the tradition of Puškin's days is repeated by the same philistines of Moscow stock who immediately try at all costs to replace the live image of the poet by a canonic saint-like mask. And even earlier. . . . But of what went on earlier Majakovskij himself related a few days before his death in a talk at a literary gathering: "So many dogs snipe at me and I'm accused of so many sins, both ones I have and ones I am innocent of, that at times it seems to me as if all I want to do is go away somewhere and sit still for a couple of years, if only to avoid listening to barking!" And this harrassment, framing the poet's demise, was precisely described in advance by Majakovskij:

> Yellow rag after yellow rag
>   of curses be raised!
> Gossip for your ears!
>   Gossip and bite!
> I'm like a cripple in the throes of love.
> Leave a tub of slops for your own.
> I'm not a hindrance.
>   But why all these insults?
> I'm only a verse
>   I'm only a soul.

While below:
    No!
        You're our century-old foe.
One such turned up—
        A hussar!
Have a sniff of powder,
    a little pistol lead.
Fling open your shirt!
    Don't celebrate the coward!

This is just another example of what they call the "incongruity" between Majakovskij's end and his life of yesterday.

Certain questions are particularly intriguing to journalists. Who was responsible for the war? Who was to blame for the poet's death? Biographers are amateur private detectives, and they will certainly take great pains to establish the immediate reason for the suicide. They will add other names to that variegated assemblage of poet-killers, the "son of a bitch D'Anthès," who killed Puškin, the "dashing Major Martynov," who killed Lermontov, and so forth. People who seek the explanation of various phenomena will, if they bear Russia a grudge, readily demonstrate, citing chapter, verse, and historical precedent, that it is dangerous to practice the trade of poet in Russia. And if their grudge is only against contemporary Russia it will also be quite easy to defend such a thesis with weighty arguments. But I am of another mind. It seems to me that the one nearest the truth was the young Slovak poet Novomeský who said: "Do you imagine that such things happen only there, in Russia? Why that's what our world is like nowadays." This is in answer to those phrases, which have alas become truisms, concerning the deadly absence of fresh air, certainly a fatal condition for poets. There are some countries where men kiss women's hands, and others where they only say "I kiss your hand." There are countries where Marxist theory is answered by Leninist practice, and where the madness of the brave, the martyr's stake, and the poet's Golgotha are not just figurative expressions.

In the last analysis what distinguishes Russia is not so much the fact that her great poets have ceased to be, but rather that not long ago she had so many of them. Since the time of the first Symbolists Western Europe has had no great poetry.

The real question concerns not causes but consequences, however tempting it may be to protect oneself from a painful realization of what's happened by discussing the reasons for it.

It's a small thing to build a locomotive:
Wind up its wheels and off it goes.
But if a song doesn't fill the railway station—
Then why do we have alternating current?

Those lines are from Majakovskij's "Order to the Army of Art" [*Prikaz po armii iskusstv*]. We are living in what is called the "reconstruction period," and no doubt we will construct a great many locomotives and scientific hypotheses.

But to our generation has been allotted the morose feat of building without song. And even if new songs should ring out they will belong to another generation and a different curve of time. Yet it is unlikely that there will be new songs. Russian poetry of our century is copying and it would seem outdoing that of the nineteenth century: "the fateful forties are approaching," the years, in other words, of lethargic inertia among poets.

The relationships between the biographies of a generation and the march of history are curious. Each age has its own inventory of requisitions upon private holdings. Suddenly history finds a use for Beethoven's deafness and Cézanne's astigmatism. The age at which a generation's call to service in history's conscription comes, as well as the length of its service, are different for different periods. History mobilizes the youthful ardor of some generations and the tempered maturity or old wisdom of others. When their role is played out yesterday's rulers of men's minds and hearts depart from the proscenium to the backstage of history to live out their years in private, either on the profits from their intellectual investments, or else as paupers. But sometimes it happens otherwise. Our generation emerged at an extraordinarily young age: "We alone," as Majakovskij put it, "are the face of our time. The trumpet of time blows for us." But up to the present moment there are not any replacements, nor even any partial reinforcements. Meanwhile the voice and the emotion of that generation have been cut short, and its allotted quota of feeling—joy and sadness, sarcasm and rapture—have been used up. And yet, the paroxysm of an irreplaceable generation turned out to be no private fate, but in fact the face of our time, the breathlessness of history.

We strained toward the future too impetuously and avidly to leave any past behind us. The connection of one period with another was broken. We lived too much for the future, thought about it, believed in it; the news of the day—sufficient unto itself—no longer existed for us. We lost a sense of the present. We were the witnesses of and participants in great social, scientific, and other cataclysms. *Byt* fell behind us, just as in the young Majakovskij's splendid hyperbole: "One foot has not yet reached the next street." We knew that the plans of our fathers were already out of harmony with the facts of their lives. We read harsh lines alleging that our fathers had taken the old and musty way of life on a temporary lease. But our fathers still had left some remnant of faith in the idea that that way of life was both comfortable and compulsory for all. Their children had only a single-minded, naked hatred for the ever more threadbare, ever more alien rubbish offered by the established order of things. And now the "efforts to organize a personal life are like attempts to heat up ice cream."

As for the future, it doesn't belong to us either. In a few decades we shall be cruelly labeled as products of the past millennium. All we had were compelling songs of the future; and suddenly these songs are no longer part of the dynamic of history, but have been transformed into historico-literary facts. When singers have been killed and their song has been dragged into a museum and pinned to the wall of the past, the generation they represent is even more desolate, orphaned, and lost—impoverished in the most real sense of the word.

The Language of Schizophrenia

Hölderlin's Speech and Poetry

Roman Jakobson and Grete Lübbe-Grothues

TWO KINDS OF THE DEMENTED POET'S UTTERANCES

Conversation

In 1802, at the age of thirty-two, Hölderlin, who had already previously suffered several attacks, fell ill, "with an acute schizophrenic psychosis" according to the medical diagnosis. In a letter to Hegel dated July 11, 1803, Schelling describes him as "mentally quite unhinged," and though "still capable" of producing some literary work "at least up to a certain point, his mind is completely deranged in all other respects." In August 1806, Hölderlin's mother received a letter from his intimate friend, Isaac Sinclair, warning her that it was no longer possible that "my unhappy friend, whose madness has become extreme, should [. . .] stay in Homburg any longer," and "that if his freedom were prolonged, this might endanger the public at large." After a few agonizing months in the mental hospital of Tübingen, the patient was taken in by a Tübingen cabinet-maker Ernst Zimmer "for board and supervision" till the end of his life. Thus the poet's premonition came true that he would be held for altogether "one half of life — woe is me, where do I take, when // winter comes, the flowers." According to the reminiscences of parson Max Eifert (published 1849), "till a few years ago the unhappy poet Hölderlin," the resident of the little room in the tower of the cabinet-maker's house at the old Zwinger, "walked [. . .] up and down [. . .] his mind astray, engaged in an eternal and confusing dialogue with himself." According to Wilhelm Waiblinger's information, he was not allowed to leave the house alone, "but could only go for a walk in the outer courtyard in front of the house."

The numerous declarations of the poet's visitors to the cabinet-maker's house,

This chapter is excerpted from "Ein Blick auf *Die Aussicht* von Hölderlin," in Roman Jakobson, *Selected Writings III: Poetry of Grammar and Grammar of Poetry* (The Hague-Paris-New York: Mouton, 1981), 388-446. The German text includes an exhaustive study of Hölderlin's poem *Die Aussicht* ("The View"). All references have been omitted in the translation; interested readers should refer to the German original. Omissions have not been indicated. The translation by Susan Kitron previously appeared in *Poetics Today*, Vol. 2, No. 1a (1980): 137–144.

from K. A. Varnhagen's observation of December 22, 1808, up to the year of Hölderlin's death, contain valuable information now collected in the *Great Stuttgart Edition.* They draw attention to the patient's persistent reluctance and harrowing inability to converse with people, which led to the "unbridgeable abyss" between him and his human surroundings.

From the poet's early youth till the development of his acute illness "the blissful give-and-take," as Nussbächer correctly perceives, was a vital need for him. "His dialogue-oriented nature sought out conversation and his poetry arose from the dialogue with the 'you.' In the love encounter with Diotima, Hölderlin experienced the fulfilling and answering 'you,' and from his early youth till the years of his illness he held a dialogue with true friends." It is precisely the loss of dialogue that leaves its peculiar mark on the behavior of the hermit of Tübingen. He became embarrassed when addressing people as well as when attempting to reply, so that "even his former acquaintances," according to Waiblinger's evidence, found "such conversations too weird, too depressing, too dull and too meaningless." He would receive strangers with a flood of meaningless words: "One hears some words which, though comprehensible, cannot possibly be answered in most cases," while he himself usually remains "altogether heedless of what is said to him."

Under persistent questioning Hölderlin became extremely agitated and the questioner was answered with "an absolutely nonsensical and incoherent flood of words." Another possibility was that Hölderlin would simply refuse to reply at all: "Your Majesty, I must not, I cannot answer this." Finally, the reply might be shifted to the questioner himself: "You have not been to France for quite some time, have you?" — "Oui, monsieur, that's what you assert." A similar subterfuge is: "You may be right." The fear of responsibility for an independent affirmation or denial becomes manifest in an attitude phrased by Hölderlin more or less like this: "It's you who say so, it's you who assert this, so nothing can happen to me." This was allegedly every "third sentence spoken by Hölderlin." Thus, the reaction to an invitation for a walk was "an extremely odd form" of affirmative opposition: "You command that I should stay."

Indeed, the continual clash between "yes" and "no" in Hölderlin's speech, such as between a statement "man is happy" and its retraction "man is unhappy," was noticed by Waiblinger "countless times." As noted by Christoph Theodor Schwab in his diary of the year 1841, the patient invented the expression *pallaksch* and was fond of using it. It could be taken to mean either "yes" or "no" and served him as a means of avoiding "yes" or "no."

The same uncertainty is reflected in the "polyglot flood of titles" and empty phrases of politeness, which, as noted by observers at various times, the patient used to utter on every occasion, especially as words of welcome. According to the information of the editor Gustav Kühne describing his impressions of Tübingen in 1838, Hölderlin "bandies about words such as 'Your Highness' and 'Your Grace' when receiving visitors, and he is even generous with 'Your Holiness' and 'Your Majesty'," as if, in this way, he anxiously wished — according to an earlier assumption made by Waiblinger — to keep everybody at an unbridgeable distance, since there was no question that he really believed he had actually anything to do with kings. According to Gustav Kühne, Master Ernst Zimmer asserted with regard to this that Hölderlin thus remained "a free man, who won't let nobody pick holes in him." The "give and take" vanished from the schizophrenic poet's daily speech. He obstinately refused to accept any gifts of books of whatever kind, even if these were editions of his own works, and Waiblinger's diary noted "a frightful oddity" in his behavior: as soon as he had finished his meals, Hölderlin simply put the dishes behind the closed door.

The disavowal of his own name and the assumption of a loan name or an invented expression is mainly an attempt to eliminate his 'I' from conversations and, later, from his writings as well. He had already told Waiblinger that he was now called Killalusimeno. According to Johann Georg Fischer, the patient disavowed the name Hölderlin on the title page of his poems and asserted his name was Scardanelli or Scaliger Rosa.[1]

Poetry

There are only fragments, preserved by chance, of the poems of the last years; yet, a study of them provides rich and suprising information about the poet's work of the last decades of his "serious psychosis." There are valuable reports concerning both the later stages of his internment of nearly forty years and the poems which the aged Hölderlin wrote down *ex tempore* in the presence of visitors who had asked him to do so. These he would then hand to the person who had made the request. In 1835 Ernst Zimmer informed an unknown correspondent: "I requested he should also write something for me, and he only opened the window, looked out at the view and in twelve minutes it was ready."

We find in the poet Gottlob Kemmler's obituary of Hölderlin a few significant points with regard to his last creative attempts: "When standing at his desk he strove to collect his thoughts for his 'poetic prayer.' All anxiety was gone from his dejected forehead, and a quiet joy spread over it, instead; though people around him would talk very loudly or look over his shoulders, nothing could

---

[1] [Though he identified himself as Scardanelli or Scarivari or Salvator Rosa,] the only name Hölderlin adopts when signing his poems is 'Scardanelli.' [. . .] If the first vowel and the letters preceding it are left out in the name of both 'Scardanelli' and 'Hölderlin,' we find that the eight letter series of - r d a n e l l i repeats all seven letters of the sequence - l d e r l i n.

| 1 2 3 4 5 6 7 | 4 2 - 7 3 1 5 6 |
| - l d e r l i n | - r d a n e l l i |

The omission of the first letter occurs quite frequently when one wishes to conceal one's name. Besides, the name of 'Scardanelli' seems to derive from another source, i.e., the well-known character of Molière's, Sganarelle, all of the nine letters of which, apart from the unstressed final vowel, are to be found again in the form 'Scardanelli,' while only the lax 'g' is replaced by the tense 'k' ('c').

The 'd' and 'i', absent in 'Sganarelle,' appear both in 'Scardanelli' and 'Hölderlin.' The ritual of using courtly, preferably French, words and servile phrases adopted by Hölderlin during his illness could easily remind him of the stage role of Sganarelle, which in many varieties develops a similar stock of clichés as well as similar gestures of bowing and scraping (Seigneur Commandeur; Je suis votre valet; Je baise les mains à M. le Docteur; Monsieur, votre serviteur . . .).

disturb him [. . .] He wrote poetry whenever he was asked to, perhaps also to isolate himself somewhat from the company of people affectionately thrusting themselves on him." The frantic and artificial dialogue and its participants would vanish before his rapture during the creation of his poetic monologue. The idea "nothing can happen to me," a formula of exorcism during Hölderlin's dialogue, now becomes a welcome and blissful experience.

Christoph Theodor Schwab, the editor of the posthumous edition of Friedrich Hölderlin's *Collected Works* (1846), asserts that he had never seen a meaningless line written by the ill poet, though he composed his verse right after "no sensible word had been spoken by him for days and weeks on end," and that he wrote these poems "without re-reading them afterwards or correcting anything at all." However, in his biography Schwab confines himself to quoting only samples of the poems "from the period of Hölderlin's depressed moods."

In spite of the enthusiasm felt by Waiblinger at the beginning of the twenties for the "intoxicated and divinely inspired man," he was nevertheless inclined to expose meaningless verse lines, errors and evidence of a "terribly bad style" in the "last fruits" of Hölderlin's pen, though the creative works of the demented poet were far superior to those of his judge.

Only a few contemporaries of the suffering artist were capable of understanding and appreciating his late poetry. Even on reading the ill poet's most recent verse in 1841 Gustav Schwab, Christoph's father, who together with Uhland had edited the first edition of Hölderlin's poems in 1826, still persisted in his conviction: "All of Hölderlin's genius is still revealed here." Gustav's wife, Sophie Schwab, added: "How wonderful to see in Hölderlin's work that even after forty years of the darkest madness the spirit is still there manifesting itself . . ."

In Bettina von Arnim's opinion of the same period, Hölderlin "has been lost to the ordinary life of human beings for forty years [. . .] oppressed by an unspeakable fate; his mouth only utters confused sounds and the presence of any other person embarrasses him and fills him with anxiety. Only his muse is able to speak to him, and in rare hours he writes verse — little poems in which the former depth and grace of his spirit are reflected, although suddenly and quite abruptly, they are transposed into verbal rhythms inaccessible to human understanding." If even this bold admirer of the poetic search believed that those poems "lead to the border where the word eludes reason," it goes without saying that the quite unexpected artistic creations of Hölderlin's late poetry gave rise to philistine censure.

As Böschenstein rightly emphasizes, the inquiries into Hölderlin's last works are usually conditioned by the prejudice that the poetry of a lunatic cannot be interpreted in any other way but as evidence of his spiritual and linguistic degeneration, though "insanity and valid poetry need not be mutually exclusive."

Probably the most ferocious attempt to devalue Hölderlin's poetry "of the years during the final stage" was made by the physician Dr. Wilhelm Lange of Tübingen in his *Pathography* (p. 137). He sees in the patient's creative works a "catatonic form of imbecility." The clinical prejudice of this scientist was apparently deepened because of his deafness to art. The deranged poet's poems are here dismissed with the following remarks: "Stiffness and constraint, an affected language, neologisms and mannerisms of language, a childish tone are their common denominators as well as absentmindedness, stereotypes and the empty play with sounds together with banal expletives and interpolations; the poet has quite lost any feeling for the difference between the language of poetry and that of daily speech; neither has he any feeling for style; plain concepts have been supplanted by mere empty phrases [. . .] the circle of his interests has narrowed; his verse contains only a gleam of rather paltry emotional relations." Even in 1921 a similar position was taken: "A systematic inquiry into these poems would be at most of interest to pathologists or to seekers of curiosities" (Viëtor).

Speech and Verbal Art of Schizophrenia
In 1816 Waiblinger's poem to Hölderlin, the "pitifully holy" poet, was published in the *Midnight Paper for the Educated Classes* carrying an editor's note concerning the celebrated author of the novel *Hyperion*, "now a man spiritually dead — a lunatic for many years." The man who was "spiritually dead" went on being poetically creative for another seventeen years. One question often asked in studies about Hölderlin, especially by psychiatrists, concerns the relations between the development of his illness and his poetry. Any fruitful answer to this question actually requires the interdisciplinary work of psychiatrists, linguists and experts in poetics and could, as Jaspers foresaw, "shed light on the character of the schizophrenic patient [though only one particular type within the wide range of this disease]. It could also clarify the concept of the schizophrenic patient" and advance the diagnosis of psychological attacks of this kind. This would be an achievement such as interdisciplinary studies in the field of aphasia have already attained.

The basic fact underlying the schizophrenic poet's verbal art and creative power is their dichotomic character — the stark contrast between the immense loss of his ability to take part in conversations with people around him and his strangely unimpaired eagerness and talent for effortless, spontaneous and purposeful improvisations. Anything connected with dialogue — the mutual address, the exchanges with questions and answers, the speaker's achievement, and the hearer's attention, the endowment of meaning to one's own utterances and the ability to grasp those of one's partners — the whole technique of conversation — could only be imitated with great effort and even then, not completely; it was confused and had mainly been lost.

Out of the madman's drive "to cancel out the partner, as it were" and hold conversations "with himself day and night" out loud, emerges a type of partner-directed conversion in spite of the intrasubjective character of such utterances; and in Hölderlin's verbal activity this conversation is marked by the same pathological degeneration as his intercourse with any other partner.

The true and pure monologues are the verses created in the poet's old age. In amazing contrast to the poor remnants of Hölderlin's usual empty prattle, these demonstrate an inviolable unity and wholeness of verbal structure. As Schwab had already mentioned in this connection, "the charm worked on Hölderlin by the poetic form was astonishing," while in prose he easily became "altogether confused."

Scardanelli's poems with their standardized meter and their regular variation between lines of ten or twelve syllables are quite the opposite of Hölderlin's helpless and unsuccessful conversations. As Ruth Leodolter has emphasized in her careful observations, the schizophrenic patient "avoids dialogue as well as any confrontation with his surroundings, whether consciously or unconsciously"; in such a syndrome the "patient's ability, or willingness to communicate," i.e., his "dialogic competence," is more or less destroyed, while his "monologic competence" is still left intact. Hölderlin's language clearly constitutes a classical example of a dialogic competence which is destroyed alongside an unimpaired and even heightened mastery of what is distinctly monological.

Scardanelli's poems are distinguished from any verbal intercourse by their systematic surrender of basic forms of conversation. In contrast to the patient's usual verbal behavior, these poems have no deictic language signs or any references to the actual speech situation. It was Charles Sanders Peirce who particularly stressed the vital importance of the various "indices" for daily speech: "If, for example a man remarks, 'Why, it is raining!' it is only by some such *circumstances* as that he is now standing here looking out a window as he speaks, which would serve as an Index (not, however, as a Symbol) that he is speaking of this place at this time, whereby we can be assured that he cannot be speaking of the weather on the satellite Procyon, fifty centuries ago" (1933: 4.544). In contrast to this, it has been repeatedly observed with regard to Hölderlin's poetry of his last years, and has been clarified by F. Beissner in particular, that the immediate visual perception does not stimulate the poet's mind, so that, accordingly, "he never describes a unique event in its peculiarity [. . .] Evidence to this effect is his strange predilection for the generalizing conjunction *when*," with which more than a third of the so-called "Late Poems" open. As Beissner says, Hölderlin scrupulously keeps out of his poetry anything connected with himself, anything personal, which means, according to an earlier utterance of the poet, anything "accidental."

The Scardanelli poems as well as Hölderlin's other later poems lack the grammatical class of "shifters," which characterize the reported event with reference to the speech act and its participants. The absence of this basic category is especially striking in comparison with the poet's earlier dialogue-oriented works, where it was efficiently prominent. In contrast to the complete absence of marked classes of both actual persons, the first and second, in Hölderlin's final period, the Diotima elegy (*When from Afar*), composed around 1820, has in its 51 lines 26 pronouns of the first and second person in various case forms as well as six possessive pronouns *my* and *your* and a large number of verbs of the same two persons. Corresponding to the later strict monopoly of the unmarked present tense there is in the Diotima elegy a competition between the present tense and 26 examples of the marked past tense, while the modal relations, later degraded to the unmarked indicative, were also represented in the elegy by imperative and subjunctive forms (such as "Be content and think / Of the [. . .]," "Though wert so alone"). Such dialogue-oriented utterances as questions ("Was it spring? was it summer?"), affirmations, addresses ("Oh, thou sharer of my sufferings!"), exclamations ("Ah, woe to me!") are no longer to be found in Hölderlin's poems of his last period. The participation of the *verbum dictionis* in its *dictum*, giving prominence to the speech act as such, is a device which also characterized the Diotima elegy but was abandoned in the further development of Hölderlin's poetry: "Say, then, how is your friend awaiting you?" — "This I must say, some good there was / In your eyes" — "Yes, I confessed it, I was yours" — "You wert so alone in the beautiful world / You've always said so, beloved!"

The very last poetic monologues of the "greatest of the schizophrenics" (as F. L. Wells called Hölderlin) are marked by the suppression of any allusion both to the speech act and its time as well as to the actual participants. The taboo name of the sender is resolutely replaced by *Scardanelli*; the author remains rather indifferent both to the consumer of the verse and to the fate of the manuscripts. The grammatical tenses of the text are limited to the unmarked present. The "absolute rule of the present," as Böschenstein called it, abolishes the sequence of tenses and reveals "the whole of the cycle of time throughout each season." Hölderlin's essay, *Concerning the Procedure of the Poetic Spirit*, which proves to be illuminating as regards the poet's further development, sheds a new light, especially on Scardanelli's symbolism. This essay written in Homburg warns poetry against the empty "infinity of isolated moments (a sequence of atoms, as it were)" and, at the same time, against the belief in a "dead and deadly unity." "The representation of the infinite" is recognized in the poetic present tense, and in order to illuminate afterwards: "What is opposed and what is united is inseparable in it."

Scardanelli's poetry completely eludes Hölderlin's vain and painful efforts to say something abstract to visitors, as Thürmer shrewdly perceived: "Effortlessness, a way of speaking which rejects the mere suggestion of effort — this is the essential point." Because of the abandonment of deixis, the nouns of such poems as *The View*, released from any deictic function, turn into uniformly ordered chains of *abstracta*, and it is to be noted that many purely conceptual nouns, which had been unknown in Hölderlin's poems of the first two decades of the 19th century, only emerged in the late poems "of the period of the poet's madness" (cf. Böschenstein): *view, sublimity, apparition, spirituality, friendliness, inwardness, humanity, pastness, familiarity*, etc.

Hölderlin and the Essential Character of Poetry is the title of a speech delivered by Heidegger in Rome forty years ago on April 2, 1936. Five key words from the poet's posthumous works were selected by the philosopher and commented upon, among them the ending of the poem *Remembrance* so typical of Hölderlin (dated 1803): "But what remains is brought about by poets" — and, immediately preceding this, four lines with which the last draft of the incompleted poem *Conciliator, Who Had Never Believed* (1801) breaks off. The most significant of these lines, "Since a dialogue we are," gives rise to the following reflection by Heidegger: "We — people — are a dialogue. Man's being is rooted in language; but language really occurs only in dialogue. This, however, is not only a way that language comes to pass, but it is solely as dialogue that language is essential. Any other meaning given to language, i.e., a store of words and of rules for the arrangement of words, is only a foreground of language. Now, what does 'dialogue' mean? Apparently the speaking with each other about something. In the course of this, the speaking mediates the coming together." Whatever Hölderlin's view of the world and of language was in the 18th century, his later path is, at any rate, an inversion of the conception quoted here. Language — with its immense store of words and its exciting rules for the arrangement of words — is essential for him not in the form of dialogue, but only in the form of a poem, while the speaking with one another and the coming together is rejected by him as a mere anteroom of language — a stand which later becomes increasingly more determined: "But what remains is brought about by poets." The reported event excludes any reference to the speech act from the solely poetic report.

REFERENCES

ARNIM, BETTINA VON, 1848. *Ilius Pamphilius* 2 (Leipzig).
BEISSNER F., 1947. "Zu den Gedichten der letzten Lebenszeit," *Hölderlin-Jahrbuch* 2, 6–10.
BÖSCHENSTEIN, B. 1965/66. "Hölderlins späteste Gedichte," *Hölderlin-Jahrbuch* 14, 35–56.
HEIDEGGER, M., 1971. *Erläuterungen zu Hölderlins Dichtung* (Frankfurt/M, 4th ed.).
HÖLDERLIN, F., 1846. *Sämtliche Werke,* ed. Chr. T. Schwab (Stuttgart-Tübingen).
    1943–1974 *Sämtliche Werke* (Grosse Stuttgarter Ausgabe), ed. F. Beissner (Stuttgart), 8 vols.
JASPERS, K., 1926. *Strindberg und van Gogh: Versuch einer pathographischen Analyse unter vergleichender Heranziehung von Swedenborg und Hölderlin* (Berlin, 2nd ed.).
LANGE, W., 1909. *Hölderlin: Eine Pathographie* (Stuttgart).
LEODOLTER, R., 1975. "Gestörte Sprache oder Privatsprache: Kommunikation bei Schizophrenen," *Wiener Linguistische Gazette* 10–11, 75–95.
NUSSBÄCHER, K., 1971. *Friedrich Hölderlin—Gedichte: Auswahl und Nachwort* (Stuttgart).
PEIRCE, C. S., 1933. "The Simplest Mathematics," in: *Collected Papers* 4 (Cambridge, Mass.).
THÜRMER, W., 1970. *Zur poetischen Verfahrensweise in der spätesten Lyrik Hölderlins* (Marburg).
VIËTOR, K., 1921. *Die Lyrik Hölderlins: Eine analytische Untersuchung* (Frankfurt/M.).
WELLS, F. L., 1946. "Hölderlin: Greatest of 'Schizophrenics,'" *Abnormal and Social Psychology* 41, 199–206.

Jakobson's Legacy

The Poetic Function and the Nature of Language

Linda R. Waugh

To Roman Jakobson, the master-explorer of the Poetic Function, on the occasion of his 84th birthday.

0.0 "WHAT MAKES A VERBAL MESSAGE A WORK OF ART?" (RJ 1960:350) What is it that differentiates a poetic text from a non-poetic text? What makes poetic discourse different in kind from other types of discourse? In other words, what are the *intrinsic linguistic properties* of the text which make it a poem: what is there about the *internal structure* of a poem which 'announces' that it is a poem? What is characteristic of 'poetic' elements in prose and in 'ordinary' language? What in fact is the *poetic function* of language?

1.0 FOCUS ON THE MESSAGE

> "The Set (*Einstellung*) toward the MES-SAGE as such, focus on the message for its own sake, is the POETIC function of language" (RJ 1960:356).

1.10 As Roman Jakobson has shown (1960), if we take any given act of *verbal communication* (=speech event), there are six fundamental factors which must be present for it to be operable:

(1) addresser (speaker, encoder, emitter; poet, author; narrator)
(2) addressee (decoder, hearer, listener; reader; interpreter)
(3) code (system, *langue*)
(4) message (semelfactive *parole*, the given discourse, the text)
(5) context (referent)
(6) contact ("a physical channel and psychological connection between speaker and addressee").

Each of these factors may be further subdivided and separated out in various ways. For example, in a literary text, there may be a differentiation between

This chapter is reprinted from *Poetics Today,* Vol. 2, No. 1a (1980): 57–82.

author and narrator and the narrator in turn may give way to several other 'speakers.' In addition, the lack of or trouble with or ambiguity about any one of the factors may have various effects on the communication itself. For example, it should be noted that without a message, there is *no* act of verbal communication.

Corresponding to these six factors are six major *functions*, each assuming an orientation within the verbal message on one of the factors:

(1)   emotive (expressive)
(2)   conative (appellative)
(3)   metalingual (metalinguistic, 'glossing')
(4)   *poetic* (aesthetic)
(5)   referential (cognitive, denotative, ideational)
(6)   phatic.

(For futher discussion and elaboration, see RJ, 1960 and Holenstein, 1979). In this formulation, the *poetic function* comprises the *focus within the verbal message on the verbal message itself*. It is, in fact, "un langage qui met l'accent sur le langage" (Todorov, 1978). Of course, most verbal messages do not fulfill only one function. Rather, they are *multifunctional* (see Waugh, 1984; Holenstein, 1979): they usually fulfill a variety of functions, which are integrated one with another in hierarchical fashion with one function being predominant: "the verbal structure of a message depends primarily on the predominant function" (RJ, 1960:353).

Jakobson christened the set toward the message—toward the single and unique *parole* as such — as the *poetic function* in accord with his belief that poetry is the major example of this function. The poetic function can be found elsewhere and poetry includes other functions; but poetry is that use of language *par excellence* in which the dominant function is the orientation toward the message. (RJ, [1935]/1971, 1960). Now, the definition of the poetic function should, as with all statements by Jakobson, be taken as relational: in the poetic function, *in relation to and as against* the five other functions of language, there is a dominance of a focus upon the message. In the referential function (its most clearly delimited opposite), there is a dominance of focus upon the context. Poetry, then, consists of texts in which the poetic function is the dominant function, but by no means the only function. Dominance presumes a hierarchization of functions, not an absolutization of functional differences. I will be opposing here, for the most part, the poetic function to the referential function, since the referential function seems to be that function which is the unmarked one in the system of six (for a definition of markedness, see 3.31 below). As evidence of the unmarked nature of the referential function, we may cite the fact that in many linguistic and philosophical studies of language, the referential function has been said to be the *only* function of language; or, if (some of) the other functions have been discerned, they have been declared to be 'deviant' or 'unusual' or needing special consideration. And even in our parlance about language, the referential function is spoken of as 'ordinary language.'

The relational definition of the functions allows for differences between the particular manifestations of the poetic function within a culture and, more importantly, between cultures, without destroying the viability of the difference itself. In other words, it is the relations between the major functions which are relevant, rather than any absolute and isolationist definition of any particular function. Given this, Jakobson's six functions are meant to be universal in scope — they apply to all cultures at all times — but they apply only as a set of six relational (not absolute) categories.

1.11   Now, the predominance of the poetic function and the subordination of the other functions does not mean that the other functions are subordinated to the extent of being excluded. On the contrary, any one or more of the functions may be present in a variety of ways and with more or less importance vis-à-vis the poetic function. And in fact, one could make a typology based on which other function(s) assume some importance, as in the following statement by Jakobson: "Epic poetry, focussed on the third person, strongly involves the referential function of language; the lyric, oriented toward the first person, is intimately linked with the emotive function; poetry of the second person is imbued with the conative function and is either supplicatory or exhortative, depending on whether the first person is subordinated to the second or the second to the first" (RJ, 1960:357).

Prose — for example, 'oral narrative,' 'practical prose,' 'scientific writing,' 'journalistic prose,' 'legal discourse,' 'literary' and 'fictional' prose, etc. — is a transitional phenomenon (RJ, 1960:374), admitting of various gradations on the continuum between 'ordinary' language with an orientation toward the referential function and the poetic function. As a transitional phenomenon, prose evidences a more complex type, a type in which the poetic and referential modes are intertwined in various ways and to varying degrees (RJ, 1960, 1935, 1969). 'Literary prose' is, presumably, closer to the poetic end, while 'practical prose' would be closer to the referential end. This means that the 'poetics of prose' (see Todorov, 1971/1977) and in general the analysis of literary, non-poetic discourse is more complex than the analysis of either 'true' poetry or of decidedly referential discourse. 'Free verse' (*vers libre*) on the other hand, is a complex superstructure based on the co-presence of both poetry and prose for its existence and definition; moreover, it too uses patternings based on such factors as intonation and pause.

1.12   Of course, as has been pointed out, the poetic function is not confined to poetry, although all poetry has a dominance of the poetic function: "même là où la fonction poétique est soumise à d'autres fonctions, [. . .] elle ne disparaît jamais totalement" (RJ, 1978:18). The poetic function occurs elsewhere, for example in 'applied verse' (see RJ, 1960:359) of various kinds where it plays a subsidiary though important role (e.g., *thirty days hath September*, [. . .]). Moreover, in the referential function, it may assume a secondary but still important role. Thus, such phrases as *through thick and thin, horrible Harry, lucky Lucy, innocent bystander*, etc., owe their success as much to their poetic basis (alliteration, paronomasia, dactylic meter, etc.) as to their referential basis ('Harry really is horrible'). The poetic function is by no means foreign to the referential use of language, but rather is simply subordinated to the overall referential thrust. Nor, as should be obvious, is the poetic function to be equated with 'great' poetry; the poetic function may also occur in 'doggerel.' Moreover, the term 'poetry' covers both oral poetry and written poetry, although of course there may be important differences between these two (differences which have, unfortunately, not yet been systematically explored). Furthermore, we know (see Čukovsky, 1966/1971; RJ & LW, 1979) that all normal children in all cultures go through a stage in the language acquisition process in which they invent or repeat rhymes, play with sound, etc. — in other words, they play with the poetic function, both as the dominant function and as a subordinate function. Jump-rope rhymes, counting-out rhymes, street games of all sorts, as well as pre-sleep soliloquies (see Weir, 1962) all attest to the importance of the poetic function in language learning. In fact, while adult speech evidences the six basic functions in varying degrees of hierarchization and combination, they each occur as well as part of the child language learning process (see for example RJ & LW, 1979:217–220 and RJ, 1978:19 for the poetic function; RJ, [1956]/1980 and RJ, 1978:19 for the metalingual function, RJ, 1960:356 for the phatic function).

1.20   The set toward the message brings forth the question of the nature of the message *per se*.

1.21   In answer to a statement by Degas that he was full of ideas but couldn't manage to say what he wanted to say in a poem, Mallarmé's reply was: "My dear Degas, one does not make poetry with ideas but with *words*" (Valéry, 1939/1958:63). We may modernize his reply and state that poetry is made not with ideas but with *signs*, words being only one of the types of signs (and further state that poetry is not about the real world or life, but about itself).

Language — both code and message — is a *system of systems of signs*, a sign being an intrinsic and indissoluble combination of a perceptible *signans* and an interpretable *signatum*. Some linguistic signs occur both in the code and in messages; other occur only in messages. In fact, given this definition of sign, the *message itself* is a system of systems of signs and at the same time a *sign* (of some complexity) with both a *signans* and a *signatum*. The act of verbal communication is, in effect, *an exchange of signs* between speaker and address-ee.

Linguistic signs form a *part-whole hierarchy* from the ultimate units (the distinctive features) to the largest units (discourses); furthermore, they are divided into three main types (see RJ, 1956/1971 and 1962/1971 and Waugh, 1976b: 60). The first type comprises those signs (distinctive features, phonemes, syllables, morphemes, words) which are codified as such, as *prefabricated wholes*, and whose occurrence in individual messages is an example of a direct type-token relationship. In fact, the 'word' is the largest such linguistic sign. But there are other signs — phrases, clauses, sentences, utterances (sets of sentences produced by one speaker), discourses (exchanges of utterances by two speakers) — which are not usually codified as such, yet the structures and possibilities of their formation are provided by the code. These are signs which occur *in* or *as* messages, but which are not necessarily given fully prefabricated in the code. (Of course, there are some examples of prefabricated or ritualized phrases, clauses, sentences, utterances, but these remain by far in the minority.) In the case of the second type of sign — phrases, clauses, sentences — the rules of combination (*syntactic matrices*) are obligatorily codified. For example, in the nominal phrase of French, the possibility of combining an article, a noun, and an adjective (in that order) is provided for by the code (both in terms of the *signans* and in terms of the *signatum*). But the fact of using a particular adjective with a particular noun is left to the creativity of the individual speaker, who constructs her/his (potentially unique) message (see Waugh, 1976a, 1977). Of course, there are many transitional types, but in general, the differences between the word (as an example of the first type of sign) and the phrase (the second type) is that the former is codified as such; the latter, on the other hand, is not. Rather, it is codified only as a general matrix or pattern of combination. This means that the particular combination of article + noun + adjective (in the French case cited above) may be new or unique (never heard before), but the general matrix upon which that combination is built is of course not unique or new. We have then a direct relation between a potentially new message-sign based on a codified, and thus 'old,' code-sign:

un journal important   article + noun + adjective
(message-sign)   (code-sign-matrix)

The third type of sign — utterances, discourses — consists of signs which are codified only as *generalized* and *optional patterns of combination* (except for certain anaphoric terms which may be used to interrelate between sentences). Such message-signs bear a more indirect relation to the code; and although they do not belong to the code as such, they nevertheless do attest to the existence and internal nature of the code. (For example, the utterances of this paper are based on optional patterns of combination in the code of English and attest to the fact that I am using the code of English and not, for example, the code of French for their construction.)

While, in particular, sentences, utterances, and discourses (i.e., those higher in the hierarchy), may be unique signs which have never occurred before, they are nevertheless *intersubjective signs* common to speaker and addressee. They may be transitory signs, especially if they occur in spoken language, and semelfactive signs which have never occurred as such before and may never again, or intermittent signs, reoccurring at various times but without necessarily being codified; but they *are* nevertheless signs, capable of being interpreted, due to the code which guarantees that interpretation. Thus, while language— both code and message, both *langue* and *parole* — is a hierarchized system (of systems) of signs, it is simply *not* the case that all linguistic signs belong to the code. *Many* belong only to the message. Thus, the equation between code and sign, which is assumed in some linguistic and literary studies, is not valid.

Now, if we take the hierarchy of signs such as phrases, clauses, sentences, utterances, discourses, not only is this a part-whole hierarchy of ascending complexity, but also one of ascending freedom or *creativity*. While the sentence is the largest sign for which the rules of combination are obligatorily codified, it is still the case that the speaker has more freedom in creating sentences than in creating phrases. Of course, there are more sentence types than phrase types (i.e., more different syntactic matrices of sentences than of phrases) and the number of possible sentences is a function of the number of possible phrases as well as of the number of possible combinations of those phrases. Consequently, the freedom of the speaker to be 'creative,' to construct new and unique messages (i.e., new signs) is greater.

1.22   From this point of view, a poem is a *message-sign* (a sentence, an utterance, or even a discourse — for the sake of brevity I will use the term 'discourse' and sometimes 'text' in the discussion to follow), the possibilities for the creation of which are provided in the code. Yet the particular poem is generally not given in the code but rather only as the specific message. A poem is generally a new intersubjective sign. Of course, this does not deny that a poem could become codified (see Barthes, 1978) or could be important in terms of changes and redefinitions in the code itself, but rather stresses that a given poem (e.g., in English) bears to the code of English the same relation as any particular instance of the use of English bears to the overall system itself.

Since a poem is a sign, it is a combination of a *signans* and a *signatum*; it is *not*, as some studies of poetry have seemed to suggest, a *signans* only. A poem is a *new intersubjective message-sign whose dominant function is an orientation toward the message-sign as a message-sign*. A poem is also a *system of systems of signs*, a complex and hierarchically ordered sign, made up of a variety of sign types, each with both a *signans* and a *signatum*, and in which the various signs are subordinated to the overall poetic function and coherence of the whole sign. As such, a poem is a *structure*, "not a mechanical agglomeration but a structural whole and the basic task is to reveal the inner [. . .] laws of this system" (RJ, 1971:711). These words, while they were written in 1929 by Jakobson about *structuralism,* fully define, in general, the poem. All of the properties discussed here, including the fact that the poem is centered on its very sign properties, are immanent structural laws of the poem as a system. From this point of view, the notion of closure (of self-limitation) evident in the poetic (but not necessarily in the referential) function, the relative autonomy of the poem as a dynamic structure, the autotelic and autoreferential nature of the poem—all of these are related to the fact that the poem-sign is a structural whole.

1.30   A distinction between message (*parole*) and the usage to which a given message may be put has to be made.

1.31   The 'function' of a given message is, in Jakobson's terminology, an *intrinsic quality* of the message itself; thus, the focus upon the message is an inherent quality of a poem. Now, it is quite obvious that a poetic text can be 'used' in various situations which do not take into account this inherent quality of the text, e.g., the Longfellow poem "Hiawatha" can be recited in the Senate by a filibustering Senator. Such a recitation does not cancel the poetic quality of the text: "poeticalness still remains the primary intent of this text itself" (RJ, 1960:359), but shows rather that any linguistic discourse may be used in a variety of ways different from its internal structure. Thus, to take another example, a linguist may analyze a glossolalic pronouncement, attempting to discern certain sound patterns but in no way correlating them with the intrinsic 'magical' function, and may even cite such a pronouncement at a scientific meeting. Such usage does not, however, cancel its intrinsic glossolalic character. In fact, if such were not the case, it would be hard to see how much of linguistic (metalingual) discourse could proceed. Recent speech act theory has focussed on certain specific examples of this divorce between internal structure and 'usage.' For example, *it's cold in here* and *please close the window* are, from the point of view of their internal structure, different in function. The former is a declarative sentence, predominantly referential in function, while the latter is an imperative sentence, predominantly conative in function. And yet, in certain situations (in the case where one is in a room with a window open and cold air is entering through the window), the referential sentence may be taken as having conative import. There is, so to speak, a conative overlay on the referential basis. Moreover, such a conative usage could be based on the substitution of one part of an utterance for the utterance itself: *It's cold in here. The window's open and it's letting cold air in. Please close the window.* The substitution of the first part of this chain for the last part is based on a series of contiguity relations and can be seen as a typical example of elliptical speech. Furthermore, rules of such elliptical substitutions may be to a certain degree (optionally) codified, much in the same way as various metonymic transfers are codified. And of course, the success of such substitutions depends to a very large extent on the right linguistic context (preceding and succeeding sentences), as well as the correct situation and, in addition, the proper relation between speaker and addressee (the speaker should have a position which allows her/him to use such a sentence in this way). All of this shows that we must differentiate sharply between the primary 'function' of a given text and its secondary 'usages,' between the internal structure of the text and external factors influencing other functions, between the basic structure of the text and secondary and figurative codifications.

2.0   EQUIVALENCE, SIMILARITY

> "The poetic function projects the principle of equivalence from the axis of selection into the axis of combination" (RJ, 1960: 358).

2.10   Message construction is based on a complex interaction between two different interrelated and mutually implicating operations of *selection* (or substitution) and *combination* (or contexture), wherein selection (from a repertory of codified signs and sign-matrices) generally precedes (and is usually complemented by) a succeeding combination. Now, the signs and sign-matrices selected from are usually (but not always) related to each other by a variety of *similarity* relations, including equivalence, similarity, dissimilarity, contrast (see below, 2.12), antonymy (see below, 3.32), synonymy, opposition (see below, 3.32), etc. On the other hand, the signs and sign-matrices combined are usually (but not always) related to one another by *contiguity* (see RJ, 1955/1971, 1956/1971, [1963]/1971; RJ & KP, 1980).

2.11   "Equivalence in difference is the cardinal problem of language and the pivotal concern of linguists" (RJ, 1959a/1971), where the equivalence is a *relational equivalence* based on sameness within a system. While the choices (signs and sign-matrices) in a selection set are bound by various types of equivalence relations — e.g., the synonymous expressions *ill, sick, indisposed, not healthy, ailing,* etc. — it is generally not the case in referential speech that the elements combined are related to each other by any (strong) equivalence relation — e.g., with *Joe was too ill to eat dinner last night,* the relation between *Joe* and *dinner* is hardly describable in any strong way by equivalence, except insofar as they are both concrete nouns. In poetry, the projection of the principle of equivalence from the axis of selection into the axis of combination means quite simply that such sameness is used as (the major) means of constructing the whole sequence. This projection is in fact the defining characteristic of poetry: "Cette thèse entre tout simplement dans la définition même du vers" (RJ & KP, 1980:124). Thus, syllable is equated with syllable (in syllable-based meter for example), whereas in 'ordinary' speech (the referential function) "speakers do not measure the number of syllables" (RJ & LW, 1979:216). Or stress is equated with stress, thus becoming a unit of measure, whereas again in ordinary speech stresses are not measured; long vowels are equated with long vowels, word boundary with word boundary, pause with pause, etc. In like fashion, finite verb is equated with finite verb, comparative degree with comparative degree, noun with noun, affix with affix, past tense with past tense, subject-verb word order with subject-verb word order, or spatial noun with spatial noun, temporal adverb with temporal adverb, verb of motion with verb of motion, etc. (RJ, 1959a/1971, 1960, 1968). The verbal material displays overall a hierarchical structure of *symmetries,* based on repetitions, regularities, and systematizations of various kinds. There is, in other words, a radical parallelistic reorientation of all the verbal material as it relates to the building of the sequence. Such *parallelisms,* whether based on sound (see RJ, 1979) or on grammatical categories (see RJ, 1966b) or on various lexical categories, are a 'natural' result of the raising of equivalence to the constitutive device of the sequence, as against any sort of non-poetic counterparts (see Lodge, 1977). Moreover, such parallelisms create a network of internal relations within the poem itself, making the poem into an integrated whole and underlining the poem's relative autonomy.

    This is not to say that in prose there are no parallelisms or repetitions or any other of the devices particularly associated with poetry; but rather to say that such symmetries are not the constructive device of prose and are not as systematically used. A single repetition or a single instance of parallelism in a given text does not, thereby, make the text a poem, although such use may evidence an importance (but not predominance) granted to the poetic function. Such parallelisms as may occur in prose are subordinated to the referential (or other) function. And they are used (often to make the prose more 'aesthetically pleasing') only when their use would not contradict or combat the main referential thrust of the discourse (see Lodge, 1977). Similarly, equivalence relations of various sorts (such as the equivalence between an anaphoric, relative pronoun and any of its potential antecedents) may be important for relations within prose, but again it should be repeated that equivalence does not thereby become the constructive device of the sequence.

2.12   Of course, the other side of equivalence is difference and the other side of similarity is dissimilarity. By projecting equivalence (and perforce difference) into the axis of combination, the *contrast* between or within parallelistic elements comes to the fore and indeed contrast, as much as equivalence, becomes an important part of the structuration of the poem. Contrast includes contrast within equational elements (e.g., rhyming words may contrast the rhyming portion and the non-rhyming portion; or two synonymous expressions may also be contrasted through their difference of perspective). Or contrast may occur between one equation set and another (e.g., the contrast between strophes one and three on the one hand and strophes two and four on the other hand in the Cummings poem discussed later in 3.32; or the contrast between stressed syllables and unstressed syllables in meter). Indeed, such observations may be extended to all the equational devices mentioned earlier; it is rare that such equivalence relations should not also include non-equivalence and contrast. "In addition to the projection of the principle of equivalence from the axis of selection into the axis of combination, there is also in poetry a projection of the principle of contrast from the significative, selective, and combinatorial operations into the level of a patent, 'palpable,' and 'perceptible' form." (Holenstein, 1974; see also RJ & KP, 1980:130–1). Moreover, contrast is another means by which the selectional axis and the combinatorial axis are intertwined. In the referential use of language, contrast very often resides not in elements linked by various equivalence relations but rather in elements which are in simple contiguity with each other. The poetic function is different from the strictly referential function by the strong *linkage of contrast with equivalence*.

This projection of both equivalence and contrast is not only a way of giving an internal, autonomous structure to the poem, but is also a way of *transcending the linearity* proper to any linguistic text. Through parallelisms the text is no longer a linear string but is subdivided in various ways. Furthermore, parallelisms help to recall an earlier passage in a later passage, may return to the beginning in the end, may align strophe one with strophe three, etc. Again, the more strictly linear character of prose is separated from the more non-linear character of poetry.

2.20   As was pointed out above, selection or substitution is based to a large extent on similarity between the selectional units, including similarity, dissimilarity, contrast, antonymy, synonymy, opposition, etc. In this case, equivalence is a (strong) type of similarity relation. Combination on the other hand, in the referential use of language, is based on and creates (Holenstein, 1974) contiguity relations between the combined elements (see my example earlier of *Joe was too ill to eat dinner last night.*) Now, of course, there are many exceptions to this generalization (see for example RJ, [1963]/1971). The conjunction *and* for example may often be used to conjoin elements from the same selectional set which are based on similarity (*Harry and Tom and Ben*). In metalinguistic usage, the sequence (combination) is used to build an equation (*a bachelor is an unmarried man*). In a sentence such as *the keels ploughed the deep*, the figurative transfers are based on similarity for *plough* (a metaphor based on the similarity relation between the motion of a ship and the motion of a plough), and contiguity both for *keel* (a synecdochic substitute for *ship*) and for *deep* (a metonymic equivalent for *sea*) (see Lodge, 1977 and the preface to the second edition, 1979). Thus, the metonymic substitution — based on a *contiguity* relation — of one term for another is founded on an *equivalence* relation.

   Such exceptions (which still need further examination and classification) do not alter the main difference between, on the one hand, referential discourse, in which the combination is built upon and/or produces for the most part non-equivalence and contiguity relations between the combined elements, and, on the other hand, poetic discourse, in which the combination is built upon and/or produces equivalence and similarity relations between the combined elements. Thus, for example, synonomy, antonymy, homonymy, *homeoteleuton* (words sharing a given suffix), heteronymy, opposition, paraphrase, circumlocution, analogy, metaphor, etc. become the major semantic relations underlying a poetic text; and the phonetic similarity relation of paronomasia "reigns over poetic art" (RJ, 1959a/1971). This is not to deny that contiguity relations play a role in the poetic use of language, for they clearly do — e.g., *paregmenon* (same root combined with different derivational suffixes), *polyptoton* (same root combined with different grammatical meanings), conjunctions, prepositions, pronouns, metonymy, synecdoche, etc., may play a wide role in the construction of a poem. But, even in such cases, the tendency is to invest such evident contiguity relations with similarity and equivalence. Thus, a preposition may become important not so much because it creates a contiguity relation between the two interrelated elements but rather because it is equated with another preposition. And the equivalence between one preposition and another as parts of speech may be as important as the interrelation between the given preposition and its context. So, as Jakobson says, "in poetry where similarity is superinduced upon contiguity, any metonymy is slightly metaphorical and any metaphor has a metonymical tint" (RJ, 1960:370); but it remains the case that the metaphoric is the dominant mode. "This emphasis on metaphorical or paradigmatic relationships in the discourse leads correspondingly to a weakening of metonymic or syntagmatic relationships — i.e., the relationships of contiguity in time and space, and of cause and effect" (Lodge, 1977:104).

3.0 SIGN VS. OBJECT

> "Il s'agit dans la langue poétique d'un changement essentiel du rapport entre le signifiant et le signifié, ainsi qu'entre le signe et le concept" (RJ. 1966/1979:542).

3.1 The dominance of the orientation toward the message-sign by the message-sign and the use of equivalence relations between signs as the constitutive devices of the message-sign lead to a reevaluation both of the message-sign with respect to its internal nature as a sign and of the sign-sign relationship in the linguistic code as well as in the message. In referential speech, the relation between the linguistic sign (in particular, the *signatum*) and extra-linguistic 'objects' (sometimes called referents) would seem to be a close and almost automatic one. In the referential use of language, the word is evaluated as a proxy for the denoted object, or for the idea/concept and in emotive use as an outburst of an emotion — the word is, so to speak, a 'verbal shadow' of the object or of an idea/concept or of an ambition (see Erlich, 1955:187). Of course, we should not let the terminology 'object,' 'idea,' 'emotion' lead us astray; as C. S. Peirce has shown, emotions and ideas are themselves signs (albeit potentially non-linguistic signs — see Savan, 1980), while objects are generally semiotic or capable of being semioticized (see Waugh, 1979b). The bond between word and object or word and emotion then is the bond between a linguistic sign and another sign (from another semiotic system). (Of course, in referential language, the bond is one which was called 'arbitrary' by Saussure, while in emotive language it is based on immediacy — see 3.2 — and in particular on a similarity relation — see RJ, 1980b; Waugh, 1979b.) One may say, with Peirce, that in the referential or emotive use of language, the linguistic sign and the non-linguistic sign are in interpretive relation with one another. It is this status of interpretation which is broken in poetic discourse, for here it is the *interpretive relation between linguistic signs* which is important.

Now, this close connection between word and object is an illusory one, even in the referential use of language, as I have tried to show; but it is a powerful illusion (see Waugh, 1979b). And it is an illusion which the poetic use of language attempts to point up, for in poetry the relation between word and object is called into question. Since the poem as a whole is a sign as well as any of its parts, the differentiation between sign and object pertains at all levels. It is in this sense that a poem may be said to be perceptible and palpable 'form' as against 'content' (='objects,' 'referents,' 'ideas,' etc.). "Whenever we cut into the literary text, and in whatever direction, we expose, not 'content,' but a systematic structure of signs in which content is made apprehensible" (Lodge, 1977:xvii). Thus, a 'literal' (i.e., a referential) reading of a poem must be subordinated to a 'poetic' reading (just as the referential function is subordinated to the poetic).

Given that the bond between sign and object is brought into question, the *inner relation* between *signans* and *signatum* and between sign and sign is focussed upon and strengthened. A poem is a message-sign in which the type of sign relations is focussed upon, both the 'vertical' relation of *signans* to *signatum* and the 'horizontal' relation of sign to sign, especially with respect to equivalence, similarity, and contrast. In fact, one could say that since the poetic function dominates the referential function and since the sign is focussed on as a sign vs. its referent, in poetry a given sign is used more because of the equivalence relations it contracts with other signs in the same poem, whereas in prose a given sign is used more because of its referential qualities. In the poetic text, a given word may be chosen not only because of its paradigmatic associations with other words in the linguistic code, but also because of its equivalence relations with other words in the text itself. The choice of one word may dictate the rest of the poem (see RJ, 1964); in non-poetic discourse, the words must 'make sense' in terms of external factors. In poetry, the "internal relationships of the component parts are far more significant than their external references" (Lodge, 1977:12). In poetry, the word has to 'fit' with other words; in prose, the word has to 'fit' with the referent. Again, all such statements about the difference between poetry and prose (and ordinary discourse) should be taken as relational statements of the relative differences between the two categories. Furthermore, it should be remembered that poetry has a dominance of the poetic function, but this does not exclude the presence and importance of other functions; and likewise, prose may exhibit more or less importance of the poetic function, even though subordinated to the referential function. In the poetic function, however, the subjugation of the referential function and the predominance of the poetic function mean, not that reference is done away with altogether, but rather that there is a totally different relation to external signification, a profound alteration of the referential function.

Now, as mentioned above, while the poem is itself a discourse-sign, it is a whole made up of other signs — sentences, phrases, words, etc. — in a hierarchically ordered structure; it is at any of the levels of sign that the *focus on the sign* becomes relevant. A poem may be (simultaneously) oriented upon signs such as distinctive features (e.g., the sound symbolic use of given featural relations), phonemes (e.g., repetitions of phonemes in various patterns), syllables (e.g., rhyme), morphemes (e.g., grammatical parallelisms), words (e.g., repetitions of grammatical or lexical words), phrases (e.g., the construction of the English comparative construction in the Cummings poem to be discussed below), clauses (e.g., the linguistic 'fictional' difference between the two coordinate clauses in Majakovskij's poem: "both life is good and it is good to live"), sentences (e.g., in the Cummings poem, each strophe is a sentence), etc. And of course, the poem is oriented upon itself.

3.2 *Sound:* "in poetry speech sounds spontaneously and immediately display their proper semantic function" (RJ & LW, 1979:222).

In the poetic function, the focus on the linguistic sign as a sign and the divorce of the sign from its referent means that the texture of the sign in all its aspects (see Èjxenbaum, 1927/1965) is made perceptible, including that aspect of the sign which is by its very nature perceptible, namely the *signans*. Sound as such, in and of itself, becomes one of the patent carriers of poetic meaning: there is a kind of 'verbal magic' in sound itself. Various *sound figures* are used for the construction of the sequence. We have already discussed the role of equivalence relations between sounds — relations such as rhyme, meter, alliteration, assonance, etc.—and have stated that, for example, the sound figure of paronomasia (the poetic pun), based on similarity between the correlated words or word groups, is most important for the construction of the poetic text. (For the use of sound in verse, see RJ, 1979; see also Rudy, 1976.) But there is more, for such use of sound — given the close interrelation between *signans* and *signatum* in the poetic function as well as the breaking of the connection between sign and object — focusses on the potentiality of sound to directly signal meanings. For example, rhyme between two words points out either a similarity of meaning between the words or various relations of semantic contrast. But rhyming words are never indifferent to the question of meaning relations; the focus on the *signans* and on a relation between two words based on the *signans* immediately brings forth questions about a possible relation based on the *signatum*. A parallelism in sound (e.g., rhyme) is often taken as a sign of a concomitant parallelism in meaning: equivalence in sound is assumed to signal equivalence in meaning. Or on the contrary, equivalence in sound is a reversal-signal of non-equivalence in meaning. Or, as Jakobson (see 1960:368) has put it, "rhyme is either grammatical or anti-grammatical but it is never agrammatical." In fact, in the poem — with on the one hand its focus on the sign as sign and on the other hand its use of equivalence as the main device — the direct connection between sound and meaning and the ability of the sound shape of given units to inform unequivocally about their correlated meanings are brought to the fore.

One consequence of this is that the mediacy — the indirect connection between a given aspect of sound and a given meaning — generally typical of the distinctive features in their use in building words, is combatted by and to a certain extent overcome by *immediacy* — the direct and close relationship between sound and meaning. Generally speaking, the distinctive features and their combinations (phonemes, syllables) do *not* carry meaning directly, but are rather used to differentiate between signs (such as morphemes, words) which *are* different in meaning. Thus, distinctive features, phonemes, and syllables, may be said to have a mediate, indirect connection with meaning (see RJ & LW, 1979; Waugh, 1979a, 1980; RJ, 1980b). However, even in the distinctive features there is a tendency for a direct and immediate relation to meaning. Immediacy is apparent in such diverse factors of language as sound symbolism, synesthesia, sound symbolic ablaut, word affinity relations, glossolalia, children's play with sound, anagrams, reduplication, poetry, etc. (see RJ & LW, 1979: chap. 4). In all of these cases (and all of these can form an integral part of poetic texture), the "speech sounds have an immediate relation to meaning or [. . .] they function as direct carriers of a latent, concealed imaginary meaning" (RJ & LW, 1979:215). In *sound symbolism*, for example, there is an iconic (similarity) relation between certain aspects of sound and meaning. In particular, it has been found that there is a latent tendency, which may become patent in certain circumstances, for the sounds of a given word to be congruent with (similar to) their meanings. Such correspondences are often built on the phenomenal interconnection between the different senses — synesthesia, including the most difficult facet of 'colored hearing' (the relation between sounds and colors). Thus, the difference in French between the vowels /u/ and /i/ tends to be associated with the oppositions bigger-smaller, darker-brighter, softer-harder, heavier-lighter, slower-quicker, etc. (see Chastaing, 1958, 1961, 1965; Peterfalvi, 1970; also RJ & LW, 1979). Another tendency of sounds toward independent signification can be noted under the general heading of *word affinities* (see Bolinger, 1940/1965; RJ & LW, 1979:194−200): features, phonemes, collocations of phonemes, which are common to a set of words with like meaning, may come to be associated with that meaning. For example, in the series of words *nip, clip, tip, sip, grip, pip, quip, yip, flip, drip,* the post-vocalic stop is (synesthetically) sensed to be like a 'blow,' and the (sound-symbolic) /ɪ/ seems to suggest a briefer focus upon the action (vs. /ae/ in *slap, clap, rap, tap, flap, lap*). Compare the use of /u/ to suggest foolishness in *rube, boob, faloot, loon, nincompoop, stooge, coo-coo, goof, spoof* (see Bolinger, 1940/1965:200), and *fl-* as expressive of movement in *flow, flutter, flitter, flirt, flap, flake, flicker, fling, flurry, flit* (see Jespersen, 1922; Bolinger, 1940/1965 and 1950/1965). Such sound-meaning associations can become the basis of a *sui generis* synchronic etymology and may lead to the survival of certain members of the general class and to the addition of new members to the class (see RJ & LW, 1979). Moreover, such associations go even further than the 'word families' described here; essentially, any association between two (or more) words which share some aspect of their *signantia* may become the basis for a sharing of some aspect of their *signata*. This is the general principle of language structure: any similarity of *signans* may be viewed as a cue to a similarity of *signatum*.

In the referential function, such similarity relations remain latent and may be overruled by the imputed contiguity relation between *signans* and *signatum* (Saussure's 'arbitrariness' — see RJ, 1975/1980, 1968/1971). But in the poetic function, similarity relations may become patent and may overrule the imputed contiguity relation. In other words, with the emphasis upon equivalence and similarity relations for the *signans*, the immediate relation between *signans* and *signatum* leads to an evaluation of the similarity relation as evidencing a similarity in the *signatum*. "This propensity to infer a connection in meaning from similarity in sound illustrates the poetic function of language" (RJ, 1964). What in the referential use of language remains latent and subordinate can become in the poetic function patent and predominant. Of course, such a relation between *signans* and *signatum* means that the given *signans* is 'motivated' insofar as the particular linguistic system is concerned. This leads of course to a questioning of the 'arbitrariness' of the connection between *signans* and *signatum*. And indeed, poetry is based to a large extent on *iconicity* — a factual similarity relation between *signans* and *signatum* either with respect to individual components (Peirce's images) or with respect to the internal relations (Peirce's diagrams) — or on *artifice* — an imputed similarity relation between *signans* and *signatum* (see Peirce, 1867/1960; RJ, 1966/1971, 1968/1971, 1975/1980). If in the referential function the imputed contiguity relation is uppermost, in the poetic function it is closely combatted both by factual similarity (iconicity) and by imputed similarity (artifice), thus creating a highly complex and hierarchized system of internal relations. Similarity proves to be the constructive device not only of the sequence but also of the internal relation within the sign as well as the relations between the signs as they occur contiguously in the sequence. In this fashion, the *signans* plays an active and constructive role in the creation and communication of meaning.

3.30 *Meaning*

3.31   The actualization of the linguistic sign as a sign leads also to a focus upon the *signatum* both in its relation to the *signans* and in terms of its own structural nature. If we take the *signatum* of any linguistic sign, it evidences a continual dichotomy between a *relational invariant* — sometimes called a *general meaning* (*Gesamtbedeutung*) — and a variety of hierarchized *contextual variants* (specific meanings) including the basic variant (=*Grundbedeutung*), that is, that variant which is 'typical' for the given sign and is least conditioned by the environment (see RJ, 1932/1971 and 1957/1971). In the English past tense, for example, the 'past time' interpretation is the basic one: *he* CAME *yesterday*; its hypothetical usage is a figurative, contextual variant due to its contextualization in an *if*-clause: *if he* CAME *today;* other, more peripheral variants include 'polite' usage: I WANTED *to ask you a question* ('right now'), sequence of tenses: *Galileo said that the earth* WAS *round*, etc. Variants thus include diverse literal interpretations as well as figurative transfers, both metaphoric and metonymic. The contextual variants, both basic and non-basic, are more specific than the more general invariant, but they are not the same as a given object or idea. It is these variants, not the general invariants, which are correlated with reference. The variants are themselves linguistic phenomena (e.g., the hypotheticalness of *if he* CAME is due to the interaction of the past tense and *if*), and as such are different from either the ideas they are meant to interpret or the situation they are meant to describe (also an interpretation). They are to a certain extent codified, although not completely, since the creativity associated with clauses, sentences, utterances, discourses means the possibility of providing new contexts and thus new variants. There are both habitual associations and novel associations. In fact, 'poetic creativity' largely resides in the exploitation of such possibilities.

Now, while the potential for ambiguity resides in the relation of contextual variants to the invariant, generally contextual meanings are discernible both from surrounding linguistic context (e.g., other words in the same discourse) and from the general situation (the non-verbalized context but capable of being verbalized) in which the speech event takes place. In any given context, in referential speech, it is quite often the case that the particular variant meant is evident to speaker-hearer; while speakers may at times be deliberately vague (ambiguous), in general this vagueness may touch only certain parts of a discourse, while other parts remain well-defined. Referential speech tends less to multiplicity of meaning and more to denotative precision. In the poetic function, however, the breaking of the tie between contextual variant and object/idea is interconnected with the *multiplicity of meanings,* the inherent ambiguity, the split reference and multiplicity of *denotata* of the poetic text. "The oscillation between several semantic planes, typical of the poetic context, loosens up the bond between the sign and the object. The denotative precision arrived at by 'practical language' gives way to connotative density and wealth of associations" (Erlich, 1955:185). The breaking of the tie between sign and object/idea, characteristic of the poetic text, means that a particular contextual variant may be correlated with a variety of different referents. And the potentiality of various figurative transfers leads to the 'levels of meaning' inherent in the text. Furthermore, the multifunctionality of the text may lead to a variety of different interpretations depending on the hierarchization of the various functions (see Holenstein, 1979).

The multiplicity of meanings is also due to the *relative autonomy* and *decontextualization* of the poem. "Puisque les rapports des signes esthétiques au *denotatum* sont beaucoup plus diffus que le rapport des signes non esthétiques au concept ou à l'objet signifié, l'attention du récepteur est dirigée sur la composition du texte esthétique lui-même. Le signe esthétique est ainsi polysémique autant qu'auto-orienté" (Winner, 1975:60). A poem is to a certain degree decontextualized: it is a system of systems which is more self-contained than referential discourse. One could say that the poem provides its own 'universe of discourse.' The orientation of the poem upon itself as a message-sign has the effect of making more of a break between the poem and its context than in referential discourse and results in a relative self-sufficiency of the poetic text. As a message-sign the poem exhibits *closure* with respect both to its beginning and to its end. Indeed, such closure is a result of the focus upon the message and is the means whereby there is focus. The use of equivalence relations and the resultant parallelisms and symmetries give a tight, interwoven structure to the poem and enhance its self-sufficiency. The loosening of the relations based on contiguity—including beginning and ending closure—seal the poem off from immediately preceding and succeeding verbal contexts.

To a certain extent, then, the poem is a relatively autonomous structure. But a poem does not exist in a vacuum: it is part of a general historico-cultural context and indeed depends on that context for its interpretation. Nor is it sealed off from a literary context. It may adhere to or, on the contrary, combat literary norms and values, but in some way the literary conventions of the times are relevant; the poetic code or codes which coexist with the poem provide an important, overarching context; and a given poem may be meant for certain kinds of readers and certain kinds of readings, etc. In this respect, the poem is highly contextualized. Thus, it is a relatively autonomous, closed structure, which is decontextualized vis-à-vis the referential context but contextualized vis-à-vis the literary and historico-cultural context.

Despite all the contextualizations there may be in terms of literary and cultural norms and values, it is the internal structure of the poem itself which provides the major context for its parts. The focus on the message, the use of equivalence relations to construct the sequence, etc. — all of these mean that the poem does not rely on outside context, as would a referential text, for the fixing of the particular meaning(s) intended, but rather that the poem must provide the major context for its own parts. But the poetic context is also cut off from reference; there is a self-reflexivity among the parts, none of which can be firmly fixed, thus resulting in ambiguities and multiplicities of meaning. A poem, as an ambiguous context, provides many 'levels of meanings,' many indeterminacies with regard to interpretation.

In any linguistic discourse, there is a constant interplay of two major dichotomies: *explicitness* vs. *ellipsis* on the one hand and *redundancy* vs. *ambiguity* on the other hand. Moreover, these two dichotomies share the common property of posing the problem of the amount of information conveyed by the given discourse (a general semiotic problem) or to put it in another way, the relation between the *signata* of the signs in the given text with respect to the amount and kinds of information they supply. Redundant signs are those signs which inform about other signs in the text and thus cannot be said to provide independent information; they are used in a sense to ensure that the given information is provided (see RJ & LW, 1979:36–38; Waugh, 1979a, 1979b on redundant phonological features). Ambiguous signs are those which, even when in context of other signs, provide more than one interpretation; the potential for such ambiguity is inherent to *any* general meaning. In this case, they are indeterminate with respect to the particular contextual variant meant. Elliptical structures are those in which certain signs have been left out, but are assumed to be known to the addressee, while explicit structures are those fully replete with signs (see RJ & LW, 1979). Now, the poem, which is focussed upon itself and upon the sign as sign, plays with both of these dichotomies, and while on the one hand poetic expression may be elliptic, on the other hand it extracts from the reduced expressions a multiplicity of meaning (ambiguity). "By ambiguity, the message is rendered creative in relation to the acknowledged possibilities of the code" (see Eco, 1976). The ambiguities result from the potentialities inherent in the partially codified contextual variants. Thus, with a minimum of means a maximum of meanings is generated. In other words, a paucity of signs is used to bring forth the fullest possible variation in the interpretation of the *signata:* "la poésie est orientée vers la variation" (RJ & KP, 1980:145).

3.32   But the other side of contextual variation and multiplicity of meanings is *relational invariance* (see Waugh, 1976b:68–89). As the basis for the meanings which a given sign may evidence in its various contextualizations, there is the *general meaning*, the common denominator of meaning, which remains no matter what alterations of or influences on that item there may be as it is used in various contexts. Now, relational invariance is, in effect, equivalence in difference or equivalence under isomorphic transformations. It is this relational equivalence of meaning which underlies the ability of the speaker to create and of the hearer to apprehend, any (especially new) contextualizations of a given *signatum*, for the general meaning belongs to the code and is presumed known to both speaker and addressee. And the general meaning is, in effect, relational — signs signify in terms not of their relation to extra-linguistic objects but rather in relation to each other (especially in grammatical categories — see 3.33). The system is a relational system, made up of terms (e.g., *signata*) defined and created by their relation to each other. Thus the relations are primary and the given terms are secondary. This means in particular that any sign (of whatever complexity) which occurs *in* or *as* a poem implicates — by its relational nature — other signs to which it is closely tied but which may not be in the poem. This also means that the *signatum* of any sign whatsoever, while it evidences contextualization, also owes its nature to its close *relata*.

One similarity relation which is extremely important in linguistic structure is that of *opposition*; opposition is a binary relation of mutual implication in which there is an inherent asymmetry between the two choices, an asymmetry known as *markedness*. Markedness entails the fact that in two choices, one is the more focussed, the more narrowly constrained, the more concentrated than the other (see RJ, 1932/1971; RJ & LW, 1979; Waugh, 1982). This means, especially in regard to the *signatum,* that the unmarked pole of any opposition evidences greater contextual variation than the marked pole and in particular may evidence two major contextual interpretations. One contextual interpretation is that in which the marking characteristic of the unmarked pole is specifically denied. For example, in the opposition of *high-low*, where *low* is the marked element and specifies reduced extent, *high* may be used to specify the non-reduced extent: *this table is too low and that one is too high* (see, for example, RJ, 1975). On the other hand, the unmarked pole may also be used in contexts where the marked term is neither explicitly nor implicitly denied and is often improper; in such a case one has a zero sign (RJ, 1939/1971; Waugh, 1982): for example: *this table is two feet high.* Such oppositional relations underlie the whole of the grammatical pattern (about which more later) and some of the lexical pattern of the language, in particular the relation of antonymy.

One series of graded antonyms based on oppositional pairs was the subject of an E. E. Cummings poem (see below; for a discussion of the sound texture of the poem, see RJ & LW, 1979:226–28; for other uses of opposition in poetic analysis, see for example RJ & CL-S, 1962/1973). In addition to the pairings of such obvious opposites as *thick-thin, forget-recall, seldom-frequent, always-never, big-little* (in strophes one and three), Cummings pairs *deep* with *high* (in strophes two and four), not a normal pairing in the English lexicon, but perfectly understandable in the context of the poem. The general code of English opposes as contradictories *deep* to *shallow* (unmarked to marked) and *high* to *low* (unmarked to marked), where *deep* and *high* are, so to speak, similar to each other through their designation of a cognate spatial relation and through their unmarked status within that relation. The pairing of *deep* with *high* is a latent possibility of the English code which is fully utilized in this specific poetic message, for here the similarity relation between *deep* and *high* is turned into one of antonymy (based on a relation of contraries), paralleling *moon-sun, sea-sky, mad-sane*. In fact, one could say that *deep* provides in this case an even more striking opposite to *high* than does *low*. The relational nature of these oppositional pairs proves to be both underscored by and created by the structuration of the poem.

1. love is more thicker than forget
    more thinner than recall
    more seldom than a wave is wet
    more frequent than to fall

2. it is most mad and moonly
    and less it shall unbe
    than all the sea which only
    is deeper than the sea

3. love is less always than to win
    less never than alive
    less bigger than the least begin
    less littler than forgive

4. it is most sane and sunly
    and more it cannot die
    than all the sky which only
    is higher than the sky

e. e. cummings

(*Some* of the semantic parallelisms within the poem based on antonymy are marked by connecting lines.)

3.33   *Grammar*: "la 'sorcellerie évocatoire' de la structure grammaticale, la force expressive des catégories grammaticales" (RJ & KP, 1980:119).

The *signata* which are focused upon and which provide the meaning of the poem are both grammatical and lexical. The grammatical elements — both morphological such as tense, and syntactic such as word order — are those which are, according to the code of the given language, obligatory in the construction of messages (see RJ, 1959b/1971). Any message-sign in the given language must be built around and with such grammatical categories, while lexical categories are optional. The message-sign, as a highly complex, hierarchically ordered sign, includes elements which recur, obligatorily, in all other message-signs of the same language. This means that, with respect to the *signatum*, there are certain elements of meaning which are always communicated in every message, no matter whether they are strictly 'needed' or not. Given that the poem is characterized by a focus upon the message and that grammatical categories are those which must be used if the message is to be acceptable, it is 'natural' that such categories should become the focus of poetic structure. Moreover, "le réseau des catégories grammaticales détermine toute la tournure d'esprit de notre langage, et les traits caractéristiques de ce réseau qui restent latents dans notre langage habituel deviennent dans la poésie infiniment plus expressifs et plus importants." (RJ & KP, 1980:120.)

Grammatical categories which may figure in a poem include (in a variety of languages) "all the parts of speech both mutable and immutable, numbers, genders, cases, grades, tenses, aspects, moods, voices, classes of abstract and concrete words, animates and inanimates, appellatives and proper names, affirmatives and negatives, finite and infinite verbal forms, definite and indefinite pronouns or articles, and diverse syntactic elements and constructions" (RJ, 1968:604). The grammatical categories of English include for example (with the marked category given first): past vs. non-past, passive vs. active, progressive vs. non-progressive, in the verb; plural vs. singular in the noun; person vs. non-person, first vs. second, plural vs. singular in the pronouns and animate vs. inanimate, feminine vs. masculine in the third person singular pronouns; definite vs. indefinite in the article, etc. While languages may differ (and they do) as to which categories are grammatical and which are lexical, all languages have some obligatory categories and it is these categories which provide the material for the *grammar of poetry* and the *poetry of grammar*.

The grammatical elements are also those which form a *closed system*, much as the poem itself is a closed system; the lexical categories form an open system. While the lexical categories are concrete and material in nature, the grammatical categories are *formal* and *relational* in nature; and "it is quite evident that grammatical concepts — or in Fortunatov's pointed nomenclature 'formal meanings' — find their widest applications in poetry as the most formalized manifestation of language" (RJ, 1968:599). Furthermore, the grammatical categories form a highly patterned network, based to a high degree on the similarity relation of opposition, including markedness. They are thus fitting material for the domain of similarity, poetry. The grammatical categories have a more indirect connection with the extra-linguistic world than the lexical categories and depend for their inherent nature as well as for their interpretation in given messages on their relations with each other. For example, it is not at all clear what referential difference the active vs. passive opposition could be said to conform to. And yet it is a highly significant difference for the patterning of the English predicate (and one which is salient to any speaker of English). Indeed, many of the grammatical differences in a language make up what Jeremy Bentham called the *"linguistic fictions"* (see Ogden, 1932) of language: categories based not so much on any difference in reference but rather on the linguistic "shape" of such differences. And they are categories which are indispensable for the functioning of the language. *Grammatical figures* then may be centered on such linguistic fictions: in fiction (verbal art), linguistic fictions assume an important role (see RJ, 1968, also 1959b/1971; and Waugh, 1979b). And given the fact that the poetic function is based on the projection of equivalence relations into contiguity and on the sign as sign rather than the sign-object relation, it is not surprising that grammatical parallelisms and grammatical figures and tropes of various kinds should be widely used. The poetic function is based not only on 'sound form' but also on 'grammatical form.' And while it would be a mistake to say that a poem is only sound or only grammar, it would be just as much a mistake to deny the part which both sound and grammar play in the construction of poetic meaning.

The focus on grammatical meaning does not of course exclude *lexical meaning* as important to the structuration and the 'meaning' of the poem. We have already seen how antonymous lexical pairs help to structure the Cummings poem. Moreover, certain kinds of lexical items will (especially in the context of a particular type of poem or poetic tradition) have a 'favored interpretation' or a long chain of associative links — e.g., the use of the sea, the moon, flowers, etc. in lyric poetry. (But see Cummings' surprising use of 'wetness' as a means of comparison between a *wave* and *love*, "instead of their changeability, inconstancy, mobility, and similar properties familiar to poetic tradition"; RJ & LW, 1979:227). Furthermore, proper names (especially well-known proper names) may entail the linguistic and cultural encyclopedia (cf. Eco, 1976) for their interpretation (e.g., the use of Napoleon or of Greek mythological figures in Western poetry or the use of the Yangtze River in Chinese poetry: see Kao and Mei, 1978), although only certain aspects may be relevant and these very often are dictated by various linguistic and poetic conventions. As with grammatical categories, lexical categories must be carefully scrutinized for their contribution to the internal structure of the poem rather than or at least in addition to their tie with objects outside of the poem.

Now, of course, not only grammatical figures but also *lexical figures* are important in the creation of poetic meaning and especially in the construction of the ambiguities inherent in the text. Such lexical figures have been the subject of much of the study of rhetoric, but much more work needs to be done for a thorough, structural reanalysis of those figures. Such a reanalysis would be based, for example, on the general differentiation of metaphor as an equivalence figure of substitution based on similarity (including both similarity and dissimilarity and contrast) and of metonymy as an equivalence figure based on contiguity. Metonymy, further, is differentiated into 'inner' types of contiguity, such as synecdoche (both part-whole and whole-part relations of various sorts) and 'outer' types, such as 'metonymy proper' (cause-effect, temporal and spatial contiguity, etc.) and includes nearness and farness (adjacency and *éloignement*) (see RJ & KP, 1980:123–132). Of course, poetry does not depend on these lexical tropes (some poems use only grammatical figures); and of course the use of lexical tropes *per se* does not make a text a poem. Ordinary language is full of such tropes; indeed, they seem to be necessary for the use of language in all its functions. What is important in terms of lexical figures is their overall relation to the equivalences, parallelisms, etc. of the poem as well as their contribution to the overall meaning of the poem.

3.4   The sound shape of a poem is provided by all the elements — phonological, grammatical, lexical — which help to build the structuration of the poem. The meaning of a poem is provided by all those same phonological, grammatical, lexical elements. Just as for the linguistic sign, so for the poetic text as a whole, the *signans* and the *signatum* are indissolubly linked with one another; thus sound implies meaning and meaning implies sound. But the poem-sign is made up of a complex hierarchy of signs from the smallest (the distinctive features) to the largest (the poem itself). The poem is a *whole* made up of a variety of parts. As in any such case, the whole cannot be understood without an understanding of the parts and the parts can only be understood in terms of their contribution to the whole (see RJ, 1962/1971). Thus, the meaning of the whole poem depends upon the meanings of all the elements making up that totality. Likewise, all of the specific aspects of the poem, rather than being goals in themselves, are mutually related to each other and at the same time are interdependently linked with the whole. They are only understandable in the light of that whole. And since the whole poem is dominated by a focus on the message itself, the contribution of the parts is radically altered, as against their contribution to a message dominated by the referential function. The exchange of the one for the other does more than alter the whole as a whole; it also has the effect of altering each of the parts both in relation to the whole and in relation to each other. As stated earlier, there may be certain aspects of the total contextualization of a poem which are due not to the strictly linguistic facets of the poem but rather to general semiotic aspects, including the totality of the historico-cultural and literary context; these must be taken into consideration also for a total contextualization of the poem, for the poem itself is also in its turn not only a whole, but also a part of a larger, *semiotic whole*.

4.0   In our discussion of the intrinsic, *linguistic* properties of poetic texts and of the poetic function as a whole, we started with a very general statement about focus upon the message and ended with such specifics as the grammar of poetry and lexical tropes. However, the discussion could just as well have gone in the opposite direction, beginning with grammar of poetry and proceeding to the focus on the message. It is because there is grammar of poetry that the focus on the message exists and because there is focus upon the message that the grammar of poetry exists. Just as for any *structure*, all the elements of the poetic function imply and implicate each other; none is privileged. They form a relational system in which one part of the system implies the other parts. Should any of the parts be missing, the system itself would thereby be intrinsically changed. The focus on the message, the use of equivalence relations as the constructive device of the sequence, the closure and the relative autonomy of the poem, the delimitation between sign and object, the multiplicity of meanings in poetic discourse, the use of sound figures and especially of paronomasia, the immediacy characteristic of the distinctive features, the poem as an autotelic system of systems of signs, the poem as a structure, the grammar of poetry and especially the use of grammatical parallelisms and figures, the constructional use of lexical figures and tropes, etc. — all of these are definitional for the poetic function as a whole. And as Roman Jakobson has shown and has exemplified in his own work (see RJ, 1979, 1980), the *structuralist* and *scientific* study of poetry and of language as a whole is concerned with deepening and expanding our understanding of the poetic function in all its aspects: "The ubiquity and mutual implication of Verb and Verbal Art impart a seminal unity to the forthcoming science of the two inseparable universals, *Language* and *Poetry*" (RJ & LW, 1979:231).

REFERENCES

BARTHES, R., 1978. "Avant-propos," *Cahiers Cistre* 5: *Jakobson* (Lausanne), 9–10.

BAUDOUX, L., 1962. "Linguistique structurale et poésie," *Logique et analyse* 19, 122–142.

BOLINGER, D.L., 1940/1965. "Word Affinities," in: I. Abe and T. Kanekiyo, eds., *Forms of English* (Cambridge, Mass.), 191–202.

1950/1965. "Rime, Assonance, and Morpheme Analysis," in: I. Abe and T. Kanekiyo, eds., *Forms of English* (Cambridge, Mass.), 203–206.

BROOKE-ROSE, C., 1976. *A Structural Analysis of Pound's Usura Canto; Jakobson's Method Extended and Applied to Free Verse* (The Hague).

BUXÓ, J. P., 1978. *Introducción a la poética de Roman Jakobson*, Mexico.

CHASTAING, M., 1958. "Le symbolisme des voyelles: signification des 'i'," I & II, *Journal de psychologie* 55, 403–423, 461–481.

1961 "Des sons et des couleurs," *Vie et language* 112, 358–365.

1965 "Dernières recherches sur le symbolisme vocalique de la petitesse," *Revue philosophique* 155, 41–56.

CULLER, J., 1975. *Structuralist Poetics* (Ithaca, NY).

ČUKOVSKY, K., 1966/1971. *From Two to Five* (Berkeley).

DELAS, D., 1973. "Phonétique, phonologie, et poétique chez Roman Jakobson," *Langue française* 19, 108–119.

ECO, U., 1976. *A Theory of Semiotics* (Bloomington, Indiana).

EJXENBAUM, B., 1927/1965. "The Theory of the 'Formal Method'," in: I. Lemon and M. Reis, eds., *Russian Formalist Criticism: Four Essays* (Lincoln, Nebraska).

ERLICH, V., 1955. *Russian Formalism* (The Hague: Mouton).

1973a "Roman Jakobson: Grammar of Poetry and Poetry of Grammar," S. Chatman (ed.), *Approaches to Poetics* (New York), 1–27.

1973b "Russian Formalism," *Journal of the History of Ideas* 34, 627–638.

FOKKEMA, D. W. AND E. KUNNE-IBSCH, 1977, *Theories of Literature in the Twentieth Century* (New York).

FOX, J. J., 1977. "Roman Jakobson and the Comparative Study of Parallelism," D. Armstrong and C. H. van Schooneveld (eds.), *Roman Jakobson, Echoes of his Scholarship* (Lisse, the Netherlands), 59–90.

HAWKES, T., 1977. *Structuralism and Semiotics* (London).
HOLENSTEIN, E., 1974. "A New Essay concerning the Basic Relations of Language," *Semiotics* 12, 97–128.
1974/1976 *Roman Jakobson's Approach to Language* (Bloomington, Indiana).
1976 "Einführung: Linguistische Poetik," to Roman Jakobson, *Hölderlin, Klee, Brecht* (Frankfurt am Main).
1979 "Einführung: Von der Poesie und der Plurifunktionalität der Sprache," to Roman Jakobson, *Poetik* (Frankfurt am Main).
RJ=JAKOBSON, R., 1921/1971. "On Realism in Art," in: L. Matejka and K. Pomorska, eds., *Readings in Russian Poetics*, 38–46.
1932/1971 "Zur Struktur des russischen Verbums," *SW II*, 3–15.
1934/1973 "Qu'est-ce que la poésie?" *Questions de Poétique* (and *SW III*, 740–750).
[1935]/1971 "The Dominant," in: L. Matejka and K. Pomorska, eds., *Readings in Russian Poetics*, 82–90 (and *SW III*, 751–756).
1935/1969 "Marginal Notes on the Prose of the Poet Pasternak," in: D. Davie and A. Livingston, eds., *Pasternak* (Glasgow), 135–151.
1939/1971 "Signe zéro," *SW II*, 211–219.
[1942]/1978 *Six Lectures on Sound and Meaning* (Cambridge, Mass.).
1955/1971 "Aphasia as a Linguistic Topic," *SW II*, 229-238.
1956/1971 "Two Aspects of Language and Two Types of Aphasic Disturbances," *SW II*, 239–259.
[1956]/1980 "Metalanguage as a Linguistic Problem," in: *The Framework of Language* (Ann Arbor, Michigan).
1957/1971 "Shifters, Verbal Categories, and the Russian Verb," *SW II*, 130–147.
1959a/1971 "On Linguistic Aspects of Translation," *SW II*, 260–266.
1959b/1971 "Boas' View of Grammatical Meaning," *SW II*, 489–496.
1960 "Linguistics and Poetics," in: T. Seboek, ed., *Style in Language* (Cambridge, Mass.). 350–377 (and *SW III*, 18–51).
1962/1971 "Parts and Wholes in Language," *SW II*, 280–284.
[1963]/1971 "Toward a Linguistic Classification of Aphasic Impairments," *SW II*, 289–306.
1963/1971 "Efforts towards a Means-Ends Model of Language in Interwar Continental Linguistics," *SW II*, 522–526.
1964 "Language in Operation," in: *Melanges Alexandre Koyré; I: L'aventure de l'esprit* (Paris). 269–281 (and *SW III*, 7–17).
1966a *SW IV=Selected Writings IV, Slavic Epic Studies* (including the "Retrospect") (The Hague: Mouton).
1966b "Grammatical Parallelism and its Russian Facet," *Language* 42, 399–429 (and *SW III*, 98–135).
1966/1971 "Quest for the Essence of Language," *SW II*, 345–359.
1966/1979 "Vers une science de l'art poétique," *SW V*, 541–544.
1968 "Poetry of Grammar and Grammar of Poetry," *Lingua* 21, 597–609 (and *SW III*, 87–97).
1969/1971 "Language in Relation to Other Communication Systems," *SW II*, 697–708.
1970 "Subliminal Verbal Patterning in Poetry," in: R. Jakobson and S. Kawamoto, eds., *Studies in General and Oriental Linguistics Presented to S. Hattori* (Tokyo), 302–308 (and *SW III*, 136–147).
1971 *SW II=Selected Writings II: Word and Language* (including the "Retrospect").
1972a "Verbal Communication," *Scientific American* 227, 72–80.
1972b "Louvain Lectures," edited by M. van Ballaer as *Aspects of the Theories of Roman Jakobson* (Memoir Katholieke Universitet te Leuven).
1973a "Postscriptum," *Questions de poétique* (Paris), 485–504.
1973b "Si nostre vie': observations sur la *composition et structure de motz* dans un sonnet de Joachim du Bellay," *Questions de poétique* (Paris), 319–355 (and *SW III*, 239–274).

1975 "Spatial Relationships in Slavic Adjectives," in: *Scritti in onore di Giuliano Bonfante* (Brescia).

1975/1980 "A Glance at the Development of Semiotics," in: *The Framework of Language* (Ann Arbor, Michigan), 1–30.

1976 "Diskussion von Roman Jakobson mit Professoren und Studenten der Universität Köln," *Arbeitspapier* Nr. 32 (Köln) (cf. 69–78 above).

1978 "Entretien" (avec R. et R. Georgin), *Jakobson*, Cahiers Cistre 5 (Lausanne), 11–27.

1978/1980 "On the Linguistic Approach to the Problem of Consciousness and the Unconscious," in: *The Framework of Language* (Ann Arbor: Michigan), 133–132.

1979 *SW V=Selected Writings V: On Verse, Its Masters and Explorers* (including the "Retrospect") (The Hague: Mouton).

1980a "A Postscript to the Discussion on Grammar of Poetry," *Diacritics* 10, 22–36.

1980b *Brain and Language* (Columbus, Ohio).

1981 *SW III=Selected Writings III: Grammar of Poetry and Poetry of Grammar* (including the "Retrospect") (The Hague: Mouton).

RJ & CL-S=JAKOBSON, R. and C. LEVI-STRAUSS, 1962/1973. " 'Les Chats' de Charles Baudelaire," *Questions de poétique* (Paris), 401–19 (and *SW III*, 417–446).

RJ & KP=JAKOBSON, R. and K. POMORSKA, 1980. *Dialogues* (Paris).

RJ & LW=JAKOBSON, R. and L. WAUGH, 1979. *The Sound Shape of Language* (Bloomington, Indiana).

JESPERSEN, O., 1922. *Language: Its Nature, Development, and Origin* (New York).

KAO, YU-KUNG AND TSU-LIN MEI, 1978. "Meaning, Metaphor, and Allusion in T'ang Poetry," *Harvard Journal of Asiatic Studies* 38, 281–356.

KRUCKENBERG, A.B., 1977. *Roman Jakobsons Poetik*. (Uppsala).

LAURENT, J.P., 1971. *L'Analyse de la poésie selon Roman Jakobson* (Louvain).

LEVIN, S., 1962. *Linguistic Structures in Poetry* (The Hague).

LODGE, D., 1977. *Modes of Modern Writing: Metaphor, Metonymy, and the Typology of Modern Literature* (Ithaca, New York) (second edition 1979² including preface).

MAYENOWA, M., 1977. "Comparative Slavic Poetics in the Work of Roman Jakobson", D. Armstrong and C.H. van Schooneveld (eds.), *Roman Jakobson: Echoes of his Scholarship* (Lisse, the Netherlands).

MORRIS, W., 1979. *Friday's Footprint* (Columbus, Ohio).

MOUNIN, G., 1968. "Baudelaire devant une critique structurale," *Baudelaire: Actes du Colloque de Nice-Annales de la Faculté des Lettres et Sciences Humaines de Nice*, no. 4–5, 155–160.

OGDEN, C.K., 1932. *Bentham's Theory of Fictions* (consisting of an introduction by Ogden, and Bentham, *Theory of Fictions)* (London).

PEIRCE, C.S., 1867/1960. "On a New List of Categories," *Collected Papers* I. C. Hartshorne & P. Weiss, eds. (Cambridge, Mass.).

PETERFALVI, J.M., 1970. *Recherches expérimentales sur la symbolisme phonétique* (Paris).

POMORSKA, K., 1968. *Russian Formalist Theory and its Poetic Ambiance* (The Hague).

1977 "Roman Jakobson and the New Poetics", D. Armstrong and C.H. Schooneveld (eds.), *Roman Jakobson: Echoes of his Scholarship (Lisse, the Netherlands).*

PRATT, M.L., 1977. *Towards a Speech Act Theory of Discourse* (Bloomington, Ind.)

RAIBLE, W., 1974. "Roman Jakobson oder 'Auf der Wasserscheide zwischen Linguistik und Poetik'," Roman Jakobson, *Aufsätze zur Linguistik und Poetik* (München), 7–37.

RIFFATERRE, M., 1966. "Describing Poetic Structures—Two Approaches to Baudelaire's 'Les Chats'," *Yale French Studies*, 200–242.

RUDY, S., 1976. "Jakobson's Inquiry into Verse and the Emergence of Structural Poetics," in: L. Matejka, ed., *Sound, Sign and Meaning* (Ann Arbor, Michigan), 477–520.

SAVAN, D., 1980. "Peirce's Semiotic Theory of Emotion," *Proceedings of the C.S. Peirce Bicentennial International Congress* (Texas Tech UP).

STANKIEWICZ, E., 1974a. "Structural Poetics and Linguistics," *Current Trends in Linguistics XII.* (The Hague), 629–659.

1974b "The Poetic Text as a Linguistic Structure," *Sciences of Language* (Tokyo).

TODOROV, T., 1971. "Roman Jakobson poéticien," *Poétique* 7, 275–286.

1971/1977 *The Poetics of Prose* (Ithaca, New York).

1973 "Structuralism and Literature," in: S. Chatman, ed., *Approaches to Poetics* (New York).

1977 "Poétique générale," in: D. Armstrong and C.H. van Schooneveld, eds., *Roman Jakobson: Echoes of his Scholarship* (Lisse).

1978 "L'Héritage formaliste," *Cahiers Cistre* 5: *Jakobson* (Lausanne), 47–51.

VALÉRY, P., 1939/1958. "Poetry and Abstract Thought," *The Art of Poetry* (New York).

WAUGH, L.R., 1976a. "The Semantics and Paradigmatics of Word Order," *Language* 52, 82–107.

1976b *Roman Jakobson's Science of Language* (Lisse).

1977 *A Semantic Analysis of Word Order* (Leiden).

1979a "On the Sound Shape of Language," *Proceedings of the Deseret Language and Linguistic Society* (Annual Meeting), Provo, Utah.

1979b "Some Remarks on the Nature of the Linguistic Sign," in: *The Sign and its Functions,* ed. J. Pelc et al. (Berlin-N.Y.: Mouton).

1980 "Form as a Cue to Semantic Structure" (manuscript).

1982 "Marked and Unmarked: a Choice between Unequals in Semiotic Structure," *Semiotica* 38:3–4, 299–318.

1984 "The Multifunctionality of the Speech Sound," in: F. B. Agard et al., eds., *Essays in Honor of C. F. Hockett* (Leiden), 288–302.

WEIR, R.H., 1962. *Language in the Crib* (The Hague: Mouton).

WERTH, P., 1976. "Roman Jakobson's Verbal Analysis of Poetry," *Journal of Linguistics* 12.

WINNER, T., 1975. "Grands thèmes de la poétique jakobsonienne," *L'Arc* 60, 55–64.

Poetics of Prose

Krystyna Pomorska

> Formalism is a child's
> illness of structuralism.
> —Roman Jakobson

The Russian Formalists undertook, for the first time, an analysis of prose encompassing all of its structural components; significantly, some of these components had until then not been considered "structural," or, to use terminology more in keeping with the OPOJAZ, had been viewed as incapable of being formalized. These young Russian scholars explored several areas in an entirely new way. First, they showed *sjužet* ("plot") and *fabula* ("story line") as related but not at all identical factors. Second, they introduced the idea of *skaz* (oral narration) and consequently the idea of the narrator as a mask, which entailed a clear-cut delineation of the narrator as a pure device in opposition to the author. Note further the related idea of oral narration as a system of sound patterning (Ejxenbaum). Finally, the protagonist was viewed as a "device," or more exactly as a component of a larger unit, namely a parallelistically patterned *sjužet* (Šklovskij).

Among the many critics and adversaries of the theories of the OPOJAZ, two outstanding men should be recalled: Vygotskij and Baxtin. These scholars looked upon art from the larger perspectives of psychology and philosophy, respectively. From their standpoint, the theory of the OPOJAZ was essentially taxonomic and therefore inadequate, even contradictory. But another outstanding figure—who, unlike Baxtin and Vygotskij, was a prominent member and a cofounder of the group in question—must also be mentioned, namely Roman Jakobson. Jakobson was not merely a member and cofounder but the group's critic and "corrector" as well: it is thus natural that Jakobson's theories, rather than those of Baxtin and Vygotskij, underlie the system of the Tartu-Moscow school, which is the continuation and corrective of the OPOJAZ today.

Before considering Jakobsonian theoretical principles and their application to the analysis of prose, let us examine a scientific methodology as such from the point of view of its operational fruitfulness and applicability. First and foremost, a proper method must not offer ready-made solutions but must present, rather, an open set of analytical possibilities. To possess such a capacity, the method should fulfill certain criteria. First, it must be founded on well-defined general principles permitting the elaboration of terms suitable for analyzing both extant and forthcoming phenomena in their mutual interrelation. Second, a proper methodology should be capable of opening up new vistas, thus allowing for connections with other appropriate methods, but without mutual contradictions. Several inter-methodological relationships are possible. Let us mention two of them. One method can elucidate another and provide it with a new dimension. Thus structuralism, for instance, has revitalized the old biographical approach. There can also be a relationship of inclusion, i.e., when one method becomes a part of another. Thus structural linguistics, in our time, has become a part of the semiotic approach. Structural linguistics, in its turn, makes use of both information theory and communication theory for its purposes. (To illustrate: Jakobson's model of the speech event makes use of principles of communication theory; and he employs probability theory in the analysis of metrics.) Methodology conceived and used in this way therefore allows us both to generalize and to individualize the phenomena under investigation.

A basic problem for any methodology is its definition of the ontology of art, i.e., the mode of the latter's existence. How does Jakobsonian methodology deal with this issue? It shows that the poetic function, with other functions of language, is present in the speech of every human being from early infancy and plays a crucial role in shaping discourse; this proves that art and literature are among the most important "institutions" in human life, since they exist potentially in everyone. Scientific proofs for this assertion come from at least three areas: from the linguistic study of infants and aphasics; from social anthropology, which shows that every social group has art, and especially poetry; and finally, from the most recent neurological studies of the brain and its topology (see Jakobson, 1980).

According to Jakobson's earliest works, "nothing exists as an absolute" (1919/1981). Accordingly, Jakobson views artistic prose not as a phenomenon in itself, but in relation to another major form of artistic discourse, namely poetry. This relationship has both historical and structural foundations. Modern anthropology and linguistics have established that poetry in various forms (including syncretic forms) existed prior to prose. As Vittorio Strada recently reminded us, remnants of the historical primacy of poetry can be seen, for example, in Russian prose of the nineteenth century, which is notable in this respect for its irregular and late development. The first two Russian novels actually combine principles of both poetry and prose. *Eugene Onegin* bears the defining subtitle *A Novel in Verse,* while *Dead Souls,* a novel based on the picaresque, is subtitled *A Poem.* (Strada, 1980.) Moreover, the fundamental poetic principle of parallelism is prevalent in Russian artistic prose, as opposed to the use of plotting in the Western European norm. This phenomenon is evidently traceable to the folk poetic tradition.

Jakobson established that both prose and poetry, as the fundamental forms of verbal art, depend on two basic axes at work in every type of discourse, namely the axis of selection and the axis of combination (1956). These two axes are related, respectively, to the principles of similarity and contiguity. Similarity or equivalence is responsible for the metaphoric pole in language, while contiguity pertains to the metonymic pole. As a general principle, both of these forces are also present in every speech act. Jakobson claims that in poetry, which involves the specific structuring of linguistic categories, the metaphoric pole is dominant, whereas the metonymic pole prevails in prose. Jakobson's critics—especially those insufficiently acquainted with modern linguistics—have singled out this idea for attack. But their misunderstanding stems from two sources: on the one hand, they usually mistake metaphor and metonymy for mere figures of speech, as opposed to pervasive forces organizing language in operation; on the other hand, they fail to appreciate that the metaphor/metonymy opposition is not an absolute one, but rather a tendency.

Not only is the basic distinction between metaphor and metonymy essential for delineating the type of information imparted, but it is also important for the process of reading (decoding) each verbal mode. In poetry the crucial question is not "what happened?"; there is no chain of *events* and therefore no suspense based on the expectation of an outcome. Poetry in its epitome—the short lyric poem—involves rather a system of equivalent pieces of information expressed in various symbolic forms, the most characteristic of which is *rhyme*. The salient feature of rhyme is that in order to perceive it, we must remember the first member of a pair. In Jakobson's approach, rhyme serves as a model for the process of perceiving a poem in general. The reader retains the beginning of a poem in his immediate field of perception as he reads its end. Indeed, we cannot easily interrupt the process of reading a poem by setting it aside, to be continued later, as we do with narratives. The factor that prevents us from so doing is the force of simultaneity, which in poetry prevails over that of successivity.

In prose the reverse process is at work: successivity prevails over simultaneity. Here we find no such basic elements as rhythm or rhyme; the fundamental factor, rather, especially in narrative fiction, is a chain of events moving forward in time, with the question "what happened?" foremost in the reader's perception. As we have already stated, however, this is not the only force, but merely the *prevailing* force in prose. The force of simultaneity—of repetitive, equivalent elements—*coexists* in it. The equivalent elements, however, are distributed differently than in poetry; they encompass larger semantic units, and their organization is not as strict.

Note first that protagonists themselves are structured as equivalent elements. Palpable examples can be drawn again from Russian literature, among them the following. In *Eugene Onegin,* the oppositions Onegin-Lenskij and Tatjana-Olga are emphasized; on the level of plot, a comparison by contrast is stipulated for both pairs in the initial description and then carried through the entire story.

The principle of equivalence is still more evident in *Dead Souls*. Here the juxtaposed "monsters" that Chichikov meets during his journey show a perfect balance between similarity and contrast. As in most narrative prose with a subdued plot line, the parallelistic structure of the Gogol example is particularly evident. But even in strongly plotted prose, protagonists can clearly be structured according to the principle of equivalence. Consider two further examples from classical Western novels: in Maupassant's *Pierre et Jean,* the title itself signals an equivalent juxtaposition, and in Stendhal's *La Chartreuse de Parme,* the two dramatically contrasted heroines vie for the hero's heart.

A second unit of equivalence is the plot line, the *contextual field* of the protagonists, which is therefore a corollary of the first type of juxtaposition. Among the members of the OPOJAZ, it was V. Šklovskij who first pointed out this analytical possibility, in his examination of the parallel plot lines in *Anna Karenina* (1923). Today, scholars stimulated by the Jakobsonian school adopt this mode of analysis as a natural way of examining the text (see Stenbock-Fermor, 1975); *Anna Karenina* simply cannot be understood without considering the family stories in their relation to each other.

No less than *Anna Karenina, War and Peace* has also been considered, traditionally, as a novel whose structure is "secondary" to its "content." But it is not accidental that Šklovskij also wrote a study on "material and style" in *War and Peace* (1928). Not only do both novels display an elaborate parallelism in their protagonists and their stories, but they are also saturated with rich symbolic systems. These symbolic systems can be analyzed successfully and convincingly only if we take into account the issue of equivalence. This is clearly the case with the symbol of the circle, of "rotation," disclosed first in *War and Peace* and subsequently in *Anna Karenina.* The image of rotation becomes symbolic and thus meaningful only if comparable images are juxtaposed in terms of contrast or similarity. In *War and Peace,* an entire network of such symbols is in play. The novel begins with a simile of a spindle, paralleled by the image of a lathe with its turning wheel, and then with a clock paralleled by a turning screw that does not find its proper path. Another set of imagery involves a more abstract idea of rotation, such as the changing seasons, the famous symbol of an oak, or the succession of generations who experience exactly the same phenomena of life, and so on. Moreover, the symbols so conceived are in opposition to one another within the author's artistic system: idle rotation, the "vicious circle," is opposed to "natural" rotation, the circle of life itself.[1] In Turgenev's *Rudin,* both at the beginning and at the end of the novel, the protagonist appears in a cart—a symbol of his mobile, homeless life.

This last example of symbolic parallelism has another important implication. The opening of a novel lends itself to a further principle of analysis after the model of poetry, pertaining to the very special, marked character of the

---

[1] See Pomorska and Drazen, 1970–72, and Vetlovskaja, 1979. Independently of our article, Vetlovskaja disclosed in *Anna Karenina* essentially the same symbolic system.

beginning. As Jakobson has shown, the first line of a poem functions as a kind of tuning fork: it signals the rhythmical pattern, the cadence, even the sound pattern, the *paronomasia,* of the entire poem. As it turns out, prose behaves in a similar way, even though it operates with a different set of constituents. The first chapter of a novel, usually even the first scene, introduces all of the protagonists as well as all the general themes. L. Ginzburg, whose contributions to the study of prose are invaluable, has shown that the protagonist is marked at his very first appearance: he is usually introduced as a value x, to be specified later as a value $(+ $ or $-) $ x. Ginzburg refers to this process as the "hero's exposition" (1973). Her investigation emphasizes once again the special importance of the beginning of a prose piece.

Further analogies with poetry can be sought in the sphere of grammar, in the generalized sense of the term. The "grammar of poetry" (Jakobson, 1968) behaves as a specific trope owing to the force of equivalence projected from the axis of selection onto the axis of combination (Jakobson 1960/1981: 27). Thus in prose, a trope that stems from a grammatical model can become the basis of an entire piece. For example, in Gogol's "Tale of the Two Ivans" the entire story is a realization of an oxymoron, implemented in the plot line itself (see Pomorska, 1980).

Earlier in this article we defined a fruitful and sound methodology of literary study, in part, as one that opens up new vistas and possibilities. Structural analysis, as demonstrated above, not only delineates poetry and prose, by designating the central tendency of each of these modes, but also opens up new vistas for prose by correlating both types of discourse. Nevertheless, the status of artistic prose remains a fundamental question facing structural analysis. It becomes evident that what makes narrative prose a form of art is parallelistic patterning; for it is only such patterning that reveals a deeper, symbolic dimension and thus transforms the "life" material into a higher level. The real "message" can only be decoded through access to this level of perception. In fact, pure contiguity manifests itself only in causation and temporal sequence. In fictional prose these two forms of sequencing dominate our perception in the process of reading. This is why we do not keep the beginning of a piece in our immediate field of perception, where it can be correlated instantly to the ending. Instead, we follow the rendered "natural" flow of time, thereby identifying our ontological perception of time with its fictitious model. In this way, we identify our own life with the life of fiction. But it is only by disclosing all the elements of equivalence, that is, the *symbolic* system in prose, that we can grasp its deeper dimension. Suddenly, those elements that we perceived in their referential functions—the protagonists, the plot lines, seemingly disparate episodes and images—acquire a new meaning, for in relating them to each other we see their "third dimension," we see in them a *system.* To analyze such elements as constituents of verbal art is not at all to "reduce literature to linguistics," as some badly informed critics would have us believe (see, for example, Gray's voluminous work, 1975). Far from "reducing," we are actually *extending,* since we find new dimensions in elements that were earlier confined to a single aspect only. Language as a system serves here merely as a *model* for explanatory purposes, and hence the role of linguistics in the analysis. As David Lodge puts it in his latest book (1981), this model offers "rules and constraints within which, and by virtue of which, meaning is generated and communicated."

The second fundamental principle, after parallelism, is that of markedness, introduced by Jakobson as early as the 1920s in his *Recent Russian Poetry* (1921; see also 1966 and 1974). The main concepts underlying this principle are correlation and hierarchy. Two mutually related elements are compared as to the amount of information they carry. The one that carries more information is the marked one, as opposed to the other element bearing less information; examples include the marked time in a verse, the downbeat versus the upbeat, or a long syllable versus a short one. A marked element can also carry a *maximum* value of some feature(s), as opposed to the other element carrying a *minimum* value of the same feature(s).

The principle of markedness can be very fruitfully applied to prose. First of all, prose and poetry as two basic types of discourse can be juxtaposed according to this principle with respect to the semiotic character of each. Poetry, being strongly semiotic, is marked, as opposed to prose, which is unmarked within this framework. Prose tends to "hide" its semiotic makeup; in general, the more camouflage we find, the more referentiality occurs, depending on historical periods, literary schools, or the individual artistic inclinations of the authors. Thus, within prose itself a more detailed classification can be made using the principle of markedness.

Let us examine a particular tendency in prose by applying this principle. At the turn of the century, within the stream of "realistic" prose, we can observe a certain persistent trend. Prose tries to represent life in its everyday monotony; nothing extraordinary happens. To put it more formally, prose perceived as "eventful" is now opposed to prose perceived as "eventless." Thus the task arises of how to define an event in a piece of narrative fiction, and how to distinguish it from a "non-event." Consider as a sample for analysis a short story by Čexov, a pioneer and master of "eventless" prose. He constructs his stories in such a way that combinatory units in a sequence are not perceived by the reader as discrete units. In other words, they are not in fact perceived at all; they are *unmarked,* and the chain of combination is experienced as an uninterrupted stream. Popularly speaking, life rendered in this way is "eventless." In traditional, pre-Čexovian prose the combinatory sequence was patterned on several basic principles: first, as a chain of cause-and-effect relations; second, and consequently, this chain involved protagonists in such a way that their basic situations became changed; and third, as a result of this, the chain so constructed formed a highly marked outcome, interpretable as the final result of a set of causal relations. In this way, the causal relations themselves did in fact form discrete units in a chain. The material, the "stock" for such units, was a set of "situations," the most usual ones being engagement, marriage, assault, death, and so on. We often believe that it is these inherently dynamic situations that render the structure "eventful"; in other words, that it is thanks to this stock of ready-made events that we obtain discrete units. But when we look at Čexov's prose from the standpoint of markedness, we learn that this is not so. In his famous story "The Darling," he portrays a woman whose most characteristic feature is that she must have someone to love in order to be a person. Once left without anyone to love, she becomes empty ("without opinions"), that is, she ceases to be a person. This peculiar portrait (so much admired by Tolstoj) is constructed as a sequence of two basic alternating situations:

Olen'ka with a man to love/Olen'ka without a man to love

These two elements constitute a structural invariant. The variations—how each man leaves Olen'ka, or who he is—are unimportant. What is important is that the heroine manages to fill her personality with the life force of each man she happens to love. Without a man, the heroine's personality is nothing but an empty frame, a shell. The telling fact is that death and marriage, items from the traditional stock of situations hitherto perceived as marked, function here as unimportant, i.e., unmarked, elements. The reason for this is that such moments are now equivalent to *any form of departure or appearance* and are thus stripped of their special, dynamic function. The deaths of Olen'ka's two consecutive husbands are mentioned as occurrences equivalent to a number of other everyday details; indeed, the announcement of the demise of one of them even has humorous overtones: the telegram about his death is delivered with a funny distortion in the text (the key word *poxorony* 'funeral' appears as *xoxorony,* a nonsense word), and it is *this* fact that catches our attention, rather than the contents of the message. The same can be said about marriage, which amounts to just another case of the appearance of a man in Olen'ka's life. Thus formerly marked situations now become dissolved in a continuum, an uninterrupted stream; they bear no *extra information* and therefore function as unmarked units.

There is yet another reason for this phenomenon. In the story, the moments of causation are all structured in precisely the same very special way; each moment in the chain of this perpetual alternation is caused by the preceding one as follows: Olen'ka gets together with a man *because* otherwise she is empty/ she is empty *because* a man has left her. This sameness in the moment of causation—the perpetually equivalent reason for the perpetually equivalent result that it generates—has the effect of obliterating the very moment of causation. There are no fluctuations, no suspense, no ups and down, no big gaps in time, no diversified changes. The only palpable change is the swing of a pendulum from "empty" to "filled," and vice versa. The chain of perpetually equivalent alternations, as so constructed, does not *change* the heroine's life but rather keeps it in a steady balance. In fact, the entire story ends at one of these moments. Therefore the ending is not perceived as an outcome: the story is not so much "ended" as "interrupted," since the heroine's life presumably continues in just the same fashion as before.

We can observe a second way in which Čexov neutralizes a potentially marked situation in another of his well-known stories, "In the Cart." The heroine, Marja Vasil'evna, on her tedious way from the village to town, suddenly meets a young landowner whom she had previously considered a potential husband. The meeting catches the reader's attention and seems to promise some development; but it dissolves into nothingness as the young people part at the crossroads. This occurrence is only a *signal* for a possible event, i.e., a possible marked unit, but it is extinguished on the spot. Thus Čexov as a writer is "playing" with an old stock of "marked" situations, which he either functionally shifts, assigning them roles as unmarked sequential variants, or else presents as potentialities or signals that draw attention to a standard pattern that is never developed as a marked unit, thus leaving the reader with a sense of "frustrated expectation." The same phenomenon can be traced in the prose of a number of twentieth-century writers of different orientation, e.g., Pasternak, Dąbrowska (see Pomorska, 1973).

Thus the principle of markedness helps us see that the notion of event, which is basic for classical prose fiction, is not an absolute but a relative component. It is only a potential for any structure and can function as a marked element only as appropriate to the general direction of the structure as a whole.

As one investigator of Jakobson's method puts it, "his commitment to linguistics is not merely as a methodology or a model but as a way of understanding and describing phenomena in the world" (Hrushovski, 1980:10). We have tried to show only one important aspect of such an understanding.

The Polish poet Jarosław Iwaszkiewicz, in one of his last poems, asks: "Czy badania Jakobsona zmienią strukturę 'Pana Tadeusza'?" ("Will Jakobson's investigations change the structure of 'Pan Tadeusz'?"). The question, posed in this way within the context of the poem—and in the context of some theoretical trends, we may add—is intended to be rhetorical, or empty, or to presuppose a negative answer. But in view of the method demonstrated here, the answer to the poet's question is: yes, Jakobson's investigations do change the structure of any artistic message, because they give us a clue about its proper decoding. One and the same message can have a number of decodings that would "change its structure" accordingly, in the sense that in each instance the structure would be perceived differently. But in any number of variations there is an invariant to be found; similarly, among various decodings, we can choose the one that is most appropriate or the common denominator. With its help, a work of art can be reestablished beneath a cliché, or the truth discovered underneath a shell of falsehood.[2]

[2] For exhaustive and original research on the principle of similarity in prose, see Menakhem Perry, "The Metaphor Behind Metonymy: Fictional World as a Network of Similarities," to appear in the materials from the conference on fictionality, held on Ossabaw Island, Georgia, 1981.

REFERENCES

GINZBURG, L., 1973. "O strukture literaturnogo personaža," in *Iskusstvo slova: Sbornik statej k 80-letiju D. D. Blagogo* (Moscow), 376–388.

GRAY, BENNISON, 1975. *The Phenomenon of Literature* (The Hague: Mouton).

HRUSHOVSKI, BENJAMIN, 1980. "Roman Jakobson in his 85th Year," *Poetics Today* 2/1a, 9–14.

JAKOBSON, ROMAN, 1919. "Futurism," *Iskusstvo* Nr. 7 (Moscow, August 2); reprinted in *SW III*, 717–722.

   1921   *Novejšaja russkaja poèzija. Nabrosok pervyj.* (Prague); reprinted in *SW V*, 299–354.

   1956   "Two Aspects of Language and Two Types of Aphasic Disturbances," in *SW II*, 239–259.

   1960   "Linguistics and Poetics," in: T. A. Sebeok, ed., *Style in Language* (Cambridge, Mass.); reprinted in *SW III*, 18–51.

   1966   "Grammatical Parallelism and Its Russian Facet," Language 42, 399–429; reprinted in *SW III*, 98–135.

   1968   "Poetry of Grammar and Grammar of Poetry," *Lingua* 21; reprinted in *SW III*, 87–97.

   1971   *SW II = Selected Writings II: Word and Language* (The Hague-Paris: Mouton).

   1974   "Mark and Feature," in: *World Papers in Phonetics, Festschrift for Dr. Onishi's Kiju* (Tokyo: The Phonetic Society of Japan), 37–39.

   1979   *SW V = Selected Writings V: On Verse, Its Masters and Explorers* (The Hague-Paris-New York: Mouton).

   1980   *Brain and Language: Cerebral Hemispheres and Linguistic Structure in Mutual Light* (Columbus, Ohio: Slavica).

   1981   *SW III = Selected Writings III: Poetry of Grammar and Grammar of Poetry* (The Hague-Paris-New York: Mouton).

LODGE, DAVID, 1981. *Working with Structuralism* (Boston: Routledge and Kegan Paul).

POMORSKA, K., 1973. 'O členenii povestvovatel'noj prozy," in: J. van der Eng and M. Grygar, eds., *Structure of Texts and Semiotics of Culture* (The Hague: Mouton), 349–371.

   1980   "On the Problem of Parallelism in Gogol's Prose: 'The Tale of the Two Ivans,' " in: A. Kodjak, M. Connolly, and K. Pomorska, eds., *The Structural Analysis of Narrative Texts* (Columbus, Ohio: Slavica).

POMORSKA, K., and M. DRAZEN, 1970–72. "Tolstoj's Rotary System," *Ricerche Slavistiche*, 17–19.

ŠKLOVSKIJ, V., 1923. "Paralleli u Tolstogo," in his: *Xod konja* (Moscow-Berlin), 115–125.

   1928   *Material i stil' v romane L'va Tolstogo "Vojna i mir"* (Moscow).

STENBOCK-FERMOR, E., 1975. *The Architecture of "Anna Karenina"* (Lisse: Peter de Ridder Press).

STRADA, VITTORIO, 1980. "K teorii russkogo romana," *Rossija, Russia* 4, 49–63.

VETLOVSKAJA, V. E., 1979. "Poètika *Anny Kareninoj* (sistema neodnoznačnyx motivov)," *Russkaja literatura*, nr. 4, 17–37.

Three Main Features, Seven Basic Principles, and Eleven Most Important Results of Roman Jakobson's Morphological Research

Igor A. Mel'čuk

> The three, the seven . . . the ace!
> —A. S. Puškin, *The Queen of Spades*

This paper is intended to be a beginner's guide to Roman Jakobson's insightful, variegated, and multifarious *morphological research*. There is, to be sure, no shortage of scholarly works that concentrate on the fascinating and intriguing phenomenon which is Roman Jakobson. Let me mention at least Holenstein 1975 or Waugh 1976 (a very clear and well arranged survey), where further relevant references are found, not to speak of the four *Jakobson Festschriften* (Halle et al. 1956; *To Honor Roman Jakobson* 1967; Gribble 1968; and Armstrong—Schooneveld 1977), which include a number of articles dedicated to Jakobson's scientific creation (cf. also Halle 1979). However, to the best of my knowledge, no one has yet attempted to analyze monographically his achievements in the domain of morphology. (The only exception is probably my own essay in Russian—Mel'čuk 1977—which serves as the basis for the present paper.)

In a single article of reasonable size it is impossible to give a developed and substantiated account of the enormous contribution that Roman Jakobson has made to the general theory of morphology, as well as to the morphological description of specific Slavic languages, primarily of Russian. Therefore, I have chosen to try to do something else, namely, to list, stating them in the most compact form, those factors in Jakobson's morphological publications that have had the greatest effect on me personally as a linguist. Thus my account lays no claim to discussion of detail, or completeness, or—most importantly—to objectivity.

The factors that are of interest to me and my readers are formulated as *seven* basic principles, which, in my opinion, constitute the very foundation of

This chapter originally appeared in Russian in D. Armstrong and C. H. van Schooneveld, editors, *Roman Jakobson: Echoes of His Scholarship* (Lisse: Peter de Ridder Press, 1977). Translation by Gerald R. Greenberg, Cornell University, Ithaca, N.Y.

Jakobsonian morphological research, and as *eleven* important results to which this research has led. It seems imperative to start with *three* main features of Jakobson's morphological studies; although these are characteristic of all his linguistic work rather than limited to his explorations in morphology, they are needed to provide the necessary background. (I admit that the delineation of the results, as opposed to the principles or to the main features and vice versa, is, to a certain degree, arbitrary. I simply was under the magic of numbers: $3 + 7 + 11 = 21$; cf. the winning number in the card game "21" and the epigraph.)

I. THREE MAIN FEATURES OF ROMAN JAKOBSON'S MORPHOLOGICAL RESEARCH

1. The broadest view of natural language and linguistics, both of which Jakobson has always regarded in close connection with other spheres of human knowledge and with the general scientific picture of the world—and the most precise delimitation and observance of the proper boundaries of language and linguistics.

On the one hand, it is hard to name any linguist who has studied the relations between linguistics and other sciences as intensively and as deeply as Jakobson. Linguistics and poetics (the title of one of RJ's articles: 1960), linguistics and musicology (the title of another of his articles: 1932a), linguistics and anthropology (1953), linguistics and communication theory (1961a), linguistics and mathematics, linguistics and psychology, linguistics and neurology (1980), linguistics and semiotics, and many other similar topics all are continually in the active zone of Jakobson's attention. His outstanding linguistic analysis of aphasia has determined the development of modern aphasiology; and he was one of the first to advance the profound analogy between natural language and the genetic code (1967a: 678–79). It is by no means accidental that Jakobson has been repeatedly invited to make the opening or closing reports at so many interdisciplinary conferences with a massive participation of linguists. Language viewed against the background of other communication systems, that is, as a particular case of semiotic device, is the fundamental direction of Jakobson's research (1968).

   On the other hand, Jakobson is uncommonly attentive to every, albeit small at first glance, linguistic fact, and at the same time, extremely scrupulous with respect to the sovereignty of His Majesty Natural Language. "Linguista sum; linguistici nihil a me alienum puto!"—he writes with pride and complete justification (1953: 555). Language, according to Jakobson, must be examined against the background but not through the prism of other semiotic and social institutions. In this connection, his article on the imperative (1963) is especially noteworthy, for it convincingly defends the immanent linguistic criteria for isolating the imperative as a grammatical category. Jakobson points out, for example, that an imperative utterance cannot be transformed into a question: *He works* ⇒ *Does he work?, I would work if* . . . ⇒*Would I work if* . . . *?,* while *Work!* ⇏. . . , and he repudiates purely philosophical considerations which tend to subsume under the imperative all utterances expressing commands, orders, requests, appeals, etc. (1963: 190–191).

Another point of utmost relevance for today's linguistic science is Jakobson's emphasizing that the nonexistence or the fictitiousness of the entities denoted by natural language expressions has nothing to do with language as such and "has no bearing on the question of their semantic significance" (1959a: 495). *Colorless green ideas sleep furiously, A pregnant male,* or *Golf plays John* are fully grammatical and therefore as linguistically valid as any less strange sentence is. Linguistics should not be interested in *what* is expressed but only in *how* it is expressed.

Note that in one of the well-known scientific battles of the forties— hocus-pocus linguistics vs. God's-truth linguistics, that is, giving the description a maximal uniformity and formality at any cost vs. making it maximally faithful to the facts and to the "soul" of the language—Jakobson was, and has remained, on the side of God's truth from the very beginning: "code-given truth," as he himself puts it. His determined support undoubtedly promoted the triumph of the latter orientation.

> 2. The most general and abstract formulation of linguistic problems—and their solutions based on the most concrete and specific linguistic material.

On the one hand, practically all of Jakobson's morphological papers are devoted to one or another important question concerning the very essence of language. In the above-mentioned article on the Ukrainian imperative (1963), the connection between the semantico-logical nature of grammatical categories and the linguistic means used for their expression is investigated; a small note (1959e) touches on the enigma of the zero *signata*; another article (1935) examines the interdependence of different levels of language; and so on. The relation of the phenomena under analysis to the general linguistic problems standing behind them is always masterfully accentuated by Jakobson himself.

On the other hand, Jakobson's studies in morphology are, as a rule, extremely concrete and specific. Here are some examples: the particularities of the genitive case in Russian (1957c); the neuter gender in Rumanian (1959d); Slavic clitics (1935); grammatical categories of the Russian verb (1957b); the structure of the imperative endings in Ukrainian (1963); the meaningful alternation "voiceless stop—voiceless spirant" in Gilyak (1957a); etc. (I could also mention such works as 1932b, 1936, 1948a, and 1958.) It is this specificity that makes Jakobson's theories so convincing, while at the same time the generality of the problems he formulates ensures the theoretical value of his specific results.

> 3. The maximally tight link with the best linguistic traditions—and the maximally bold innovativeness of theoretical breakthroughs.

On the one hand, Jakobson, more than any other outstanding contemporary linguist, relies on the accomplishments of his predecessors. From the Stoics and Schoolmen to Charles Sanders Peirce, from the unjustly forgotten Mroziński to Baudouin de Courtenay, from Winteler, Whitney and Sweet to Saussure, Boas,

Sapir, Whorf, and Bloomfield—all of the most remarkable precursors of contemporary linguistics have been absorbed into Jakobsonian morphological studies naturally and solidly. This is particularly true of some Russian linguists—Vostokov, Potebnja, Šaxmatov, Fortunatov, Peškovskij—of whose ideas Jakobson is a prominent expert and advocate. Jakobson has stressed many times his deep devotion to "sound" traditions, emphasizing his dislike for new terminology that disguises old notions and his effort to make use of existing concepts, sharpening them when necessary rather than replacing them (cf. 1953: 557).

On the other hand, to this day many of Jakobson's results are considered in traditional Slavic and Russian studies to be the extreme of modernism. This is the case, for example, with his system of categories of the Russian verb (1957b) and with his description of Russian conjugation (1948a), both of which still have to find a place in the university manuals of Russian, let alone high school textbooks. (For example, the latest Russian reference grammar published by the Soviet Academy of Sciences—Švedova 1980—has not accepted Jakobson's approach.)

To summarize, the three basic characteristics of Jakobson's morphological (and for that matter, all of his linguistic) research are the following:

1. The scientific broadness of perspective with its utmost linguisticality.
2. The most general character of the problems stated with the most specific material drawn for their solution.
3. The loyalty to traditions successfully combined with daring innovations.

It is within this framework that the principles presented in the following section are advanced and implemented.

II. SEVEN BASIC PRINCIPLES OF ROMAN JAKOBSON'S MORPHOLOGICAL RESEARCH

As was the case with the three above-mentioned features, some of the principles that follow relate not only to morphology but to phonology or to linguistics in general as well. Nevertheless, they must be cited here: substantial parallelism of all linguistic levels is, according to Jakobson, one of the most typical properties of natural language (cf. Principle 6) and, therefore, Jakobson's principles of linguistic description are the same for all the domains of linguistics.

Several of Principles 1–7 were stated, and in a sufficiently general form, before Jakobson, or independently of him. Yet it is he who combined all these principles into a system and has consistently applied them as such in concrete linguistic research.

1. The *principle of the calculus of possibilities* is illustrated best of all by Jakobson's analysis of verbal categories in 1957b. The most outstanding feature of this analysis is its actual approach to the problem: instead of supplying an empirically obtained list of categories (as is usually done), Jakobson first of all establishes the most general logically possible pattern thereof. In doing this, he introduces two universal distinctions:

- speech itself (^{s}) vs. the narrated matter (^{n});
- the event itself (E) vs. any of its participants (P).

From, this, Jakobson constructs four basic items, in whose terms the verbal categories of any language can be described: E^s (= a speech event), E^n (= a narrated event), P^s (= a participant of the speech event), and P^n (= a participant of the narrated event). Adding the further distinction of the quantitative vs. the qualitative characterization of any entity under consideration, Jakobson is in a position to calculate all of the possible relationships between verbal categories in the following terms:

a. Categories that characterize the participants of the narrated event (either the participants themselves, P^n, or their relation to the event, P^nE^n) vs. categories that characterize the narrated event itself (either the event as such, E^n, or its relation to another narrated event, E^nE^n).

b. Categories that characterize (events or their participants) qualitatively (= qualifiers) vs. categories that characterize quantitatively (= quantifiers).

c. Categories that characterize the narrated event or its participants with reference to the speech event (either to the event itself: . . ./E^s; or to its participants: . . ./P^s), that is, shifters, vs. categories that characterize the narrated event or its participants without reference to the speech event.

It is hard to deny myself the pleasure of presenting here the universal table of verbal categories that resulted from this investigation (cf. Fig. 1, reproducing, in a slightly modified form, the table drawn by RJ in 1957b: 136).

Among the twenty-four squares of Table I, some of the empty ones seem to be impossible to fill in, even in principle: there are, so to speak, meaningless or contradictory (but this still remains to be ascertained and proven). Others predict certain still unknown verbal categories, to be discovered in languages of the world. On the whole, Jakobson's table of verbal categories may be compared to Mendeleev's Periodic Table. Just as the latter does for chemical elements, the table of verbal grammatical categories, on the one hand, reveals the relationships between known categories, and, on the other hand, it orients the linguist in the search for new categories, which, in fact, the table predicts.

With the Jakobsonian Table of verbal categories, the researcher obtains a principled basis for classifying grammatical categories when describing the morphology of a given language.

In more general terms, the very essence of Principle 1 is as follows: in approaching the description of some range of phenomena, the linguist must first of all single out the simplest items underlying these phenomena, and then by combining these items in all possible ways, construct the most general universal pattern for the totality of observable data. To examine linguistic facts against a background of universal patterns that have been established beforehand (also on the basis of facts, of course)—this is exactly what the principle of a calculus of possibilities boils down to.

There is a further point to be emphasized: the logical completeness of

Figure 1
Universal Table of Verbal Categories

	Characterizing the participants of the narrated event				Characterizing the narrated event itself			
	With reference to the narrated event		Without reference to the narrated event		With reference to another narrated event		Without reference to another narrated event	
	Qualitatively	Quantitatively	Qualitatively	Quantitatively	Qualitatively	Quantitatively	Qualitatively	Quantitatively
Characterizing with reference to the speech event — With reference to the speech event itself					E^nE^{ns}/E^s: evidential (witnessed/by hearsay)		E^n/E^s: tense	
Characterizing with reference to the speech event — With reference to the participants of the speech event	P^nE^n/P^s: mood		P^n/P^s: person					
Characterizing without reference to the speech event	P^nE^n: voice		P^n: gender	P^n: number	E^nE^n: taxis (anteriority, simultaneity, ...)		E^n: status (assertion, negation, question)	E^n: aspect (single/repeated event, ...)

descriptions entailed by Principle 1 by no means precludes substantive or factual exhaustiveness. "There should be no 'and so on' in grammars," Jakobson writes—and he means it. On the contrary, Principle 1 facilitates exhaustiveness on the factual side.

2. The *principle of intersecting classification,* or the *feature approach,* requires the detection of some basic elements (factors, features) of a description and their subsequent combination in all possible ways. Principle 2 is methodological: it points out how to construct the universal patterns and schemas that were discussed above, under Principle 1.

Note that instead of the hierarchical classifications so typical in traditional linguistics and leading to partitions (i.e., to disjunct subsets), Principle 2 puts forth an intersecting, or multidimensional, classification dealing with overlapping subsets.

The feature approach was introduced into phonology by Trubetzkoy and Jakobson and then transferred by the latter into morphology. (Later Noam Chomsky carried it over into transformational syntax: cf. his Standard Theory.) This approach enables linguists to avoid frequent fruitless arguments about the "best" partition of a set of linguistic items, and to concentrate instead on specific properties of these items representing the properties observed in terms of a few standard features.

The use of logically independent features, of which Jakobson is an outstanding advocate, makes it possible to discover and describe important underlying similarities—as if a set of objects that seem very heterogeneous at first glance were pierced through by one abstract feature. (Regarding the abstract character of features, RJ has stressed many times that one and the same feature can be realized on the surface in different ways; what he is always talking about are abstract features, those that are "emic" in character.)

A wonderful example of Principle 2 as applied in morphology is found in Jakobson 1959a, where the system of indicative forms of the English verb is fully described in terms of six basic categories; (a) passive vs. active (*is killed~kills*), (b) preterite vs. nonpreterite (*killed~kills*), (c) perfect vs. nonperfect (*has killed~kills*), (d) progressive vs. nonprogressive (*is killing~kills*), (e) potential vs. nonpotential (*will kill~kills*), (f) assertorial vs. nonassertorial (*does kill~kills*). Combining all these values in all the possible ways yields sixty-four logically possible forms ($64 = 2^6$), of which only twenty-eight actually occur. The absence of the remaining thirty-six forms has to be investigated and explained (e.g., the assertorial does not combine with the passive, the perfect, the progressive and the potential because the verb *to do* does not combine with other auxiliaries; the progressive does not combine with the perfect or the potential in the passive since two consecutive nonfinite forms of *to be* are unusual: *?has been being killed, ?will be being killed*[1] etc.).

---

[1] Yet some speakers readily accept sentences with a verb in the passive present perfect progressive:

  (i) *Her house* **has been being** *continually* **painted** *and repainted for seven years already.*

  (ii) *This mountain* **has been being climbed** *since 1893.*

I owe these examples to Th. Hofmann.

We see that Principles 1 and 2 are tightly interwoven, which is perfectly natural—after all, in a sense they are two different sides of the same phenomenon.

3. The *principle of binarism* has been very extensively discussed in the literature, and so it will be enough to briefly touch upon it here.

The requirement of reducing the description of any complex system to minimal, that is, binary, oppositions provides for high logical precision and enhances completeness of analysis: by always subdividing the area under examination into *A* and *not A*, the researcher lessens the probability of missing a phenomenon. Some facts that seem to form a linear sequence—"gradual oppositions"—may display, under the binary approach, an essential hierarchy. As a case in point, see the analysis of the category of person in Jakobson 1932b: the superficially linear series "first, second, third person" is resolved into two hierarchical categories, "personal vs. impersonal" (first and second persons vs. third person) and "participation of the speaker in the event vs. nonparticipation of the speaker" (first vs. second person). This view explains a number of particularities in the use of different persons and turns out to be very productive. Not without reason it was decisively taken up by Benveniste in his famous article on the structure of verbal persons (1966a).

Two additional comments are in order here. (a) Principle 3 does not require every classification or every system described to be necessarily dichotomous, in the sense that the set in question must be divided into exactly two disjunct subsets, each of which (independent of the other) must be divided in two again, and so on. Nothing of the sort! Principle 3 by no means contradicts the idea of intersecting classification; it demands only that the classificatory features, not the classification itself, be binary. And with the help of two-valued features, the most diverse and multidimensional relations among the objects under consideration can be easily described. Thus, in Jakobson 1958 it is convincingly shown how the meanings of the eight Russian cases (including the partitive—*[nemnogo] snégu* 'a little snow'—and the locative—*[v] snegú* 'in the snow') are represented by means of three strictly binary features: (1) directionality; (2) quantification; (3) marginality. The case meanings themselves do not give way to a dichotomous classification but form instead a three-dimensional structure—a cube (cf. Fig. 2).

The binarism of classificatory features espoused by Jakobson actually prompts the rejection of dichotomous (and, in general, of all hierarchical) classifications in favor of the feature analysis (i.e., Principle 2). Let it be recalled that it was the binary distinctive features of phonemes, as proposed by Jakobson, that allowed linguistics to overcome the traditional dichotomous chasm between vowels and consonants by describing both in terms of the same abstract features.

(b) For Jakobson binarism is by no means simply a convenient device postulated by the linguist as a useful trait of his metalanguage. Principle 3 is advanced as a reflection of the state of affairs in natural language—as a reflection of the real property of oppositions that build up any linguistic structure. Jakobsonian features are binary only because they are binary in

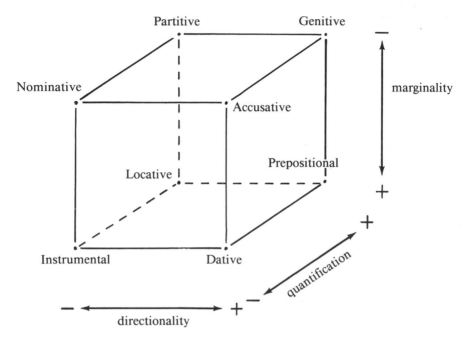

Figure 2
System of Russian Cases in Terms
of Three Binary Features

language itself. This linguistic binarism is linked by Jakobson with the binarism of the human mind in general, which is manifested not only in language, but in all other intellectual and cultural spheres as well. The neurological and psychological research of recent years supports Jakobson's view more and more; however, this is beyond the scope of my theme.

4. The *markedness principle* consists in recognizing the essential asymmetry of opposed linguistic items: one of any two opposed items is normally distinguished by the language itself in that it receives a special mark, while the other is characterized only by the absence of such a mark. The notion of markedness was introduced into linguistics by N. S. Trubetzkoy on the basis of phonemic correlations: marked voiced consonants *vs.* unmarked voiceless consonants (the mark being the vibrations of vocal chords), etc. But it was Jakobson who not only applied this notion in numerous concrete analysis, but insightfully generalized it as well, extending Principle 4 to morphology, that is, to the meaningful units of language. There are at least three respects in which Jakobson's contribution seems to be particularly valuable.

(a) Jakobson showed the necessity of distinguishing the following two oppositions (he calls them "antinomies"; see Jakobson 1932b):

- The signaling of some A vs. the nonsignaling of A (or, in the handy notation of M. V. Panov, nA vs. ñA). Example: Russian *oslica* 'animal of the species ≪asinus asinus≫ of the feminine sex' vs. *osël* 'animal of the species ≪asinus asinus≫'; here A = 'feminine sex,' so that *oslica* is nA while *osël*₁ is ñA.

- The nonsignaling of some A vs. the signaling of non-A (ñA vs. nĀ). Example: Russian *osël*₁ 'animal of the species ≪asinus asinus≫' vs. *osël*₂ 'animal of the species ≪asinus asinus≫ of the nonfeminine [= masculine] sex' (*osël*₁ is ñA, while *osël*₂ is nĀ). Cf. *Èto ne oslica, a osël* 'This is not a she-donkey, but a he-donkey'; *osël*₁ is the unmarked member in both oppositions.

(b) Jakobson stresses the important fact that the markedness of a given item can be different in different respects. Let us consider, for instance, the opposition "nominative case vs. accusative case" in Russian. With respect to grammatical meanings, the nominative is unmarked, and the accusative is marked, while with respect to grammatical means the situation is more complicated, since either case can be both marked or unmarked (1939: 214–215), cf. Fig. 3:

Figure 3
Comparative Markedness/Unmarkedness in Different Respects of the Russian Nominative and Accusative

Grammatical case	Grammatical meaning	Grammatical means	Examples
Nominative	unmarked	marked unmarked	*slug*-a 'servant' *syn*-'son' *xvost*-'tail'
Accusative	marked	marked unmarked	*slug*-u, *syn*-a *xvost*-

And that is not all. At the same time, the lexemes of the type *sluga* 'servant', *sud'ja* 'judge', *junoša* 'youth' belong to an unmarked paradigm, which comprises nouns of feminine as well as masculine gender, whereas the lexemes of the type *syn* 'son', *xvost* 'tail' belong to a marked paradigm embracing only masculine nouns.

In other words, there is no obligatory parallelism of markedness in different respects. Therefore, we cannot speak simply about markedness: it must always be specified in what respect markedness or unmarkedness is being discussed.

The elaboration of this remarkable result leads to an understanding of the fact that "to be marked" is different, generally speaking, from "to be semantically/formally more complex." To take an example: in the opposition perfective aspect *vs.* imperfective aspect (in the Russian verb) the perfective aspect is, as

Jakobson has stressed many times, marked, and the imperfective is the unmarked member. This is manifested, first of all, in the precise intuitive feeling by native speakers of the special primacy of the imperfective aspect. It is not mere chance that in foreign-language-to-Russian dictionaries the Russian equivalents of the foreign-language verbs are given in the imperfective. In the contexts where the opposition of aspects is neutralized, it is the imperfective that usually appears, for example, in the negated imperative: *vstan'!* (perf.)/*vstavaj!* (imperf.) 'get up!' — *ne vstavaj!/*ne vstan'!* 'don't get up!'; *zakrojte knigi!* (perf.)/*zakryvajte knigi!* (imperf.) 'close [your] books!' — *ne zakryvajte knig!/*ne zakrojte knig!* 'don't close [your] books!' (Actually, the perfective is also possible in the negated imperative form, but not with an imperative meaning: *ne vstan' ran'še vremeni* 'make sure you don't get up before it is time' or *ne zakrojte nečajanno knigi* 'be sure not to close accidentally [your] books' are not orders, but simply warnings.) Nevertheless, the imperfective aspect can be formally more complex than the perfective in some cases (*sbros-[it]* [perf.] 'to throw down'—*sbras-yv-[at]* [imperf.] 'idem'), simpler in others (*s-del-[at]* [perf.] 'to make'—*del-[at]* [imperf.] 'idem'); and in a third case forms of both aspects are equally complex (*bros-i-[t]* [perf.] 'to throw'—*bros-a-[t]* [imperf.] 'idem'). The same three relationships are also possible between both aspects on the semantic side (this has been noted, in particular, in Apresjan 1980: 63–66): *umirat'* (= 'to die', imperf.) is semantically more complex than the perfective *umeret'* (*X umer* = 'X ceased to live'; *X umiral* = 'X was passing through such physical states that, if nothing interfered, X *umer*'); *pet'* (as in *On pel tu samuju pesnju* 'He was singing that song') is simpler than *spet'* (= 'to complete singing'); and *mešat'* [*komu-l. čitat'*] 'to make it harder [for someone to read]' and *pomešat'* [*komu-l. čitat'*] 'to have made it impossible [for someone to read]' are equally complex.

Similarly, in the opposition of feminine gender *vs.* masculine gender, the marked member is the feminine gender. However, from the viewpoint of form or meaning, various relationships between genders are possible: *učitel'* 'teacher'—*učitel'-nic-[a]* 'a teacher of feminine sex' (a feminine noun is both formally and semantically more complex than its masculine counterpart); *vdov-[a]* 'a widow'—*vdov-ec* 'a widower' (a feminine noun is formally and semantically simpler than its masculine counterpart); *leningrad-ec* 'an inhabitant of Leningrad of the masculine sex' — *leningrad-k-[a]* 'an inhabitant of Leningrad of the feminine sex' (both nouns are equally complex formally, while semantically the feminine noun is simpler); and so on. Note that in comparing the meanings in the pairs quoted, I used the following curious fact: the meaning 'feminine sex = female' is simpler than 'masculine sex = male' (Wierzbicka 1972: 44–45). Indeed, 'feminine sex' = 'ability to create inside one's own body and bring into the world other beings like oneself', whereas 'masculine sex' = 'ability to cause a being of the feminine sex to create inside her own body and bring into the world other beings like herself.' But all this does not at all affect the markedness of the feminine gender, as opposed to the unmarked masculine.

Markedness/unmarkedness may be connected with the mode of storing the corresponding items in the speaker's memory: the unmarked member is stored as such, and its marked partner is derived from it by some rules. Thus, a number of psycholinguistic experiments show that English sentences in the passive (passive being the marked voice) are understood with a greater effort, that is, more slowly and with more mistakes, than the related active sentences. This seems to suggest that additional operations are needed to understand a passive sentence if compared to the active one.

Let it be noted also that the unmarked member of a grammatical opposition is usually characterized by a greater level of polysemy than the marked one. In Russian, the imperfective aspect in verbs and the singular nouns have a greater variety of meanings than the perfective aspect and the plural, respectively. Correspondingly, a wider sphere of usage (cf. J. Kuryłowicz's well-known thesis) and a greater frequency in texts are characteristic of the unmarked member; for example, the frequencies of the imperfective aspect and the singular in Russian texts are 53% and 72% (Šteinfeldt 1963: 44,52).

(c) Language avoids the piling up of marked categories in one item (Jakobson 1939). Therefore, in the unmarked present tense of the Russian verb, person is distinguished, but in the marked past tense it is not; the Russian adjective distinguishes gender in the unmarked singular, the neuter and the masculine being distinguished only in the unmarked nominative, but not in the marked plural, etc. In this Jakobson has proposed, following Ch. Bally, an important linguistic universal: a language avoids differentiating more entities within a marked category than in the corresponding unmarked one.[2]

5. The *iconicity principle*. Protesting against the too literal and therefore trivial understanding of the Saussurean postulate about the arbitrariness of linguistic signs, Jakobson insists on the iconic character of numerous linguistic devices — that is, on the direct resemblance between some signantia and signata. So, for example, Jakobson points out the iconicity of word order (1965): the order of conjoined verbs expresses the order of events (*Veni, vidi, vici*); the order of conjoined nouns may reflect a hierarchy of entities denoted by them (*The president and his wife*, but not the other way around, i.e. not something like *Mrs. Reagan and her husband*); the usual order of the subject and the object of an action — with the subject preceding the object — is connected with the psychological order in which the components of a situation are normally perceived. The other cogent example is provided by the degrees of adjectives: lengthening for the signans may correspond to an increase in the degree of quality, for example, *high* — *higher* /haiə/ — *highest* /haiəst/, or Latin *alt-(us)* 'high' — *alt-i-(or)* 'higher' — *alt-i-ssim-(us)* 'highest'. Similarly, plural forms of verbs are often physically longer than singular forms: French *je finis* /fini/ 'I

---

[2] This is by no means an absolute law, but rather a clear-cut tendency. Roman Jakobson indicates a counterexample himself: in the Russian verb, the genders are distinguished in the marked past tense, but not in the unmarked present. However, even in this deviation, the general tendency is observed since the genders are distinguished only in the singular (unmarked) and not in the plural (marked).

finish' — *nous finissons* /finisō/ 'we finish', *tu finis* /fini/ 'you [sg.] finish' — *vous finissez* /finise/ 'you [pl.] finish,' *il finit* /fini/ 'he finishes/ — *ils finissent* /finis/ 'they finish'; or Polish *znam* 'I know' — *znamy* 'we know', *znasz* 'you [sg.] know' — *znacie* 'you [pl.] know', *zna* 'he knows' — *znają* 'they know'. No language is known in which the nominal plural is always expressed by a zero morph and the singular by a nonzero morph, although the reverse is completely normal, for example, in English or Spanish. In general, the tendency is to use zero morphs for "zero" (= unmarked) categories (cf. the zero suffixes of the nominative and the third person in Turkic languages). (This, however, is no more than a tendency, and not an absolute law: see above, p. 186, item (b), about markedness in different respects.) Two further linguistic devices, both highly iconic, could also be mentioned: the use of reduplication for the expression of plural, emphasis, repetition, duration, or intensity, as well as the use of palatalization for the expression of diminutiveness, for example, in Basque (*zakur*/sakur/'dog' — *txakur* / čakur /'doggie', or *tanta* /tanta/'a drop' — *ttantta* /t'ant'a/ 'a tiny drop', etc.).[3]

A rich illustration of what Principle 5 entails in the uncovering of essential dissimilarities of externally similar phenomena and thus in the demonstration of their true nature is provided by Jakobson's analysis of the Russian and Bulgarian gestures for "yes" and "no" (1967b). The Russian (and in general European) affirmative nod is primary, its iconic essence being inclination, obedience, agreement. The affirmative nod goes back to a biologically programmed gesture of obedience: one's head inclined before the other. The negative shaking of one's head (from side to side) is maximally different, at the purely semiotic level, from the affirmative nodding movement, still preserving a certain iconicity: the turning of one's head from the interlocutor signifies unwillingness to listen or see. In Bulgarian, where a naïve observer could distinguish the same head movements — down-and-up jerk, equivalent to nodding, and from-side-to-side shaking — things are completely different. Here the negative gesture is primary; the "obstinate" jerking of one's head up (with its subsequent return to a normal position). The most contrastive movement to this is the turning of one's head in the horizontal plane, this gesture being also iconic: to lend an ear (Bulgarian *Az nadavam uxo,* literally 'I lend [you] my ear', i.e., 'I'm listening'). In the emphatic repetition of both gestures, the European affirmation does not differ outwardly from the Bulgarian negation, nor the European negation from the Bulgarian affirmation: one more instance of substantial deep differences that appear "homonymously" on the surface.

An important corollary of the Jakobsonian approach to the iconicity of linguistic signs is his requirement of finding and explicitly stating the most delicate parallels between the signans and the signatum. Jakobson insists on taking into account not only the full identity of morphs, which is commonplace, but also the specific situations in which, for example, some affixes share a

---

[3] This is not an absolute law either. In some languages reduplication is used for the expression of diminutiveness, of incompleteness, etc., while palatalization may well express plural, as in Rumanian: *plop*/plop/'poplar' — *plopi*/plop'/'poplars', *rak* 'lobster' — *raci*/rač'/'lobsters', etc.

certain grammatical function and one phoneme or at least one phonemic feature, which thus becomes the carrier of the above function (1965: 353). For example, in Russian the phonemes /m/ and /m'/ are found in the endings of all the marginal cases (dative, instrumental, prepositional), in nouns and adjectives (*nos*-**om** 'nose' instr. sg., *nos*-**am** 'nose' dat. pl., *nos*-**ami** 'nose' instr. pl., *dlinn*-**om** 'long' prep. sg. masc/neut), but they do not occur in the endings of any of the nonmarginal cases; in Polish, in all the endings of the instrumental case (in all parts of speech, and in all numbers and genders) the feature of nasality appears either in a consonant or in a vowel. Consequently, the phonemes /m ¦ ~ m'/ in Russian and the feature of nasality in Polish serve as the mark of case marginality and of the instrumental case, respectively. The appeal to consider any, even the most insignificant and quite particular, form/meaning correlations in a grammatical description seems to be very fruitful. To give a further example, the detailed account of the Russian declension in the terms just indicated (Jakobson 1958) has been developed by A. A. Zaliznjak (1967), who examines the connection of the vowel -*á*- with plurality in the Russian nominal declension (*ostrov-á, ostrov-á-m, ostrov-á-mi, ostrov-á-x* 'islands', nom./dat./ instr./prep.) and of the element -*in*- with singularity (*armjan-in* '[an] Armenian' vs. *armjan-e* 'Armenians', etc.).

Essentially, what Jakobson did was to give linguistics the following task, complicated but at the same time fascinating: to introduce a new, submorphic level of description, which would allow the analyst to state naturally such correlations as, for example, the following two:

(a) In Russian declension, spirants serve as a mark of quantifying cases: -*x*- of the prepositional, and -*v*-/-*f*- of the genitive (Jakobson 1958: 170).

(b) In Ukrainian conjugation, if a verbal form ends in a vowel, then the rounding (= flatness) of this vowel is a mark of the first person: in the indicative we have *pas*-**ú** 'I herd', *pas*-*ém*o 'we herd' vs. *pas*-*éte* 'you [pl.] herd' etc., and in the imperative, *kyn'*-*m*o 'let us throw' vs. *svýsn*-y 'whistle!', *kýn'*-*te* 'throw!' and so on (Jakobson 1963: 197).

At present, the majority of linguistic descriptions do not reflect similar facts. There are still no adequate formal means for the rigorous description of such submorphic form/meaning correspondences, and, most importantly, the place of these correspondences in the models of languages is still far from clear.

Jakobson's efforts to account for even the smallest manifestations of iconicity in language brings about a particular attention to all parallels and mappings between the plane of expression and the plane of content, that is, between different linguistic levels. Thereby, the iconicity principle is naturally linked to the following principle — that of interlevel connections in language.[4]

6. The *principle of interlevel connection* is solidly anchored in linguistics since Saussure, whose postulate, "La langue est un système où tout se tient," has been recognized by everyone. But the acceptance of the postulate and its consistent application are far from one and the same thing. Therefore, those of Jakobson's

---

[4] The Jakobsonian approach to the iconicity of grammar is developed at length in Haiman 1980, which tries to show to what extent this iconicity reflects the structure of reality.

numerous works that demonstrate the linguistic embodiment of Principle 6 by material of various grammatical phenomena are particularly valuable. I shall limit myself to two examples.

Jakobson 1935 offers an elegant analysis of the history and theory of Slavic verbal enclitics. The languages with free force stress (Bulgarian and the East Slavic languages) stopped obeying Wackernagel's Law (in accordance with this law, enclitics must occupy the second linear position in the sentence), and as a result, these languages lost enclitics. Therefore, the perfective (= compound) forms could no longer differentiate person: *dál esm' > dal, dál esi > dal, dál est' > dal*, making the use of the subject personal pronoun obligatory: Russ. *ja dal, ty dal, on dal.* This construction was generalized, and as a final result, "Russian lost subjectless declarative sentences; [...] sentences without pronominal subjects became just elliptical variants of full two-element sentences. Therefore, in contemporary Russian, sentences with a personal verb but without a grammatical subject are impossible. Impersonal sentences should be considered as featuring a zero subject" (Jakobson 1935: 21; the translation is mine). In this way, the intimate link of accentuation — through morphology — with syntax is exposed. (At the same time, this small paragraph 50 years ago sketched a whole program for the theory of the syntactic zero, a program which even today has not yet been completely realized. The same article [Jakobson 1935] throws light on still another facet of the phenomenon under analysis: the dependence between the abolition of Wackernagel's Law and the appearance of the zero copula in Russian.)

A paper of Jakobson's dedicated to the comparison of the grammatical and phonological aspects of language (1948b: 114) emphasizes the necessity of the parallel investigation of both aspects: "Both synchronic and diachronic studies show an intimate link of solidarity and interdependence between these two autonomous structures — the phonemic and the grammatical." There are at least two dimensions to be distinguished:

(a) Phonological units are selected and used in different grammatical contexts, items, and categories in different manners. Here are some incidental examples: the initial, middle or final position in the word-form exclusively admits (or does not admit) some specified phonemes or phoneme clusters; at prefix-root as opposed to root-suffix junctures different sandhis are normally observed; in Gilyak, certain phoneme combinations are found in proper nouns that never occur in common nouns; in Semitic languages vowels are used practically in affixes only; in languages with vowel harmony certain phonemic oppositions are possible solely in roots; in Russian, among grammatical morphs only inflectional ones (in contrast to derivational) may consist of a single vowel, and among roots only pronominal ones (in contrast to non-pronominal, "full" roots) may consist of a single consonant; etc. Jakobson's works abound in similar observations.

(b) Changes in a phonological system are, as a rule, connected with changes in the corresponding grammatical system. Jakobson points out at least four aspects of such connections (in the direction from phonology to grammar):

- Disappearance of the physical difference between two forms, for instance, second and third persons singular in the Slavic aorist, eventually leads to the loss of the corresponding category.
- An alternation that arose "accidentally" begins to be exploited as a grammatical device (e.g., meaningful umlauts).
- Phonological changes entail the complete restructuring of paradigms (specifically, the reanalysis of stems); thus, the fall of *ŭ* and *ĭ* in old Russian resulted, after a series of modifications, in the new paradigm of the type *nôs*~*nôs-a*.
- Phonological changes bring about new grammatical categories. In Gilyak, after the indefinite object prefix *i-* an initial stop appeared as a spirant: *təu-* 'to teach' but *i-rəu-* 'to teach someone', where *r* is a positional variant of *t*. But after the initial *i-* dropped, the opposition *t-/r-* was phonemicized and the corresponding alternation became a means for generating objectless forms from transitive verbs; the grammatical category of objectlessness was thus created.

Jakobson stresses that phonological changes promote the restructuring of a grammatical system only in those cases where the appropriate tendency has already taken shape in it. The reverse direction — the grammatical system determining phonological development — is given special attention by Jakobson as well. I shall not, however, concern myself with that problem.

7. The *invariance principle,* one of the main tenets of the Prague school, found in the person of Jakobson its most ardent and effective promoter: "The question of the Gesamtbedeutungen of grammatical forms is basic to the theory of any grammatical system" (1936: 23). This statement did not remain just a slogan. Jakobson devoted one of his best known articles to the establishment of the "general meaning" of each Russian grammatical case (1936); he returned to this theme later (1958). In dealing with the general meanings of cases in languages like Russian, Jakobson placed himself in a very difficult and unfavorable position. The fact is that the Russian case (and, more generally, the Slavic case) is to a considerable degree a syntactically controlled category; in other words, in many of their uses Russian case forms are markers of syntactic dependencies and may lack their own semantic values. (This consideration is the basis of J. Kuryłowicz's, A. de Groot's, and A. V. Isačenko's case theories, and of the definition of case in the so-called algebraic linguistics: A. N. Kolmogorov, I. I. Revzin, A. V. Gladkij, S. Marcus; see Gladkij 1969 and 1973 for more references; cf. also A. A. Zaliznjak's approach: 1973.) Therefore, the discovery of the general meaning of this or that Slavic case turns out to be an exceptionally hard matter, as this meaning easily dissolves in the syntactic context. Nevertheless, the general meaning of a Slavic case apparently exists, and it determines the tendency toward the use of the given case for given syntactic goals. The Jakobsonian analysis of the general meanings of the Russian cases yields interesting results, which can be roughly summarized as follows:

(a) The systemic value, or general meaning, of a case makes it possible to explain its specific uses. Thus, it is precisely the "pure" marginality of the Russian I(nstrumental), which is nondirectional, in contradistinction to the A(ccusative) and D(ative), and nonquantificational, in contradistinction to the G(enitive) and P(repositional), that determines the possibility of its various syntactic uses: the agentive instrumental (*ubit VRAGAMI* 'killed by the enemies'), the instrumental of tool (*narisovan PEROM* 'drawn with a pen'), the restrictive instrumental (*jun DUŠOJ* 'young in soul'), the comparative instrumental (*mčalsja STRELOJ* 'rushed like an arrow'), and so on. The fine shades of meaning found in cases like *On byl tituljarnyj sovetnik* 'He was a titular counselor' (an official rank of civil servants in prerevolutionary Russia) vs. *On byl tituljarnym sovetnikom* 'idem, but implying a temporary state' are due to this very marginality (1936: 49).

Even for those who do not consider the quest for the semantically invariant core for each case to be expedient, the necessity of finding some kind of invariant characteristic of cases must still be obvious. In particular, Benveniste (1966b) gave a good example establishing the invariant syntactic function of the Latin genitive: to mark the adnominal transposition of both the nominative and the accusative. But despite the difficulty of the task it sets itself, Jakobsonian case semantics — posited as underlying the syntax of cases — is a very useful, even necessary thing. The problem is that at present linguistics is still poorly equipped to find the right place for such information — in much the same way as it cannot find a place for the so-called internal form and associative semantics of words which are so actively exploited by speakers (in puns or metaphors; inferring interpretation of unknown words from the context; and so on).[5]

(b) The general case meanings allow us to formulate the laws of case syncretism operational in a given language. For example, in Serbian all the marginal cases have in the plural one syncretic form (*udar-ima* 'blows' in D,I,P), while all the nonmarginal ones maintain their differences (*udar-i* 'blows' in N, *udar-a* in G, and *udar-e* in A); Czech presents an inverse picture: *znamen-í* 'sign' in N, G, A (all nonmarginal cases), but *znamen-ím* 'signs' in D, *znamen-ími* in I, *znamen-ích* in P (1936: 69).

(c) "The connection between the components of a case meaning and phonemes or distinctive features of phonemes in the corresponding case form can be discovered: in Russian, -*m'*- (in automatic alternation with -*m*-) occurs as the mark of the case meaning component 'marginality', whereas spirancy, the common attribute of -*v*- and -*x*-, serves as the mark of 'quantification.' Phonology and grammar turn out to be tied together by an entire series of transitional, interdisciplinary phenomena" (Jakobson 1958: 177; the translation is mine. — I.M.). It has already been noted above how important it is for linguistics to take into account all regular relationships between form and

<hr>

[5] An excellent discussion of case semantics, based on an analysis of the Russian instrumental, is found in Wierzbicka 1980. The book, dedicated to Jakobson, expands the framework put forth in Jakobson 1936 and 1958.

meaning (pp. 190–191) and the interconnection of different levels of language.

The semantic invariants of the Russian cases are perhaps one of the most vivid, but by no means the only trophy of Jakobson's in his hunt for invariants. In fact, all of Jakobson's linguistic work is dedicated to the continuous search for them: invariant elements in phonology (distinctive features), semantic invariants of grammatical meanings other than case (e.g., in Jakobson 1932b), invariant factors in different types of aphasia, and so forth.

Thus, Jakobson's morphological (and not only morphological) works are based on the seven above-mentioned principles:

1. Logical calculus of possibilities as a preliminary step in the investigation of any linguistic domain.
2. Feature approach, providing for the universal pattern in the totality of linguistic items under analysis.
3. Logical binarism of classificatory features (oppositions).
4. Markedness principle.
5. Iconicity principle.
6. Interconnection of linguistic levels.
7. Invariance principle.

The introduction of these principles into general linguistics and, in particular, into Slavistics is linked forever with Jakobson's name.

I must remind my reader once again that I have not shown, of course, all the valuable theses that have been established by Jakobson in morphological studies, let alone in linguistics. Thus my list does not include, among others, the following important items:

- The strict differentiation between the linguistic proper (= Germ. *sprachwissenschaftlich*) and the cryptanalytic, or deciphering, approach to language.
- A semantic approach to linguistic correctness, or well-formedness (1959a: 494–95): any utterance that expresses any kind of meaning (including nonsense, contradiction, lie, etc.) in accordance with the norms of a given language must be considered grammatically correct.
- The insightful analysis of the notion of linguistic sign. (Cf., in particular, Jakobson's thesis that "the *signans* is perceptible, and the *signatum* is intelligible," or translatable [1959e: 267], and his review of different types of signs.)
- The promising topic of poetic use of grammatical categories and grammatical devices (1961b).
- The study of language as a teleological system: the so-called means-ends model of language, with its insistence on the fact that any device is used by language for a specific goal and that there is a continuous feedback between the devices used and the goals.

These and many other features are considered too general, relating more to the theme "Roman Jakobson and linguistics" (successfully covered, as indicated above, in Waugh 1976) than to the theme "Roman Jakobson and morphology."

III. ELEVEN MOST IMPORTANT RESULTS OF ROMAN JAKOBSON'S MORPHOLOGICAL RESEARCH

Now to a brief summary of Jakobson's positive results in the field of morphological theory and morphological description. When I say "results" I mean results such as theorems proved in mathematics, or a new species discovered by a zoologist, that is, results that can be easily counted. My summary is of necessity incomplete, including only the most essential of Jakobson's accomplishments in the field of morphology. I indicate first four general theoretical results, and then seven specific descriptive ones.

1. The definition of "grammatical" as obligatory (Jakobson 1959a: 491–492): "Grammatica ars obligatoria." "Languages differ essentially in what they *must* convey, not in what they *can* convey" (1959b: 264). A Russian, translating the English sentence *I hired a worker,* has to choose between *nanjal* 'hired [perfective]' and *nanimal* 'hired [imperfective]', between *nanjal/nanimal* [the subject is male] and *nanjala/nanimala* [the subject is female], and between *rabotnika* 'a male worker' and *rabotnicu* 'a female worker'. The Russian language demands this regardless of the speaker's personal wishes: in Russian, one simply cannot be vague on these points. This is the essence of "grammatical," precisely formulated and richly illustrated by Jakobson.

2. The definition of a specific class of linguistic signs, so-called shifters, that are very important from the grammatical viewpoint. This definition is based on the examination of all the possible relationships between a linguistic message M and the corresponding linguistic code C (1957b):

M/M, or message referring to message, covers the reported (= quoted and quasi-quoted) speech;

C/C, or code referring to code, singles out proper names, since the meaning of a proper name cannot be stated without a reference to the code;

M/C, or message referring to code, subsumes the *autonymous* mode of speech and metalinguistic expressions;

C/M, or code referring to message, is the formula of shifters, signs whose meanings are impossible to define without a reference to the message in which they are used.

Jakobson brilliantly applied the notion of shifters to the description of verbal grammatical categories.

3. The universal pattern of verbal grammatical categories (Jakobson 1957b). Besides the Hjelmslevian general pattern of case meanings, this is one of the first attempts in modern linguistics to construct a calculus of grammatical categories.

4. The sketch of a theory of linguistic zero items (1939, 1940). Actually, Jakobson was the first to propose a general picture of all those phenomena to which we apply the term "zero." In this picture, he provided a reliable basis for

the elaboration of a formalized theory of zero in language. (Unfortunately, such a theory still does not exist.[6])

5. The description of consonant alternations in Gilyak and their role in the expression of the grammatical meaning of intransitivity (1957a).

6. The system of the grammatical categories of the English verb (1959a: 489–91). Strange as it may seem, to the best of my knowledge such a system had not been proposed earlier.

7. The system of the grammatical categories of the Russian verb (1932b, 1957b).

8. The description of the Russian conjugational system (1948a). This description immediately became a classic model for morphological descriptions of verbal systems in the most varied languages, but most of all in Slavic languages. Jakobson 1948a contains a full-fledged theory of Slavic conjugation, together with its practical application. Suffice it to mention simply such crucial notions as full ~ truncated stem, basic form of the stem, etc., as well as the reduction of the two traditional stems (infinitive and present) to one, which is achieved by stating the changes of the full basic stem before different types of endings. Even to this day, the revolutionizing significance of the Jakobsonian rules of Russian conjugation, which fit into seven and a half printed pages, has not been completely realized by many linguists. Perhaps, even if Jakobson had done nothing else in morphology than write "Russian Conjugation," his name would still have had a prominent place in the annals of our science.

9. The system of grammatical gender in Russian (1959c), together with profound inquiries into the relationship of the markedness/unmarkedness of a given gender and the categories that are compatible/incompatible with it. For example, the opposition between masculine and neuter is only possible in the unmarked nominative or in caseless forms, that is, in short adjectives; or in past tense verbs, but again only in the unmarked singular; and so on. In this connection, it is worth noting another paper, Jakobson 1959d, which gives the most concise and accurate characteristics of the neuter gender in Rumanian.

10. The system of Russian case meanings (1936 and 1958), virtually representing an outline of a semantic case theory that contains, in an embryonic form, all its basic tenets.

11. The morphological description of the Russian declension (1958), about which much has already been said.

There are, to be sure, further important results in the domain of morphology, but to include them all would mean to list the complete bibliography of Jakobson's morphological studies.

Finally, all that remains is to sum everything up. Although this may seem to contradict what has been said above, Jakobson did not create his own grammatical theory nor did he establish his own linguistic school. The main point here lies in one important distinctive feature of Jakobson himself,

---

[6] For an attempt to outline a theory of linguistic zero signs, following Jakobson's principles, see Mel'čuk 1979.

opposing him to such ideologically minded linguists, creators of particular theoretical systems as, among others, Leonard Bloomfield (descriptive linguistics), Louis Hjelmslev (glossematics), and Noam Chomsky (transformational grammar). Although Jakobson is one of the founders of Prague structuralism, personally he is closer to "broad" linguists, linguists *par excellence:* for example, to Sapir or Benveniste, or to one of his teachers, Peškovskij. He is completely free of even the slightest trace of sectarianism; nothing is as far from him as any manifestation of *esprit de clocher* that is inevitable when "one's own," "particular" philosophical or theoretical system is constructed. This is why Jakobson's philological interests are so broad: he is to the same degree an authority in structural poetics and in the history of literature and mythology as he is in theoretical and descriptive morphology. Jakobson's trend in grammar, and for that matter in linguistics in general, has been and still is one of broadening and lengthening the road that had been projected by some of his forerunners, often extending it himself to boundaries where no one has ever been. In accordance with Vjač. V. Ivanov's astute comparison, from the viewpoint of the "classics vs. romantics" opposition, Roman Jakobson is a typical romantic, courageously blazing new trails, laying the foundations of new theories, and, as Lomonosov puts it, "conjoining pretty far-distanced ideas" as well as generously sowing new ones. At the same time, Roman Jakobson is a convinced realist, who always prefers the earthly beauty of linguistic facts to the cold elegance of formalistic abstractions divorced from the reality of Language.

I cannot attach the name of Roman Jakobson to a particular linguistic sect that would be his own, but there is no reason to be sorry about that. For a long time already it has belonged and will always belong to the one and indivisible field of linguistic science, for which Roman Jakobson has done so much.

I am sincerely grateful to my colleagues Ju. D. Apresjan, T. V. Bulygina, Th. Hofmann, L. N. Iordanskaja, Vjač. V. Ivanov, E. Kelly, N. V. Pertsov, V. Ju. Rozencvejg, L. Waugh, L. Wynne, and A. K. Zholkovsky, who read the manuscript of this paper. Their criticisms and advice made possible many improvements in my text.

REFERENCES

APRESJAN, JU. D., 1980. *Tipy informacii dlja poverxnostno-semantičeskogo komponenta modeli "Smysl–Tekst"* [Types of Information for Surface-Semantic Component of the Meaning–Text Model] (Vienna: Wiener Slawistischer Almanach).

ARMSTRONG, D. AND C. H. VAN SCHOONEVELD, eds., 1977. *Roman Jakobson: Echoes of His Scholarship* (Lisse, Holland: P. de Ridder Press).

BENVENISTE, E., 1966a (1946). "Structure des relations de personne dans le verbe," in: E. Benveniste, *Problèmes de linguistique générale* (Paris: Gallimard), 225–236.

    1966b (1956) "Pour l'analyse des fonctions casuelles: le génitif latin," in: E. Benveniste, *Problèmes de linguistique générale* (Paris: Gallimard), 140–148.

GLADKIJ, A. V., 1969. "K opredeleniju ponjatij padeža i roda suščestvitel'nogo" [The Concepts of Noun Case and Noun Gender], *Voprosy jazykoznanija*, No. 2, 110–123.

1973   "Popytka formal'nogo opredelenija ponjatij padeža i roda suščestvitel'nogo" [Attempt at Formal Definition of Concepts of Noun Case and Noun Gender], in: A. A. Zaliznjak, ed. *Problemy grammatičeskogo modelirovanija* (Moscow: Nauka), 24–53.

GRIBBLE, CH. E., ed., 1968. *Studies Presented to Professor Roman Jakobson by his Students* (Cambridge, Mass.: Slavica Publ.).

HAIMAN, J., 1980. "The Iconicity of Grammar," *Language* 56:3, 515–40.

HALLE, M., 1979. "Jakobson, Roman," in: D. L. Sills, ed. *International Encyclopedia of the Social Sciences, Biographical Supplement* (New York: The Free Press), vol. 18, 335–41.

HALLE, M., H. G. HUNT, H. MCLEAN, AND C. H. VAN SCHOONEVELD, eds., 1956. *For Roman Jakobson* (The Hague: Mouton).

HOLENSTEIN, E., 1975. *Roman Jakobsons phänomenologischer Strukturalismus* (Frankfurt am Main: Suhrkamp). [See also the English translation: 1976. *Roman Jakobson's Approach to Language: Phenomenological Structuralism* (Bloomington: Indiana University).]

JAKOBSON, R. O., 1932a. "Musikwissenschaft und Linguistik," in: *SW II*, 551–53.

1932b "Zur Struktur des russischen Verbums," in: *SW II*, 3–15.

1935   "Les enclitiques slaves," in: *SW II*, 16–22.

1936   "Beitrag zur allgemeinen Kasuslehre," in: *SW II*, 23–71.

1939   "Signe zéro," in: *SW II*, 211–219.

1940   "Das Nullzeichen," in: *SW II*, 220–22.

1948a "Russian Conjugation," in: *SW II*, 119–29.

1948b "The Phonemic and Grammatical Aspects of Language in Their Interrelations," in: *SW II*, 103–114.

1953   "Results of a Joint Conference of Anthropologists and Linguists," in: *SW II*, 554–67.

1957a "Notes on Gilyak," in: *SW II*, 72–97.

1957b "Shifters, Verbal Categories, and the Russian Verb," in: *SW II*, 130–147.

1957c "The Relationship between Genitive and Plural in the Declension of Russian Nouns," in: *SW II*, 148–53.

1958   "Morfologičeskie nabljudenija nad slavjanskim skloneniem" [Morphologic Observations on Slavic Declension], in: *SW II*, 154–83.

1959a "Boas's View of Grammatical Meaning," in: *SW II*, 489–96.

1959b "On Linguistic Aspects of Translation," in: *SW II*, 260–66.

1959c "The Gender Pattern of Russian," in: *SW II*, 184–86.

1959d "On the Rumanian Neuter," in: *SW II*, 187–89.

1959e "Linguistic Glosses to Goldstein's 'Wortbegriff'," in: *SW II*, 267–71.

1960   "Linguistics and Poetics," in: *SW III*, 18–51.

1961a "Linguistics and Communication Theory," in: *SW II*, 570–79.

1961b "Poèzia grammatiki i grammatika poèzii" [Poetry of Grammar and Grammar of Poetry], in: *SW III*, 63–86; English version in *ibid.*, 87–97.

1963   "Stroj ukrainskogo imperativa" [Structure of Ukrainian Imperative], in: *SW II*, 190–197.

1965   "Quest for the Essence of Language," in: *SW II*, 345–59.

1967a "Linguistics in Relation to Other Sciences," in: *SW II*, 655–96.

1967b "Da i net v mimike" [Motor Gestures for Yes and No], in: *SW II*, 360–365.

1968   "Language in Relation to Other Communication Systems," in: *SW II*, 697–708.

1971   *Selected Writings II [SW II]: Word and Language* (The Hague: Mouton).

1980   *Brain and Language: Cerebral Hemispheres and Linguistic Structures in Mutual Light* (Columbus, Ohio: Slavica). [With the assistance of K. Santilli.]

1981   *Selected Writings III [SW III]: Poetry of Grammar and Grammar of Poetry* (The Hague-Paris-New York: Mouton).

1983   *Studies in Slavic Grammar, 1931–1981,* ed. L. Waugh and M. Halle (Berlin-New York: Mouton). [Contains English translations of Jakobson 1932b, 1936, 1939, 1940, 1958, 1963, and reprinting of 1948a, 1957b, 1957c, 1959c.]

MEL'ČUK, I. A., 1977. "3 osobennosti, 7 principov i 11 rezul'tatov grammatičeskix issledovanij Romana Jakobsona," in: Armstrong—Schooneveld 1977, 285–308.

1979   "Syntactic, or Lexical, Zero in Natural Language," in: *Proceedings of the 5th Annual Meeting of the Berkeley Linguistic Society* (Berkeley, Cal.: Univ. of California).

ŠTEINFELDT, E. A., 1963. *Častotnyj slovar' sovremennogo russkogo jazyka* [Frequency Dictionary of Modern Russian] (Talinn: NII Pedagogiki Èstonskoj SSR).

ŠVEDOVA, N. JU., ed., 1980. *Russkaja grammatika* [Russian Grammar] (Moscow: Nauka), vol. 1.

To Honor Roman Jakobson: Essays on the Occasion of His Seventieth Birthday, 1967, 3 vols. (The Hague: Mouton).

WAUGH, L. R., 1976. *Roman Jakobson's Science of Language* (Lisse, Holland: P. de Ridder Press).

WIERZBICKA, A., 1972. *Semantic Primitives* (Frankfurt am Main: Athenäum).

1980   *The Case for Surface Case* (Ann Arbor, Ill.: Karoma).

ZALIZNJAK, A. A., 1967. "O pokazateljax množestvennogo čisla v russkom sklonenii" [On Plural Markers in Russian Declension], in: *To Honor Roman Jakobson,* vol. 3, 2328–2332.

1973   "O ponimanii termina padež v lingvističeskix opisanijax. I" [On the Interpretation of the Term 'Case' in Linguistic Descriptions. I], in: A. A. Zaliznjak, ed. *Problemy grammatičeskogo modelirovanija* (Moscow: Nauka), 53–87.

Contributors

Grete Lübbe-Grothues, critic and author of articles on poetics and literature in scholarly journals in West Germany and Switzerland.

Igor A. Mel'čuk, Professor of Linguistics, Université de Montréal

Krystyna Pomorska, Professor of Russian Language and Literature, Massachusetts Institute of Technology

Stephen Rudy, Assistant Professor of Slavic Languages and Literatures, New York University

Linda R. Waugh, Professor of Linguistics, Cornell University

Jurij Tynjanov (1894–1943) was an outstanding theoretician of literature and a novelist. He was a co-founder and one of the most important members of the Petersburg group OPOJAZ (the "Society for the Study of Poetic Language"), part of the movement known as "Russian Formalism." Tynjanov's most significant contributions include *The Problem of Verse Language* (1924, trans. 1981), *Archaists and Innovators* (1929), and other studies on literary dynamics and evolution.

Name Index

Name Index

Adamovič, G. V., 125
Adrianova-Peretc, V. P., 41
Aljagrov (pseudonym of Roman Jakobson), vii
Andreev, L. N., 114
Annacker, Heinrich, 76
Annenskij, Innokentij, 112
Apresjan, Ju. D., 188, 198
Aquinas, Thomas, 45
Aristov, N., 41
Armstrong, Daniel, 178
Arnim, Bettina von, 136
Aseev, Nikolaj, 112, 127
Astaxova, A. M., 41
Augustine, Saint, 32

Bailey, James, 96
Bally, Charles, 20-21, 29, 189
Baratynskij, E. A., 112
Barthes, Roland, viii, 148
Batjuškov, K. N., 129
Baudelaire, Charles, 60
Baudouin de Courtenay, Jan, 44, 74, 180-81
Baxtin, Mixail, 169
Becking, G., 73, 74
Bednyj, Demjan, 125
Beethoven, Ludwig van, 132
Beissner, F., 138
Bentham, Jeremy, x, 38, 39, 56, 163
Benveniste, Émile, 28, 185, 193, 197
Bernštejn, S. I., 17
Berry, F., 41
Beyle, Marie Henri. See Stendhal
Blake, William, xiii, 60, 72
Blok, A. A., 22-23, 71-72, 112-13, 124
Bloomfield, Leonard, 181, 197

Boas, Franz, 43, 180-81
Böchenstein, B., 136, 139
Bogatyrev, P. G., 5, 18, 41
Bogorodickij, V. A., 44
Bohr, Niels, 31, 32
Bolinger, Dwight D., 156
Bonaparte, Napoleon, 163
Bonnefoy, Yves, 82
Bragdon, Claude, 43
Braque, Georges, vii
Brecht, Bertold, 76
Brik, O. M., 63, 127
Bronstein, L. D. See Trotsky, Leon
Brooke-Rose, Christine, 41
Brown, Edward J., 111
Bulygina, T. V., 198

Cézanne, Paul, 132
Čaadaev, Petr, 115
Chastaing, M., 156
Čexov (Chekhov), Anton, 174-76
Chomsky, Noam, 184, 197
Čukovskij, Kornej, 146
Cowell, R., 83
Cummings, E. E., 151, 154-55, 161, 163

Dąbrowska, Maria, 176
Dante, Alighieri, 72
D'Anthès, G. I., 131
Davie, Donald, xii, 38
da Vinci, Leonardo, 104
Degas, Hilaire Germain Edgar, 79, 146
de Groot, A. W., 193
de Honnecourt, Villard, 44
Del'vig, A. A., 129
Dostoevskij, F. M., 14, 120, 123

Born in Moscow in 1896, **Roman Jakobson** studied at the Lazarev Institute of Oriental Languages and in the philology department of Moscow University. He was a co-founder of the Moscow and Prague Linguistic Circles and an active member of the Russian and Czech avant-garde movements. His twenty-year sojourn in Czechoslovakia, where he was a major force in building the modern science of language, included a professorship at Masaryk University in Brno. In 1939 the Nazi invasion forced him to flee, first to Scandinavia and then to the United States. In New York, Jakobson taught at the École Libre des Hautes Études, a Free French and Belgian university hosted by the New School for Social Research, and then at Columbia University. From 1949 till 1967 he was a professor of Slavic languages and literatures and of general linguistics at Harvard University, and in 1957 he was appointed Institute Professor at the Massachusetts Institute of Technology. Jakobson wrote over 650 essays in linguistics, poetics, and Slavic studies, most of which are included in his seven-volume *Selected Writings*. His work also includes *Child Language, Aphasia, and Phonological Universals, The Sound Shape of Language* (with Linda Waugh), *Puškin and His Sculptural Myth, Russian and Slavic Grammar: Studies, 1931-1981,* and *Dialogues with Krystyna Pomorska.* Roman Jakobson died in Cambridge in 1982.

Krystyna Pomorska is professor of Russian language and literature at MIT. Her publications include *Russian Formalism and its Poetic Ambiance, Themes and Variations in Pasternak's Poetics,* and *Fifty Years of Russian Prose* (an anthology). **Stephen Rudy,** an assistant professor of Slavic languages and literatures at New York University, has published numerous articles on poetics and semiotics, and has edited an anthology, *Dostoevsky and Gogol: Texts and Criticism.* He is the editor of Jakobson's *Selected Writings, Volumes III, V, VI,* and *VII* and has compiled *A Complete Bibliography of Roman Jakobson's Writings, 1912–1982.*